Bowhunting Whitetails

the Eberhart Way

Bowhunting Whitetails

the Eberhart Way

John and Chris Eberhart

STACKPOLE
BOOKS

Published by
STACKPOLE BOOKS
5067 Ritter Road
Mechanicsburg, PA 17055
www.stackpolebooks.com

Printed in the United States

Distributed by NATIONAL BOOK NETWORK

First edition

Library of Congress Cataloging-in-Publication Data
Eberhart, John.
    Bowhunting whitetails the Eberhart way / John and Chris Eberhart. — 1st ed.
        p. cm.
    Includes index.
    ISBN-13: 978-0-8117-0762-6 (pbk.)
    ISBN-10: 0-8117-0762-8 (pbk.)
1. White-tailed deer hunting. 2. Bowhunting. I. Eberhart, Chris. II. Title.
    SK301.E333 2011
    799.2'7652—dc22
                            2011008691

CONTENTS

Hunting Pressure

Like most of you readers, we love to bowhunt whitetails. We are grateful to be blessed with the opportunity to bowhunt. Bowhunting whitetails has become such an integral part of our lives you could even say it defines who we are. Chasing mature pressured bucks is a supreme challenge, and matching wits with these elusive creatures is about as exciting as it gets. Being successful requires a lot of hard work, but for us it is a labor of love.

A decade ago, when we began writing *Bowhunting Pressured Whitetails*, our goal was to help other whitetail hunters who found themselves in situations similar to our own. As natives to an area of Michigan that receives hunting pressure on par with the most intense in all of North America, we were frustrated by the often poor and even misleading hunting information in most hunting media sources. You can probably relate to this. Tactics and hunting presented on television and in magazines just didn't work in our neck of the woods and probably won't work for the majority of bowhunters around the country either. We also weren't in a position to spend big dollars on hunts. For the most part, we had to make do with the opportunities close at hand. Through decades of careful bowhunting, we have developed a bowhunting system that is unique and effective on truly pressured mature bucks. Our system is no secret and certainly isn't a shortcut. It takes a lot of hard work, time, and constant attention, but it will raise your success on mature bucks anywhere whitetails live. Nothing is static, and our system has continued to develop because of dramatic changes in the last ten years in the whitetail hunting world. Our goal is still to help you become a more successful whitetail bowhunter and accomplish your bowhunting dreams.

The misrepresentation of normal hunting conditions on television and in magazines stems mainly from the fact that the playing field in bowhunting is not level. It is easier to kill big mature bucks in some places than in others. The usual path to making a name in hunting media is having killed a lot of big bucks. The guys who kill the big deer are automatically accepted as experts, even if they are hunting the best whitetail spot on the planet. Unfortunately, the measurement of total antler mass killed has in most instances very little to do with actual hunter ability. A guy who hunts on public land in northern Michigan or Pennsylvania or New England and kills a $2^1/_2$-year-old buck every year is probably a far more skilled bowhunter than most television or magazine experts. This public-land hunter probably has a wealth of knowledge that could help his fellow bowhunters a great deal, but because his total inches of antler don't measure up, he will never get the opportunity to grace the pages or screens of hunting media. We want guys like this to know that they shouldn't be fooled by the hunting media. Bowhunters like this are every bit as adept as the experts. Here's why.

Whitetail deer are a prey species and hunters are a primary predator. Our actions as predators can have direct influence on how deer move and act in our hunting areas. The key to this influence is the amount of consequential interaction the deer have with hunters. Deer always react somewhat to a hunter's presence, but they react far more severely in areas where they have suffered consequences, or witnessed consequences, from previous encounters with hunters trying to kill them. To put it a bluntly, a deer that has suffered a wound from an arrow will be far more cautious than a deer that has never encountered a bowhunter. Also, a deer that encounters hunter presence regularly but suffers no consequences will certainly not react as severely as the deer that has been shot at. Hunting pressure is a matter of degree.

Defining heavy hunting pressure is difficult. Everyone believes they are hunting in a pressured area. At the extreme end of the scale are areas where there are a lot of hunters, say more than twenty per square mile, and most of them target all antlered bucks regardless of age and antler size. At the other end are areas devoid of hunters and that don't have heavy hunting pressure. There are many levels of pressure in between. Also, hunting pressure and hunter presence are two very different things. Understanding the differences in hunting pressures can help you define your hunting goals and help you see through the smoke and mirrors of hunting media that makes whitetail hunting mature bucks appear easy. The only way to understand hunting pressure and how it affects your hunting is to understand the following variations.

Pay-to-Hunt Ranches and Large Micromanaged Properties

The lightest hunting pressure, outside of enclosures, is found on large exclusive leases and large private parcels where deer herds are micromanaged to grow mature bucks. These places have enough acreage, quality habitat, food, and does to deter mature bucks from leaving the property. In these types of areas, most of the work done during the course of a year is done while sitting on a tractor altering the landscape or planting food plots. It is not about learning to hunt, it is about learning to manipulate the land to grow many big bucks. Hunting these places becomes a matter of averages. The more mature bucks there are, the better your chances of killing one.

Many hunters believe that no matter what the circumstances, if there are several other hunters on the same land or in the same vicinity, they are hunting pressured whitetails. This is not necessarily true. On managed properties, bucks are rarely targeted until they are $3^1/2$ years old or older. In such areas, when bucks are allowed to pass by hunters until they reach the proper age or antler size, no matter how many hunters they pass by while growing up, they haven't experienced life-threatening reasons to alter their daytime movement habits to avoid hunters. While there may be hunter presence, there is no consequential hunting pressure on subordinate bucks. Once a buck matures, or antler criterion has been met, his lack of fear of hunters makes him vulnerable and relatively easy to hunt. Another factor makes hunting easier on these properties: A herd with a somewhat balanced age structure with lots of mature bucks creates a very competitive rut. This makes bucks extremely susceptible to all hunting tactics such as rattling, decoys, calling, mock scrapes, and scents.

Hunting personalities who hunt these areas claim they are hunting wild fair-chase deer, even though these areas present grossly different hunting conditions than most hunters in this country ever experience. The vast majority of hunting personalities on TV shows, in videos, on advertisements, in magazines, and books hunt properties like these, which is understandable when you consider that they are in business. That business is entertainment, and viewers want to see lots of big antlered bucks. Recognize that this does not represent normal hunting conditions throughout the country, and the hunting techniques the personalities use where they hunt will not yield consistent results on mature bucks in heavily hunted areas. Don't be fooled by the big racks.

Of course there are a few TV shows that depict hunting under somewhat normal hunting conditions. They go out of their way to show deer hunting in as real a situation as possible and still keep it interesting. These shows are not always successful because the hunters take good bucks but not monster bucks, but they are our favorite shows.

The trend toward more of these managed properties in big buck country is obvious. After a seminar at the Wisconsin Deer Expo, a hunter from south-central Iowa lamented to John that nearly all the hunting land in his and several of the bordering counties had either been bought or leased by media personalities or wealthy hunters. Many of the purchases were thousands of acres that made it impossible to receive hunting permission. Of course, this is pure capitalism. The landowners have something that hunters value, and they capitalize on the situation. Controlling large tracts of hunting land is nearly the easiest way to be regularly successful at antler harvesting. The mainstream hunting media is largely to blame for this. Though we try to run counter to the trend, we too carry some

Bowhunter Density Per State Per Absolute Square Mile, 2006

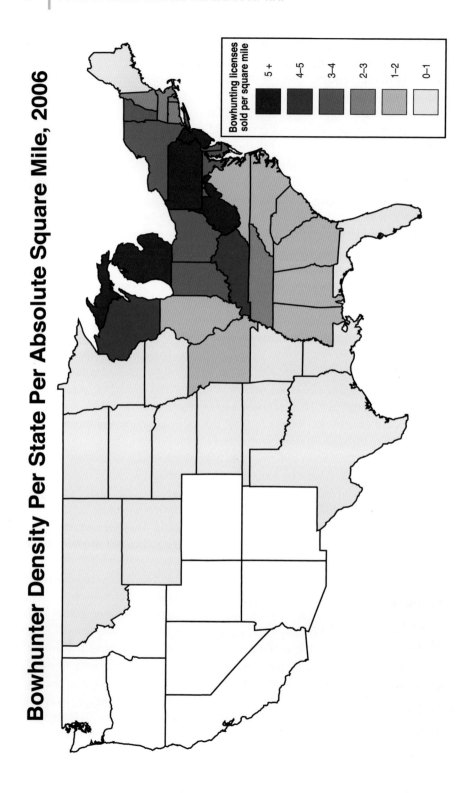

Bowhunting licenses sold per square mile

5 +
4–5
3–4
2–3
1–2
0–1

blame, as we are guilty of showing off some big mature bucks. For us, though, how we hunt is more important than how many inches. In many cases hunters don't need to learn how to hunt well in order to take a big buck; money takes care of lack of skill. Money for antlers does not bode well for the future of hunting.

Around the Country

Overall hunting pressure varies widely across the country. We calculated each state's absolute bowhunter density per square mile by dividing license sales into absolute square miles of land. We also calculated the ratio of licensed bowhunters per Pope and Young entry by dividing each state's entries by bowhunter license sales (see table, below). The span of hunter density was between .19 and almost 8 hunters per square mile. Though these are very general numbers, they should give you an idea of hunting pressure differences in various regions and an approximation of the amount of hunting pressure where you live.

Whitetail Bowhunting Data		
State	Bowhunter license sales in 2006	Pope & Young entries in 2006
Alabama	62,700	7
Arkansas**	30,000	21
Connecticut	12,314	14
Delaware	5,500	6
Florida	24,636	1
Georgia	78,641	23
Illinois**	140,000	398
Indiana**	79,000	162
Iowa	75,315	240
Kansas*	22,026	130
Kentucky**	90,000	70
Louisiana	27,413	6
Maine	15,060	2
Maryland	57,700	28
Massachusetts	26,653	15
Michigan**	310,000	85
Minnesota	81,200	108
Mississippi	41,793	20

Whitetail Bowhunting Data *continued*		
State	Bowhunter license sales in 2006	Pope & Young entries in 2006
Missouri	133,089	112
Montana*	16,000	27
Nebraska*	14,633	51
New Hampshire	19,026	4
New Jersey	34,467	26
New York	203,890	53
North Carolina*	55,000	10
North Dakota*	15,553	67
Ohio-(inc. crossbows)**	300,000	167
Oklahoma*	82,635	27
Pennsylvania	268,751	88
Rhode Island	5,041	2
South Carolina**	30,000	3
South Dakota*	26,200	47
Texas	81,238	91
Tennessee**	90,000	10
Vermont	19,173	0
Virginia	70,366	17
West Virginia**	150,000	17
Wisconsin	254,399	540
Wyoming*	16,094	11

*Figures from these Western states indicate total archery permits sold for all species.
**These state agencies have no method of accounting for only bowhunter license sales, so these numbers are state estimates.
Source of license sales: *Archery Business / Trade News*.
Source of Pope & Young entries: Pope & Young Club 26th recording period statistical summary.

A state's absolute bowhunter density doesn't account for specific areas within that state. For example, public lands near large cities receive a lot of hunting pressure, no matter what that state's statistical hunter density. And large areas of private land in states with high hunter densities may have only light hunting pressure. There are other variables in hunting pressure that are hard to account for with statistics, such as terrain form. For instance, North Dakota has statistically one of the lightest hunter densities in the country. Yet because much of North Dakota's prairie is essentially free of whitetails and the deer are concentrated in river bottoms, public land along such bottoms is hunted hard. Even Michigan has some areas in the Upper Peninsula with lower hunting pressure, due to the size and composition of the giant swamps there. So keep in mind that statewide density statistics are not area specific.

Lightly Hunted States

States with hunter densities between .19 and 2.00 bowhunters per square mile have light hunting pressure throughout most of the state and offer excellent opportunities for mature bucks. These states include Iowa, Kansas, Illinois, Missouri, Minnesota, Nebraska, and the Dakotas, to name a few. These states annually have excellent Pope and Young entry ratios, and the average P & Y entry score from the top five states is nearly 15 inches higher than the states at the opposite end of the hunter density chart.

Most lightly hunted states are located west of the Mississippi River in the farm-rich Midwest. In these states a $2^1/_2$-year-old buck commonly grows antlers that exceed the 125-inch Pope and Young minimum score, and a $3^1/_2$ year old can exceed 140 inches. Outside of this rich agricultural land, bucks generally do not reach that size at such a young age. In portions of the Northeast, East, and South it often takes a buck $3^1/_2$ years to grow antlers that exceed 100 inches. Hunter expectations can and should differ greatly from area to area, because the antlers on the heads of bucks of the same ages will vary widely in different areas. A hunter from a lightly hunted agricultural area may throw a set of antlers in the box, whereas that same rack may be taxidermist material to a hunter in a pressured, or less agricultural, area.

Overall low hunter density has a couple of different effects on deer and hunting. The first is simply that with fewer hunters more bucks grow to maturity. Local hunters see far more mature bucks. More mature bucks also means that it is common for local hunters not to target animals until they are $3^1/_2$ years old or older. Targeting only mature bucks has the same effect in these areas as on locked up managed ranches. Deer become habituated not to expect negative consequences with hunter encounters. They move more during daylight and are more susceptible to various hunting tactics.

We have had great success traveling to low hunter density states in the last decade, as have many of our friends. The difference in hunting expectations in such areas is well demonstrated by our friend Ed Simpson's experiences. Ed is a serious and skilled Michigan bowhunter. Hunting in central Michigan for forty-one years, he has killed sixty-one bucks. More than a dozen of his bucks were $2^1/_2$ year olds and three were $3^1/_2$. None of Ed's Michigan bucks net scored more than 100 inches. At the time of this writing, Ed has logged fifteen out-of-state one-week hunts, all by free permission to lightly hunted states. On those fifteen hunts, he has taken thirteen bucks scoring between 116^{1}/$_{8}$ and 168^{7}/$_{8}$ inches. Ed didn't suddenly become a better hunter, he simply used his ability in less pressured areas. Hunters from high pressure areas can usually find stellar success when they hunt low pressured areas; the opposite is usually not the case.

This example was not meant to suggest that you should not hunt in an area with heavy hunting pressure, but you should possibly reconsider your hunting goals. If you hunt in an area with light hunting pressure, consider yourself extremely fortunate. Where a hunter hunts should determine his expectation for mature bucks.

States with Moderate Hunting Pressure

The states that statistically have between 2.00 and 4.00 bowhunters per square mile have moderate bowhunting pressure. These states are middle of the road concerning pressure and hunter expectations. Some places will have high pressure and others low. Regional differences abound.

In moderately pressured areas, we have found that there is a split of opinions concerning deer hunting. Some hunters practice some form of quality deer management and some don't. There will be more areas of heavy pressure than in lightly hunted states but also more areas with low pressure than in heavily hunted states. A common trend in these states is private deer associations.

Several bordering property owners get together and devise parameters for buck harvest on their lands. Some examples of the rules might be a buck must have four points on one side, any buck you take must be mounted, the buck must have at least eight points, you have to take a doe before you can take a buck, and if you take a buck that doesn't meet the group's criteria, you have to pay a fine. We know of one group that briefly implemented the rule that your next buck had to be bigger than any you had previously taken. After a while that becomes a really tough standard. Setting rules such as these ensures that there will always be mature bucks in the area, there will be a bond among the landowners and hunters, and most hunters in the area will frequently take mature bucks without the pay-to-play mentality. The groups usually have exceptions for youths or first-time hunters.

In moderately hunted states your hunting goals should mirror the microconditions of the area you hunt.

States and Areas with Heavy Hunting Pressure

Last are states with absolute statistical hunter densities between 4.00 and 7.83 per square mile. We have hunted our entire lives in a state with hunting pressure that is second to none and have hunted moderately pressured areas as well as lightly pressured states, and we are speaking from experience when we say that heavy life-threatening hunting pressure alters buck behavior more than any other factor.

States with high hunter densities have one thing in common: They all have large general populations. In states with large general populations, there is a natural competition for available land that translates into higher property prices, which leads to small fragmented parcels. In rural areas, it is normal to have twenty or more property owners per section, with parcels ranging anywhere from 1 to 80 acres each. If each property owner allows 1 to 3 hunters on his land, it can get ugly. We consider areas with actual consequential bowhunter densities over 10 per square mile to be heavily pressured areas.

The five most prominent aspects that separate hunting in a heavily pressured area from hunting in any other area are listed below. If these apply to your hunting area, you are probably hunting truly pressured deer.

1. There are very few and occasionally no bucks that survive to reach $3^1/_2$ years old. In many areas over 80 percent of the bucks killed during bow and gun season are sporting their first set of antlers. Estimates in some areas place the survival rate of bucks reaching $3^1/_2$ years or older at less than 1 percent. That means that if there were twenty antlered bucks per 1-mile section, there would only be one buck $3^1/_2$ years old or older per every five sections.

2. The nocturnal buck is a dreaded reality in heavily hunted areas. The mature buck leaves sign but is rarely seen during shooting hours. Daytime movement habits of bucks $2^1/_2$ years old and older are usually limited to the opening day or two of the season and then during the rut phases. Even then, daytime movements are limited.

3. Mature bucks rarely expose themselves in short crop fields as is frequently seen on TV and in videos. A $2^1/_2$-year-old buck in a heavily pressured area would be less likely to step out into a short crop field during season than a $5^1/_2$-year-old buck would in a lightly hunted area.

4. The lack of multiple mature bucks creates a situation where, even during the rut phases, they do not have to wander far for receptive does or compete for breeding rights.

5. The lack of rut competition among mature bucks plays a huge role in how hunting tactics such as calling, rattling, and decoying must be performed and how bucks react to them.

To kill mature bucks on a regular basis anywhere can be a challenge, but it is far more of a challenge and requires a lot more attention to detail in areas where bucks receive life-threatening, heavy hunting pressure during the entire deer season. You can be successful on mature bucks in areas like this; hopefully we can show you how. Read on.

2

ACCESS

Before you can begin to think about the specifics of bowhunting whitetails you need a place to hunt. For those fortunate enough to own land, this is not a factor, but for the average bowhunter, access can pose a huge and frustrating challenge. Deer hunting access, bowhunting in particular, was for generations one of the last things that could be easily had for free in North America, but it is getting more and more difficult to obtain, free or not. To buck the trend you need to be smart, creative, and use every tool at your disposal. Despite astronomical hunting lease prices in some areas and a trend toward European-style land control, if you are thick-skinned and do not give up even when many property owners deny your request, free access is still possible. The good news is that you don't need to be rich to gain access to hunt big, mature whitetails, but you may have to travel to do so.

Private Land Permission

Gaining permission to hunt private property for free is getting tougher all the time. Up until the early nineties it was rather easy to just walk up to a couple of farmers, knock on their doors, and be granted permission. This has changed in the last two decades. Private hunting land continues to decrease, and the cost of leasing or buying hunting land continues to rise.

Lease and hunting property costs are driven by two main factors: location and quality. Location boils down to supply and demand. Hunting properties near areas with large general human populations are very limited, and due to sheer competition for them from both developers and hunters, the cost per acre to purchase, or lease, is extremely high when compared to more rural areas.

Over the past twenty years or so trophy whitetail hunting has become more and more popular and has transformed hunting from something that the family and neighbors did a couple days a year into a lucrative source of cash for landowners. And why give something away for free that is worth money? That idea has raised the price of ownership, leases, and guided hunts in areas well known for quality bucks all over the country. Several national real estate agencies concentrate on buying, developing, and reselling hunting land. Countless hunters have the financial means to pay large sums of money and travel long distances for the opportunity at trophy bucks in such areas. The ease of both gaining information and travel has created a large viable hunting land market. With lease rates as high as seventy-five dollars an acre in some areas, no wonder free permission is tough to come by.

Networking

Seeking hunting land access is a matter of positive attitude, determination, appearance, and communication skills. The main tenant of gaining access is to communicate your goal of gaining hunting permission to the right people, landowners. One of the first mistakes hunters make is asking hunting permission from the wrong people. Hunters tend to stick together and spend time with other hunters. Asking other hunters for hunting permission might work occasionally, but it is sort of like asking a kid for his one remaining piece of candy. The hunter will be less than excited to share, especially if he is focused on mature bucks. Although hunters associate with other hunters, good hunting spots are hard to find, special, and rarely shared. This doesn't mean you shouldn't ask, it simply means your chances of success are low.

We have found that the best people to ask for hunting permission are non-hunting landowners, and the best way to gain access is through networking. Networking sounds like something complicated, but it's not. It simply means communicating your goal of finding places to hunt to as many people as possible who may be able to help you. The first place to start is within your own family. You never know what connections that distant great uncle might have. Even if he doesn't own land, his best friend might own the property next door. Get the word out to all of your relatives, near and distant, and remind them occasionally of your wish. Be nice, but also be persistent. Get on the phone, look up long-lost aunts and uncles, go to that family reunion, and do whatever it takes to get the word out. Who knows, you might improve family relations. Borderline anti-hunting relatives may allow a family member to hunt their land.

Most of us have relatives or acquaintances scattered throughout the country, so if you are planning an out-of-state hunt, call those who live in known big buck states before applying or going. Even in states with overall low hunter densities, private lands are generally better than public. Asking distant relatives for hunting permission is important if you are planning out-of-state do-it-yourself hunts.

The next groups of people to speak to about hunting permission are those close to you. Colleagues at work, old school or college friends, members of your church, and friends from other non-hunting organizations are all good options when it comes to looking for hunting access. Many of our best hunting areas have come through this method. In 1995 John gained access to a 5-acre late-season location while his dentist was doing a root canal. His dentist didn't hunt and no one had ever asked him to hunt, so he was quite amused when John slobbered the request.

Since these people know you, they are more likely to either grant you permission themselves or put in a good word for you. Landowners are simply far more likely to grant hunting access to people they know directly or who come with a good recommendation from a trusted acquaintance. Chris gained permission to several great hunting areas through friends he met in college. Networking is far and away the most effective way to gain access to hunting property.

Networking doesn't stop with family and friends. One good place to explore hunting permission possibilities is the local farmers' hangout. This might be a local restaurant where nearby farmers gather for lunch or a coffee corner in a small-town gas station where farmers gather early in the morning to gossip. A few times we have gained permission to hunt by spending a few days eating lunch at the local farmer hangout and striking up conversations. Neutral locations like this are good places to get to know who is who in a farming community.

Cold Call

The next option is simply asking landowners for permission to hunt. This is far more difficult than networking and should be approached somewhat like looking for a new job. Remember when seeking permission in this fashion that denial is part of the game. Generally, you will be turned down far more than you'll have success, especially in areas with a high hunter density or generally high human population. Although we always leave room for impromptu situations that arise, like striking up a conversation with a farmer at a gas station or restaurant, we generally approach cold calling with a plan. The first step is to select an area in which you would like to hunt, and then purchase a plat book or visit the local government office to determine who the landowners are. In many areas, plat books list the owners of the land and even give their addresses and telephone numbers. If we don't already know the area, we compare land ownership with aerial photos from the Internet. This way we can concentrate on asking permission where we know the terrain holds deer, or at least looks promising. After deciding on a group of landowners we would like to ask permission from, we then do just that.

But before we get into the procedure of asking permission, it is important to consider timing. Just like timing is critical to successful bowhunting, it is critical to gaining access to private property. If you walk up and knock on a landowner's door the day before hunting season starts, you probably won't be granted permission. By asking for permission so close to the season, your seriousness as a hunter will immediately be questioned, and more than likely you will not have been the first to ask for that season. The best time to ask for hunting permission is in the spring or early summer. At this time of year, most landowners aren't thinking about hunting and have other things on their minds. By showing up early in the year, you show your commitment to hunting, and landowners appreciate people who are serious about their endeavors.

The best approach is to ask for permission in person. Figure out when the landowner is home before knocking on the door. You want to catch them when they have a moment. A good time of day is after work but before dinner, or just after dinner. Farmers tend to be around their farms at certain points of the day, sometimes late in the morning. Never approach a landowner early in the morning or late in the evening.

When we begin asking permission we attempt a blanket approach. We spend a couple evenings visiting the landowners in the area we have selected. If for some reason we miss one, we make an attempt to go back.

Presentation is important to gaining access to private property. Dress nicely but casually, and try to dress in a manner that is comfortable to the people you will be asking. A suit and tie probably isn't necessary when asking a rural farmer for permission, but they may be acceptable if you are asking permission in a deer-laden high-end suburb. Camouflage may be a fashion statement in your circle, but it probably won't be to non-hunters, so avoid wearing it when asking permission.

The owner of the property will consider what you drive as part of your presentation. Just as camouflage is not considered a fashion statement, neither is a dirty vehicle or a vehicle with gaudy hunting stickers pasted all over it. The owner will assume this is the vehicle you will drive to hunt there, so it will be a reflection on them as property owners when it is parked in the yard. Go to the door with a smile and be ready for anything; you never know whom you will encounter or what their views are. Remember, at the point of contact you are asking for something, and you represent all bowhunters. Do your best to make a good impression.

Many landowners themselves hunt, have relatives or friends who hunt, have already given permission, or lease their property. Their properties are tied up, and they usually have a short reply to permission seekers that is easy to understand and swallow.

To some landowners, the potential of getting sued is yet another reason they hesitate or refuse to offer permission. After all, we have become a lawsuit-happy society. Some property owners who used to grant permission now refuse or are skeptical. In areas where property owners get pounded for permission, most are not easily persuaded to give it.

Talk politely, and if a landowner invites you to come in to sit down and talk for a while, do so. We thoroughly enjoy the opportunity to sit down and talk to farmers, because they are such interesting people. When anyone takes time to talk with you, he is probably sizing you up and considering granting you permission. The other doors you were planning on knocking on can wait for another day. Even if the door is slammed in your face, be polite, and thank anyone who listens to you for their time even when you get turned down, as you most likely will be.

When we talk to a landowner we always attempt to leave a card with our name, telephone number, e-mail, hunting group affiliations, and as a reminder, a sentence or two asking for permission to hunt. This leaves something in the landowner's hands with which he can remember us or get in contact at a later date.

Ask for permission only for yourself. You can take your wife or perhaps your child, but do not show up with a group of friends, and never attempt to acquire permission for a group of hunters. A landowner is far more likely to grant a lone responsible hunter permission than an entire group. Even if you are initially turned down, you never know what might happen. Perhaps a hunter who has been hunting the property for several years relocates to another part of the country, or the farmer suddenly has a problem with crop damage. Jon Jr. has gained permission from landowners who formerly leased their land but became frustrated with the poor attitude those hunters had toward their property.

Many lease contracts exclude farmers and their families from enjoying their own land, and some people who lease land tend to treat it like their exclusive kingdom. In the past few years, we have encountered numerous landowners who previously leased their property, but now allow hunting only by free permission due to poor behavior of those leasing the property. In such a situation, a farmer is left with no recourse other than to fulfill his end of the contract. One farmer we met was actually threatened with a lawsuit if he entered his woods during hunting season. The card you leave behind may invoke a phone call at a later date, leading to hunting permission from an unexpected source.

When you are granted permission, take some time to establish a relationship with the landowner. The more trusting a relationship becomes, the more solid it is. We have become close friends with several property owners and e-mail and talk to them regularly. Always ask the property owner about his concerns and follow any directions he may give. If the landowner does not want anyone driving across his fields, make sure that doesn't happen, even if it means dragging that buck an extra half mile. Your job is to keep the landowner happy so that you retain permission to hunt his land.

A thank-you card or even a small gift (for example, a gift certificate to a nearby restaurant) to show your gratitude for permission can do wonders in keeping it. If you know the property owner have small children or grandchildren, you can really touch them by giving them something for the children. In the past, we have given Barbie and Scooby Doo fishing combos, kids folding chairs and tables, and tents.

If you kill a deer, offer some to the landowner. They may not take it, but at least you offered. We never promise work for permission, but once granted, if the landowner needs help and we have the time, we are more than willing to help. Property is expensive and there are annual taxes to be paid. Do not take permission for granted; it can be taken away as fast as it can be given.

The Back Door

Another approach to gaining permission to hunt deer is by starting from a different point altogether. Deer are something that most landowners or their families value highly and are protective of. However, landowners consider other activities less important, and those are therefore easier to gain permission for. When we find an area where we would like to bow hunt, but local farmers are not willing to grant immediate permission, we ask to predator hunt. Most farmers aren't all that fond of coyotes, particularly if they have livestock or value deer hunting, and they will often allow predator hunters access. By gaining permission to predator hunt, you have the opportunity to develop a more personal relationship with the landowner during the off-season. You can prove that you are an honest, serious hunter. If you kill any predators, make sure to show the farmer, and share both your hunting successes and failures. Your foot is in the door, so take a little time to sit down and talk, if they signal even the slightest interest to do so. Also, let him know what is happening on his land. Quite often farmers do not have the time to frequently walk their property, and your small tidbits of information about it show that you are interested in more than just killing.

Predator hunting certainly isn't the only avenue of access. Other possibilities include turkey hunting, looking for morel mushrooms, and photography. However, be careful only to ask to do activities you really enjoy. Any landowner will see through your ploy if you are merely asking for permission to eventually gain deer hunting permission with no real interest in your initially requested pursuit. The main idea is to make contact and create a relationship. After a few years of predator hunting, a landowner might reward you with your deer hunting wish. This, of course, may never happen, but on a positive note, you still have access to a piece of property on which to do other things.

Public Land

Depending on where you live, good hunting certainly isn't limited to private property. Every year a large portion of our bowhunting takes place on public ground, and many of our biggest bucks have fallen there. Since public land is often open to anyone who wants to set foot there, you might be asking why we include it in a chapter about access. The answer is that there are several forms of public property where ways of access vary, and to us, access includes using all the tools available to locate and hunt mature bucks. Compared to private land, it is indeed more difficult to find great spots; however, there are public land gems located all across the whitetail's range.

The first step to finding great public land to hunt is to locate all the public ground in the area you want to hunt. There are several tools that will help you do this. We always purchase a quality atlas of any area we intend to hunt; our favorite is from Delorme's. These usually have most public land, game management areas, and refuges clearly marked. The next tool that we use is our plat book. Sometimes tracts of public ground are not marked as such in the pages of the larger atlas. The reasons for this vary, but some areas of public land are very small; are located in close proximity to a town, city, or suburb; or simply aren't listed.

Locate every piece of public land where hunting is allowed in the general area you would like to hunt. Plat books also show the proper boundary lines, which are sometimes obscure on larger scale maps. Some of the tracts may be enormous and well known, and others may be tiny. Once you locate them, sort through the pieces of public land and decide where the best hunting is going to be.

Not that long ago the only way to figure out if a piece of property was worth hunting was to get out there on foot and investigate each tract. The Internet has greatly reduced the footwork, and saved enormous amounts of time, by allowing you to get a preview of any land you want to look at. Before you start on-foot scouting, get online and study topographical photos and maps of each of the public areas. This not only allows you to pinpoint the spots you want to investigate first on a specific piece of land, but the maps oftentimes offer enough detailed aerial photos of the property that you may decide not to even consider them or certain areas within them for deer hunting. This is usually the case on public lands designated for duck and goose hunting, where the property is made up of ponds, marsh grasses, or cattails in water that is knee deep or deeper. You can't get that kind of detailed information from a map in an atlas.

When researching public lands on the Internet to see if they are worth accessing, look for obvious terrain features where you can be certain deer will be found, along with funnels and generally secluded areas. Secluded areas are those that are either a long walk from any access point or road, or cut off from general access by water or swamp. Some obstacles as minor as a waist-deep small stream will keep a lot of hunters from crossing to the other side and therefore from hunting beyond its banks. If it is necessary to use waders or a canoe to get into an area, you will generally have the place to yourself. There is even a chance of finding a landlocked piece of public ground only accessible by boat. There is an area like this that we sometimes hunt in Michigan, and although it is a long canoe ride, the hunting is worth it a time or two each year.

Public lands are sometimes large, and unlike most areas of private property, they may not be sectioned off with roads every mile. These large areas of land keep many hunters from accessing deep into their interiors because most hunters will not walk more than a quarter mile to access a hunting site. In most instances, if you go beyond that, you will have less competition. After previewing all the public land areas, select the tracts that appear most promising and get out there and take a closer look. There are two objectives to this initial investigation. One is to locate deer sign and the other is to locate hunter sign. The goal is to find an area with mature buck sign and little or no hunter activity. We will get more into the scouting process a little later on.

Walk On

Many state DNR agencies pay farmers to open their land to hunters, and on some occasions farmers will open their land in an attempt to curb a burgeoning deer herd. These areas can change from year to year, and they will not be listed on state maps, Delorme's maps, or in plat books. Most states print a small booklet listing these properties. Booklets like these are usually available at local sporting goods dealers. These properties may also be listed on a state game agency website.

Other Land Options

There are other forms of municipal and township land where public hunting is sometimes allowed to manage the deer population, such as city and township property, waterworks property, and many state parks. You can sometimes discover areas like these by researching on the Internet. Check your state game management website or department of natural resources website. Many of these special open-to-public hunting areas will not be highly publicized and will require local research, such as contacting city hall or the local police department. You may have to jump through some hoops, but the hunting may be worth the effort.

Hunting in parks is regulated differently from state to state and even from park to park. Many parks allow hunting by permit only. Most of these are based on some kind of random draw principle. Check both state and individual park websites for detailed information. John has killed several great late-season bucks in Illinois in parks that allow limited hunting. Sometimes a barrier as simple as having to sign in before hunting, or tree step and tree stand limitations, is enough to keep the majority of bowhunters from attempting to hunt these areas.

You might also explore company landholdings. Some larger companies, such as power companies, mining operations, and lumber companies, allow hunting on their land. The systems they implement for allowing hunting are usually company specific, but sometimes they are also directed by state agencies. Any land where access is available is worth investigating. Keep in mind that a lot of areas hold mature bucks, and public land is a good option for skilled bowhunters.

Summary

Gaining access to good land is a project that never ends, because you can never have too many good places to hunt, and in many heavily hunted areas, free access to private parcels is lost at a similar rate as new access is granted, meaning you must stay proactive. Always continue to seek new property to hunt; the more places you have to hunt the more likely it is that a mature buck will reside in one of those areas.

3

SCOUTING TOOLS

Proper scouting and preparing your location play the largest role in achieving success, and both require specific tools. You need to use maps and notebooks while on-foot scouting, and preparing your location requires specific items and tools and physical labor. Like any job, the more prepared you are, the better.

Ideally, you'd be able to pack in and carry the necessary tools to totally prepare a location yet still be mobile enough to walk or crawl through any type of cover. Notice we didn't say comfortably. Scouting and preparing a location should be treated as labors of love, and while you can dress for comfort, your overall venture will likely not be comfortable. During the preparation process, there will be times that you are dead tired, drenched in sweat, filthy, and wished you had put it off for another day and stayed home, but when the final tack is placed and you are back at your vehicle, you will be extremely glad you stuck it out.

Computer

One of your most valuable scouting tools is your home computer. Up until the early 2000s we hand-drew maps, which we still do occasionally, and booked rides in small airplanes to get an overview of some hunting areas. You can do this now with a click of the mouse. A number of websites offer quality topographical maps and aerial photos. Some free online sources of maps are Google Maps, Yahoo Maps, Bing Maps, and Terraserver USA, or you can pay for more detailed higher quality images.

The computer is also a great tool for gathering information. Just a decade ago you had to mail away to states to receive regulations booklets, and now you can find them online. For general information regarding season dates, regulations, bag limits, limited draws, costs, and even locations of various tracts of public land, the computer is an invaluable tool. Every state game agency has its own website with all the pertinent hunting information.

Topographical maps are important tools for scouting. We print maps of any new property we scout and locate points of interest before entering the field.

Scouting Maps

Aerial maps

Before you hit the woods, download aerial photos, one in a small scale that shows the bordering properties and the other in the largest scale available of just the hunting property.

The small-scale aerial map may show bedding areas, funnels, crop fields, and the like on neighboring properties that are not noticeable from your side of the fence when scouting. Neighboring property layouts and terrain features will always affect movements through your land.

The large scale aerial will give a close-up overview of the property that will aid in scouting. We carry this map with us when on-foot scouting and document all pertinent information concerning every hunting location on it for future reference. You might note the type of tree (for when the tree loses foliage), number of steps, entry and exit routes, natural destination food sources such as fruit trees or oaks, scrape areas, etc.

Elevation maps

In hilly or mountainous terrain, also print topographical elevation maps to identify where saddles and ridges are. Severe terrain undulations usually confine deer movement habits in certain points. While deer will transition along the side of a steep slope, they are far more apt to travel along its bottom or top edge where the ground is level.

Map books and plat maps are important tools for locating new property to hunt. Plat maps indicate size and shape of properties along with ownership.

Plat books

Plat books are critical both for finding landowner information and deciphering the exact location of property lines. Plat book information is listed on the Internet for some areas, but the most practical information is still found in book form. Plat books are normally available from the county seat and occasionally in sporting goods stores. These books list landowner names, show the size and shape of properties, and sometimes even have addresses and phone numbers. This is valuable in both searching for new hunting ground and for gaining a bearing on a new piece of land.

We use our plat books as notebooks and on the appropriate page write where we were denied permission, the landowner's name and phone number, and the year we asked. With a yellow highlighter we mark any property we have permission on. We also keep a small legal pad in our plat books so we can go into greater detail with other information about property owners that denied and granted permission.

DeLorme state maps

DeLorme maps show most state and federal public lands, side roads, some non-maintained roads, railroad tracks, and land formations. While we are driving, nothing yet tops the ease-of-use of these maps for immediate local information. We also use these maps as notebooks and highlight any property we hunt. We stow our legal pad notebooks within our plat books, and our plat books and topo maps within their corresponding DeLorme state maps.

Clothing and Boots

Proper scouting ventures require a lot of walking, followed by climbing, cutting, and general hard chain-gang-like physical labor. You need to be in good shape to scout on foot and prepare locations, but you have to be dressed correctly too. It is always critical to match your clothing to the time of year you will be scouting and the weather conditions.

Scouting and preparing locations is mostly done in late winter and early spring, and during this time frame you do not need to be concerned with leaving odor and can wear comfortable, permeable, and durable clothing. We use surplus military pants because they are extremely comfortable, permeable, durable, and have plenty of large pockets for carrying items once the labor begins. We wear long sleeved cotton T's and a jacket to keep from getting poked and scratched when busting through brush and thorn bushes. We wear billed ball caps to shade and protect our eyes.

Gloves

Scouting and preparing locations requires you to push brush and thorn bushes out of the way, climb trees, cut brush saplings and trees, and drag them away. All of these activities are tough on your hands, so during spring scouting ventures when human odor is not an issue, wear leather gloves.

During pre- or in-season scouting, always wear a properly activated and cared-for permeable Scent-Lok suit as your outer layer and carbon-lined gloves and a ball cap to keep your human odor as minimal as possible. We have been using Scent-Lok for the better of part of two decades, and when we've worn our suits for five years, we start using them for scouting only.

If there is a chance of rain, carry a lightweight rain suit. No matter what time of year, only wear the waterproof suit when it rains. Once you start working, waterproof clothing will make you overheat, sweat profusely, and be very uncomfortable.

Boots

When scouting, wear lightweight, durable, comfortable knee-high rubber boots that are waterproof and scent-free. When you are not traipsing through heavy brush, consider knee-high boots with neoprene uppers and rubber soles and side panels, because they are much lighter in weight yet still waterproof and scent-free. Even in relatively dry springs, there will usually be areas of standing water from the winter melt-off, and in the fall you'll want to use them because they don't leave any odor.

When it comes to footwear, quality usually means comfort and durability, and with all the walking and climbing, you don't want cheap boots. Quality rubber boot makers are LaCrosse, Ranger, Rocky, and Irish Setter. On the quality neoprene side there is Muck and LaCrosse.

Tools and Other Items

Over the years we have bought and used just about every conceivable type of location preparation item and tool and have found that some brands simply perform better than others. The poor performing brands of items and tools now sit idle or have been given away or sold. We have also narrowed our tool list down to necessary items, and to save you money and time in the field, here is a list of our favorite brands and a brief explanation of why we like them.

Extendable pole saw

It is nearly impossible to properly prepare a location without a pole saw that extends to at least 12 feet. Hooyman makes a 5-, 10-, and 15-foot extendable saw specifically for the hunting industry. Hooyman uses an aluminum I-beam configuration for the frame, giving it unsurpassed strength and rigidity. The sierra-toothed saw blades are also made of higher quality stainless steel than most of

The Hooyman extension saw is one of our favorite scouting and stand prep tools. Small enough to carry comfortably, it extends far enough to get to hard-to-reach branches.

their competitors. Hooyman's 5-foot saw collapses to 12 inches, the 10-footer to 28 inches, and the 15-footer (with longer saw blade and pruner) to 5 feet.

HME makes a 6-foot extendable saw ($2^{1}/_{2}$ feet when collapsed) with a rope pruner that also works well.

Without question, Silky Saws make the best and likely most expensive saws on the market. They have aluminum frames and extra-long sierra-toothed blades. Due to their cost, Silky Saws are not commonly found in hardware stores; John discovered them in a Stihl chainsaw shop. You can also buy them online.

Corunna, which you can find at hardware stores, has a couple different extendable saws. The only one we use is the 14-footer with rope pruner and sierra-toothed saw blade. The Corunna extension frame is made of tubular fiberglass and the 14-footer collapses to about 8 feet.

Scouting Pack

On a typical scouting venture we carry everything other than our extension saws in our backpacks, and like anything else, you get what you pay for when buying a backpack. A well-made, well-designed quality backpack with padded shoulder straps and a padded waist strap will aid in overall comfort when loaded with all the items and tools you will have in it.

While you can use any backpack, our preference in a scouting pack is Badlands. While we do not use Badlands packs when hunting, for sheer scouting comfort and abuse, there are no better packs. We have been carrying pointed tools and sharp, threaded-edged steps for years and have yet to wear through or cut the reinforced fabric of our 15-year-old Badlands packs. All the major stress point straps are carried through to a second stitch point and are reinforced with Kevlar thread.

Our two favorite Badlands models are the Super Day and the 2200, and they are both tall enough to carry a sheath hand saw and hatchet.

Backpack Contents

We carry the following things into the woods in our backpacks. We are always prepared to get work done as thoroughly, quickly, and in as few trips as possible, and these items, along with hard work, have proven to do the best job.

GPS
For larger areas, we mark our hunting locations on a handheld GPS. This is mostly just a precaution in areas we won't be hunting very often or on public lands where someone may have removed our reflective tacks.

Compass

In some dense timber and swamps far from the sound of road traffic, it is easy to get turned around, so we always carry a decent compass for such occasions. We also use it to get a direct line to the road when making and marking entry and exit routes.

Sheath-carried handsaw

We always carry a long-bladed sheath handsaw when scouting. We use these saws more than any other type of saw—their long cutting stroke allows them to cut trees, saplings, branches, and tall thick-stemmed weeds much faster than a folding saw. We always strap our sheath handsaw to our belt when preparing trees and use it for cutting branches and scraping bark. We can't carry too many items, and these handsaws have replaced the machetes and sickles we carried in the past for slashing tall weeds.

Hooyman, HME, and Coghlans make similar versions of sheath handsaws with aggressive sierra-toothed blades, and they have proven to be our favorite affordable brands. Silky Saws also make several offerings of sheath saws—if you can afford it, they are the best.

Hatchet and belt holder

On severely rough-barked trees (white oak, hickory, choke cherry, etc.), we use a hatchet instead of our sheath handsaw to chop off and scrape bark. We scrape the rough edges of bark around each step so we can climb quietly. We more aggressively chop off and scrape bark at the location in the tree where we hunt with our saddles so we can move around the tree without making noise. To be prepared for this situation we carry hatchets in our vehicles for instances when it is necessary. We don't prefer any particular brands, but look for a hatchet with a wide chopping blade.

Belt

You'll need a waist belt to carry the sheath handsaw and hatchet. We use military-style nylon belts with metal slide adjustment buckles (no gapped adjustment holes) because they are strong, and you can quickly adjust them to any specific length when you are in awkward positions.

Folding handsaws

There are many brands of folding handsaws, and any one with sierra-toothed blades will work well. We like Hooyman, Gerber, Browning, HME, Coghlans, Allen, and Trophyline, for their sturdy frames and locking mechanisms.

Ratchet pruners

These work great for cutting small flimsy branches, brush, briars, and thick-stemmed weeds. Cutting any of these with a saw usually requires both hands, one to hold above the cut location and the other to make the cut. With pruners, that job can be done faster and with one hand. Florian ratchet pruners and HME's ratchet shears are good brands.

Tree steps

While we only rarely use climbing sticks when hunting, even when we do, we still scout and prepare trees using screw-in or strap-on steps because we can carry many of them in our backpacks. When we scout we usually traverse through heavy cover, and climbing sticks or any other cumbersome climbing tools are just too much to tote around and hang-up on brush. Once your scouting is done and locations prepared, you can go back to each location and hang whatever you use for climbing.

Our favorite scouting screw-in steps are based on two criteria: how easy they start and screw in. Our top choice in a non-folding step is Gorilla's $1/2$-inch diameter Vortex step. This step also has deep aggressive knurling on the foot-peg that make it a slip-resistant hand grip for climbing.

Our two top choices in folding steps are both made by Cranford (EZY). The single-fold and double-fold steps are more compact than non-folding steps and are easy to start and screw in. The Cranford and Gorilla steps all screw in without wearing yourself out to get them started.

When we place steps, we leave about 2 feet between them. If we plan on leaving steps in the trees we prepare, we pack in about twenty steps for the first tree and an additional fourteen for every other tree. That is twelve to fourteen to get to our height in the tree and four to six (depending on tree diameter) for foot-pegs around its perimeter to move around the tree while in our saddle. When finished we always take out the bottom six steps so our other steps are not accessible and difficult for other hunters to see. The six we take out and another fourteen are enough to prepare another tree.

We also carry a step starter tool by Ameristep (it is no longer offered by them) that was designed to hold and start conventional screw-in steps in hard trees. It has a long bar for extra leverage to screw in steps more easily. We only use the step starter on our older steps that don't start and screw in very easily.

Whenever you screw in steps, make sure to screw them into the trunk of the tree. In large trees with deep bark (oaks, cottonwood, hickory) always screw in the step between two sections of bark. If a tree has 1-inch deep bark and you screw a step into the bark, there is a good chance that the bark will break off when you put your weight on the step because the threads are not buried into the meat of the tree.

Folding steps are safest for deep-barked trees because the threads can be buried into the meat of the tree (between sections of deep bark) and then the step portion can drop down between the sections of bark where the threaded portion is.

There is only one strap-on step worth mentioning—Cranford's—and we only use them when they are mandatory on public lands. Cranford's seem to stay in place when climbing (they do not kick to the side).

Over time, the straps on strap-ons or on climbing sticks can fray as they slide over sharp bark. While this is rare, if you leave the straps in trees, squirrels and porcupines can chew on the straps. Make sure to check them out from time to time and throw them away if they look unsafe.

Safety climbing harness

This is by far the most important tool to carry because preparing trees is dangerous. A climbing harness has to be safe and comfortable and allow you to have both hands free for installing steps, cutting branches, scraping bark, hanging sticks, and hanging stands.

Several companies used to make safety climbing harnesses, but due to lawsuits, liability insurance rates have skyrocketed and most companies have opted out of the business. We hang from Trophyline Ambush Saddles when hunting from trees, and they also double as excellent climbing safety harnesses. All Trophyline Saddles are approved by the Treestand Manufacturer Association (TMA) and have shoulder straps, leg straps, and safety climbing straps that easily adjust to tree diameters while climbing. Saddles also have a side pocket for the lead strap, and since you will not be using the lead strap when preparing trees, you can use the pocket to store other items such as steps and a folding saw. We have been unable to find any other TMA-approved safety climbing systems on the market and wouldn't consider a non-TMA-approved harness.

Rope

A rope is another required tool because you never know when you may need your extendable saw in the tree to trim out-of-reach branches that may interfere with your shooting lanes. When you need to do this, tie the rope to the saw end and prop the saw (in the collapsed position) against the tree. Ascend the tree, and once you are securely in position, pull up the saw, use it, and let it back down. We always carry a 40-foot long, $3/8$-inch diameter nylon rope with a solid nylon core. The large diameter rope is strong and doesn't tangle as easily as small diameter ropes do.

Reflective tacks, ties, and trail markers

You never want to take one step off course when using entry and exit routes that traverse through timber, brush, marshes, or along any route that is difficult to follow, especially when it's dark, so use reflective markers to mark the course. Wherever trees, hard brush, or hard-stemmed stickweeds are available, use reflective tacks, and in limp brush, tall weeds, marsh grass or cattails, use reflective ties (similar to bread ties). We use about six tacks for every tie.

On private properties, depending on how many other hunters have permission and if we know or trust them, we generally use white reflective tacks because you can see their reflection from farther away than any other tack color.

On heavily hunted public lands (and some private properties), we use brown reflective tacks simply because they are difficult to see in dark-barked trees during daylight. White tacks would be nearly as easy for other hunters to follow as orange flagging tape is. If another hunter saw one of our brown tacks in the daytime and attempted to follow the route, in time he would find our hunting location, but it has not happened to us yet.

Since brown tacks do not reflect as far as white tacks, you need to space them a bit closer together. Use your hunting flashlight to test the reflective distance of the tacks you use before spacing them along any route.

If we need to make a hard turn in the tacking route, we usually place two tacks next to each other as turn indicators. When following tacks that you put in six-months earlier, you'll be worried when all of a sudden there isn't another tack up ahead and you forgot you had to make a 90-degree turn. The double turn indicator tacks will eliminate that anxiety and help keep you from overheating.

Years ago, before reflective tacks were available, John used to buy thumbtacks and put reflective fishing lure tape on them, but now there are many manufacturers (HME, Hunter's Specialty, Eastman Outdoors, Allen, and Primos) that market white reflective tacks. While they all seem to reflect equally well, there is definitely a difference in the strength and quality of the tacks. You may not think that means much, but on hard trees the pin portion on most manufacturers' tacks will frequently bend and have to be thrown away.

HME offers stronger pins that rarely bend as well as a new plastic-headed reflective tack called PRT (plastic-reflective tack). As far as we know, HME is the only company remaining that also offers a brown and orange tack to complement the white ones.

We have only found reflective ties in white or silver, so no matter where we are we have no alternative but to use those colors. When twisting them on, make sure the flat surface of the tie faces the direction you will be coming from; when you tie them on bushes, be sure to break off any branches that may leaf out and block your flashlight beam.

Hang-on reflective markers have a much larger reflective area than tacks, but due to their cost and how easy they are for other hunters to see, we do not use them. If you hunt where there aren't any other hunters, hang-on markers work great, and unlike inexpensive flagging tape, you can gather them after the season.

Water or drinks

We always carry water. How much depends on the weather conditions and the length of time we plan on spending in the field. When we know we are going to be gone for a long period of time in warm weather, we substitute one of our water containers with a thirst-quenching energy-replenishing drink.

Toilet paper

While this needs no explanation, it is definitely better than plucking leaves off a bush.

Chain saw

Some private property owners will allow us to use a chainsaw to prepare hunting locations, and we carry a 14-inch saw for those occasions. When cutting shooting lanes and entry and exit routes, a chainsaw can save a lot of time and energy. When you cut tall trees with 4- to 10-inch diameter bases, you usually have to cut them into manageable lengths in order to move them away from the immediate area, and a chainsaw will make that job much easier.

Neoprene hip boots and waders

By looking at your maps when scouting new properties, you can often tell if you are going to have to cross a river or creek. You can't tell, however, how deep they are or if there will be a fallen tree you can cross on, so you may need waders or hip boots.

Canoe or boat

On several occasions we needed a canoe or boat to access remote areas. One person can easily handle a foam-lined, lightweight, aluminum Radison canoe. Our Radison 15-footer only weighs 44 pounds. On a few occasions, John used a boat with an outboard motor to access his location.

Summary

The list of tools we use is quite comprehensive. You might not need several of these items, and you certainly do not need all these things for every outing. Before scouting we plan for our outing and bring along the items we think we will use.

4

Spring Scouting

Scouting is the most important aspect of hunting. Scouting is the work that makes you seem lucky during the actual hunting season. The more thoroughly and effectively you scout and prepare locations, the better your chances at having mature buck shot opportunities and capitalizing on them. We separate the hunting season into segments, and scout and plan our options for each of those segments. Opening few days, October lull, prerut, main rut, gun season (go out of state), postrut, and late season are our dividing lines, and we always have a specific plan for each.

Postseason

We get most serious about scouting immediately after the season, what we refer to as postseason. In some seasons, we have filled our tags early, and in those years we began scouting afterward, during season. But typically our postseason scouting runs from January through April. Whenever there is snow on the ground, we wait until it melts before doing any on-foot scouting for new locations. While we look for other things as well, our main scouting objective at this time of year is to locate last season's rut activity: We look for scrapes, licking branches, rubs, and converging well-used runways. Snow covers over most of the sign on the ground, making scouting rather worthless, yet as soon as it melts, the ground sign left from last fall will look just as it did before the snow covered it.

Typically Michigan has snow on the ground from late November through late February or even into mid-March. Once it melts and when time allows, we scout and prepare locations until spring green-up makes it too difficult to identify sign. When there is snow on the ground, we continue to scout, but in a different way. We concentrate our efforts on gaining new permission, renewing our old permission for next fall, and researching, via aerial photos on the Internet, new public land options that may have looked interesting during season. During some seasons, we discover new locations that need to be set up for next season, and these predetermined trees and locations can be prepared with or without snow on the ground.

During this postseason time frame, we exert more physical energy than at any other time of the year. This is the time we explore, set up most of our new hunting locations for the coming fall, and prepare our old locations again. There are two principle reasons postseason scouting is so critical to consistent success in pressured areas. The first is that nearly 60 percent of every state's Pope and Young record book buck entries are taken during the rut phases, and postseason is the only scouting time when previous rut sign is identifiable. Scouting and preparing locations during the rut phases for hunting that season is another option, but that is extremely counterproductive for taking mature bucks in pressured areas. Secondly, you can scout postseason without worrying about spooking deer or what effect your intrusion will have on your hunting. Hunting season is many months away, and intrusions in a buck's core area and bedding areas will be long forgotten by the time hunting season rolls around again. Preparing your locations at this time not only allows deer to get used to any visual alterations you make to their home range, it also gives you an element of surprise when you simply appear in a tree several months from now without giving them any prior warning signs.

During our postseason scouting ventures in Michigan, we are aware of the hard reality that the mature buck that made the sign we are studying was likely killed during one of the gun seasons. Once a buck has reached the ripe old age of $2^1/2$ in the areas we hunt, he is a target for nearly every hunter, and he seldom survives beyond that season. However, there were certainly good reasons why a certain mature buck chose his core area, destination areas, and movement patterns. This usually means that when that core area is open and another season passes, by next season another mature buck will likely move in and take it over as his core area, or as a portion of it. Whitetails are very social animals throughout the year, and the $1^1/2$ -year-old subordinate bucks are aware of the secure areas that dominant bucks use and call home, and they know when they are abandoned. And when they get another year under their belt and become more dominant, if the new pecking order allows, they will alter their core areas accordingly.

Getting started

We always begin our spring scouting ventures on new properties we have acquired permission to hunt, where we gained access too late to do a really thorough scouting job, or on new public land areas. Before scouting new property we follow a fairly standard routine. The first step is to print topographical maps and aerial photos off the Internet for any new property we are about to scout. These maps and photos are great tools that not only give us an overview of the area, but they also save us a lot of time by allowing us to pinpoint areas we want to concentrate on. On these maps, it is possible to identify stands of ma-

Before scouting any new piece of property, we consult our maps to pinpoint areas we want to investigate.

ture timber, stands of conifers, ridges, saddles, marshes, swamps, crop fields, lakes, ponds, creeks, rivers, some obvious funnels, two tracks, railroad grades, roads, and undulations in terrain. They also show the exact same features on neighboring properties, and more often than not neighboring property layouts will affect where and when deer transition through yours. Keep in mind that neighboring property layouts are usually not very obvious from ground level on your side of the fence.

What maps offer is an overview of what is on your property and how deer may use your property. Before the days of the Internet and easily available topo maps and aerial photos, we relied on our own feet to get an overview of new areas, making our own hand-drawn maps that were never true to scale. Being able to download exact scale maps not only saves a ton of time, they are much easier to understand and review.

We print two aerials of each property, one that is zoomed out so that it shows the surrounding properties, and the other in the highest zoom available of just the hunting property. While most Internet sites allow you to order a large aerial photo (at a cost), we prefer to print as many fully zoomed-in aerial pictures as necessary and cut and tape them together into one large print. We use these large aerials for scouting as well as for documenting pertinent information and marking hunting sites and entry and exit routes to each location. We only print topographical elevation maps when hunting in hilly terrain to help identify how saddles, cliffs, and ridges may affect deer movements. Some free online sites are TerraServer, Bing, and Google Earth.

We also use plat books and DeLorme maps when scouting. (See chapter 3.)

Scouting tools

During post-season scouting and tree preparation ventures we take just about everything mentioned in chapter 3, the scouting tools chapter. By looking at our maps we can tell if we are going to need waders, or a boat or canoe, and if so we will take them as well. There are very few times we are allowed to use a chainsaw, but we take that too, when we can use it.

Concerning clothing, unlike any preseason ventures into the field—when scent is a factor and we always wear an activated Scent-Lok suit, gloves, headcover, and rubber boots—when scouting after season, scent is not a concern, so we usually wear old military fatigues because they are comfortable, durable, and have lots of pockets to put stuff in when climbing trees. We also always wear knee-high rubber boots because there are usually areas of standing water from the winter melt-off.

In Season

During years we fill our tags before gun season, we scour our primary areas up until gun season in search of in-season rut activity. Since we are tagged out we have no fear of spooking deer, and there is no better time to scout than while the rut is taking place and the sign is fresh. If we find a good spot, we mark it on our maps and wait for our springtime scouting and tree preparation forays before we prepare the location. If we were to prepare the location immediately, our fresh cuttings and alterations would be obvious to other hunters scouting for gun season, who might hunt there and perhaps return the following bow season. We definitely don't want to make it easy for other hunters to find our spots.

Winter

If there is snow on the ground, we may scout immediately after the close of season or even mid to late December after gun season ends. In most areas we hunt, deer movement is altered quite markedly at the onset of deep snow. Bedding areas may change, and preferred food sources often change to places where food is more easily accessible. In certain areas, deer will travel miles from their core areas to yard for the winter, transition routes will change to accommodate new bedding and feeding areas, and daily timing will change as deer require more calories to ward off the cold weather. The better insight we have into how deer react to deep snow conditions, the better we can scout, react, and hunt when faced with similar weather conditions in future seasons.

One year during the late 1980s, we had an early blast of winter. Around October 20 about 10 inches of snow fell overnight. The deer didn't move the evening prior to the snowfall and they didn't move much the morning after, so John figured they had to move early in the evening and feed in the alfalfa field that was the only crop field within miles. He set up a Carrylite decoy about 15 yards out into the snow-covered field so that any deer entering the field would see it, and to make what was a long and exciting story short, he took a nice eight-point that evening that ventured too close to check the fake female out. This was one of the very few times John has ever hunted a short crop field edge.

Late Winter and Early Spring

Typically, our scouting begins just after the snow melts, usually in mid March or April. On new property we follow a fairly standard routine. With our maps in our pockets and our scouting tools comfortably in hand and in our backpacks, we set out to scout. Although we usually have a couple areas in mind that look best on our maps, we always take a complete look at any property we are scouting, no matter its size. Minor terrain features and undergrowth below the tree canopy that may not be visible on any map might be central to deer movement in an area. Every Internet aerial photo we have seen and printed was taken during summer when trees were in full foliage and their dense canopy left no visual clue of how dense or what type of vegetation grew below them. While technology helps, it will never replace footwork.

We move at a fairly rapid pace through open areas, through timber with little or no undergrowth, and along perimeters of crop fields. We only slow down when we get to the interesting areas we noted on our aerial maps or when we

While spring scouting, you should explore every bedding area fully.

see sign or interesting locations that were not identifiable on our maps. In any area, we try to first discover the best hunting spots and take note of possible secondary stand sites. We never prepare any locations until we have thoroughly scouted the area. In our system of hunting, we concentrate heavily on primary scrape areas and isolated mast and fruit food sources surrounded by security cover, but remember, you have to stop and consider the importance of all types of sign. Really good spots are usually a combination of things. A single stand site might be a primary scrape area, staging area, funnel, rub line, and general transition zone.

Potential Hunting Locations

The list below rates the type of sign we consider potential hunting locations. Remember, deer sign can vary enormously depending on the number of deer in the area, habitat, location, food sources, whether corn was left standing nearby throughout the previous season, hunting pressure and general human disturbance, and seasonal variations among other reasons.

1. Primary scrape areas
2. Isolated food sources and water
3. Interiors of bedding areas
4. Funnels
5. Rut staging areas
6. Scrape and rub lines
8. Other sign combinations such as brush- or weed-lined fencerows between crop fields, fingers of security cover that reach out into fields, low spots, holes or gaps in fences, and swale holes
9. Other hunting and human activity
10. Access routes

There are so many variables to consider when scouting; we'll describe general tendencies and characteristics for each of the nine types of locations in the rest of this chapter.

Primary scrape areas

Identification of a ground scrape: A scrape is an area of ground where a buck or bucks use their front hooves to clear away all or most of the grass, weeds, and dead debris, down to bare dirt. Scrapes are usually oval or circular and between 12 and 40 inches in diameter, and large perennial scrapes can be dished out as deep as 4 inches in the center. So you don't misinterpret scratches turkeys leave on the ground after searching for food or dusting themselves, remember that a buck's ground scrape will always be directly under or in front of an overhanging licking branch.

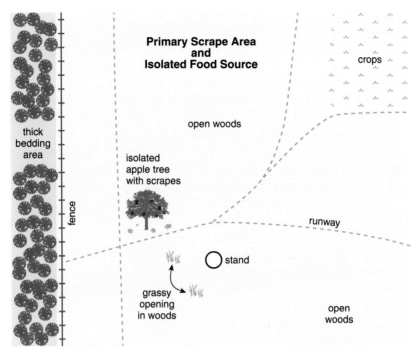

Always place your stand within shooting distance of an isolated food source (about 20 yards).

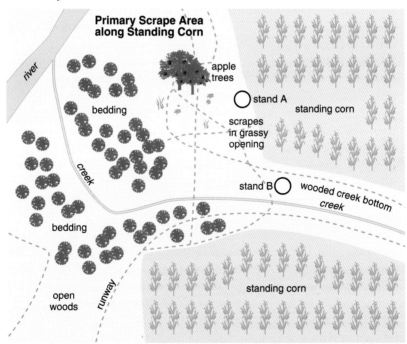

Stand A should be set up within shooting distance of the apple trees and the edge of standing corn. Stand B should be set up within shooting distance of the runway across the creek and the standing corn on either side.

A deer's main sources of communication are scent and body language. With an acute sense of smell, they literally see the world with their noses. Scrapes are scent communication centers, sort of like message boards, that are used by all deer in a population, and the most crucial element of a scrape is the social scent licking branch or branches above it. Deer can mark licking branches with any one or more of their scents. Scents or glands they use include saliva, nasal gland, preorbital gland (also known as the tear duct), and forehead gland (located between eyes and antler burrs). At some scrapes we have witnessed bucks, does, and even fawns socially scent-mark licking branches throughout the year, though the frequency increases in the fall. Though there is no way to know exactly what information is being passed along by the different scents, it certainly leaves an indication of presence, a sort of, "I was here."

Several bucks may work the same ground portion of a scrape, with some leaving a bit more of a calling card by urinating in them. Most bucks do, however, scent-mark a licking branch or several licking branches during each visit. We have also witnessed does close to their estrous cycle squat and urinate in ground scrapes. The ground portion of the scrape will also be scent-marked by every deer that steps in them with the scent from their interdigital glands located between their hooves.

A primary scrape can consist of one large dished-out ground scrape the size of a truck hood, or most commonly a group of scrapes, but either way, the scrape will be in a small, somewhat open area. We have seen scrape areas with a dozen or more scrapes scattered under trees and bushes within the small opening. It is also common to have multiple scrapes under the same tree or bush, and on occasion we have seen scrapes totally encircle the perimeter of a tree.

Each scrape will have at least one utilized overhanging licking branch, and we have often counted as many as twenty chewed, nipped, and marked licking branches over an individual scrape. We consider a scrape's overhanging licking branch or branches to be their primary social component because both genders and all age groups of deer will use them, whereas the ground scrape itself will primarily be used by antlered bucks.

The vast majority of primary scrape areas we have found in perimeter cover have been in small openings anywhere from 10 to 30 yards wide. The opening isn't a specific shape; it could be 10 yards long and 3 yards wide or 30 yards long and 20 yards wide. On one occasion we found twenty-one scrapes scattered along a two track that paralleled a crop field edge. The lane was about 20 yards off the field, the scrapes were strewn along it for about 80 yards, and the lane was a mere 6 feet wide, so that was a primary scrape area of 80 x 2 yards.

A primary scrape area will have multiple well-used runways leading to and away from it, and if the saplings and trees of the right sizes are at or near the area, there will also be signposting (buck rubs) on some of them.

This is a primary scrape area found in the spring. Notice the three large scrapes and overhanging licking branches.

The most common places to find scrape areas are in narrow transition zones between bedding and preferred feeding areas, at or near mast and fruit tree food sources, at a waterhole, along perimeters of preferred crop fields, along perimeters of clear-cuts in areas with no crops, and within the perimeter cover of corners of preferred short crop fields. All of these scrape areas have to do with feeding or drinking. Other than the brief period of when a doe is in estrus and not that interested in feeding, all doe movements revolve around eating and drinking. Scrapes are made to get the attention of does, so that is why primary scrape areas are near food and drink.

Many primary scrape areas are perennial, appearing year after year as long as the nearby food source remains a preferred source and the landscape remains somewhat static. Scrape areas along or near crop fields, for instance, will remain perennial as long as the crops planted are what deer like to eat during the rut in the fall. However, terrain alterations, such as property development or a nearby clear-cut in northern regions where there are no crops, can alter deer movement patterns, causing deer to abandon a previous primary scrape area.

Primary scrape areas located at or near mast and fruit trees can be annual or every two, three, or four years, depending on if the trees are producing and dropping food. Only during the years they produce food will they attract does, and only when they attract does will they become attractive as active scrape areas. The same holds true for water sources: If it is a long dry summer and the water hole dries up, the appeal is gone and so are the does and scrapes.

Primary scrape areas are rarely found in big timber areas with few deer, yet they are fairly common in agricultural areas with lots of deer. They become even more prevalent in areas abundant with deer and little hunting pressure because the mature-buck-to-mature-doe ratio is somewhat balanced and the bucks have to compete more for breeding rights.

The key to recognizing a primary scrape area that is worthy of hunting is to understand deer's seasonal timing, how the scrapes are used, and most important how to decipher what time of day they may be used by the location they are in.

In late summer, or early fall, bucks begin to make scrapes. Generally speaking, the earlier they appear in a hunting area, the more likely it is that a mature buck with previous breeding experience started them. Mature bucks strategically start their scrape activity where there is a natural flow of general deer traffic. Most preseason and early season scrapes will be singular scrapes, and as the season progresses and the rut approaches, the scrapes that are visited and worked by does will usually become primary scrape areas in which mature bucks will begin making more scrapes if the makeup of landscape in the immediate area so allows. The common thread among all primary scrape areas is that they are located in areas of heavy general deer traffic. Once a primary scrape area is established, it seems to attract more attention from all deer in the local herd. If preseason and early season scrapes do not receive sufficient traffic and attention from does, they will be abandoned and likely never opened again during that season.

As rut activity increases, scrape activity decreases because the mature bucks are with does and do not need to signpost as frequently. As the main rut declines into postrut, scrape activity will increase a bit. In pressured areas due to the onslaught of gun season, most rut and postrut scrape activity will be done under the security of darkness.

Does close to, or in, estrus will sometimes gravitate to a primary scrape area and either bed down near it or simply loiter around it while patiently waiting. This, of course, isn't lost on mature bucks because whenever they cruise through their core areas during the prerut while searching for the first does to come into estrus, or during the main rut in search of a new doe, they will pick up on the scent the doe left and take up chase. By no means does the majority of this behavior take place during daylight, but enough of it does that it's important to understand this behavior.

In recent years, many hunters have called scrape hunting into question; they have problems with scrapes because they are hunting the wrong scrapes, mostly short crop field edge scrapes, or their seasonal and daily timing is off.

Studies using motion cameras also call scrape hunting into question. Most studies simply show that the majority of scrape activity takes place after dark, even during the prerut and rut. We agree with those studies, but the key word in the previous sentence that supports our daytime hunting in primary scrape areas is "majority." Anytime you have a majority, there is also a minority. Not all scrape activity takes place after dark. We are more than happy to take our chances at the right types of scrape areas and at the right time of season and day. In pressured areas, that small percentage of daytime scrape visitation is often a mature buck's only point of vulnerability outside of its bedding area.

The main problem with most scrape studies is the human variables, such as the amount of consequential hunting pressure the bucks in the area receive, checking motion cameras, and the methodology that says a scrape is a scrape regardless of location. Considering all scrapes equal regardless of location is a mistake. For instance, it is common to find several singular scrapes scattered along the perimeter of a short crop field, but unless you're on highly managed property, they will only be revisited exclusively after dark. In pressured areas we wouldn't even consider setting up on a scrape along a short crop field, no matter how many scrapes there are or how active they may have appeared to be.

If you find a primary scrape area, you have found something special. To us, scrapes are by far the most complex visible signposts that deer leave. Though we understand a little how scrapes are used, there is certainly more that we don't know. What we do know is that primary scrape areas have been our absolute best hunting locations for taking mature bucks in pressured areas. Primary scrape areas are out there, and if they are in the right type of areas, and offer adequate security and transition cover, they will be your best bet too. When you discover a primary scrape area with adequate cover, mark it on your map. This is a spot where you must prepare a tree to hunt. We will delve into how to hunt primary scrape areas a bit later on.

Isolated food sources and water

Locating any isolated fruit trees, such as apples and pears, and hard mast trees, primarily white oaks, can be integral to a successful hunting season. Isolated individual trees in areas with surrounding cover are simply awesome places to hunt, as long as they are dropping food. Imagine finding an apple tree sagging under the weight of its apples along the perimeter of the best bedding area within miles and completely surrounded by good cover. It doesn't get any better than that. Situations like this can offer a fantastic opportunity at a mature buck, quite often on opening day. A lone acorn-bearing white oak offers the same chance. These food sources are available for a short time only, on a first come, first served basis. Imagine how comfortable a mature buck must feel stepping out of his bedding area and munching on a few apples before moving out into open areas to feed after dark, or stopping by to feed before entering his bedding area in the morning. Even midday forays will be quite normal.

Isolated apple trees, or other fruit-bearing trees, are excellent hunting locations for connecting with a mature buck.

Deer prefer white oak acorns to red oak acorns because they contain fewer tannins, which is the substance that gives acorns their bitter taste. If given the choice, deer will eat all the white oak acorns before touching the red oak acorns. While deer will eat red oak acorns after the whites are gone, the areas we hunt usually have some white oaks available. We concentrate on hunting white oaks.

Because white oaks are so important to our hunting, we have made an effort to understand some of their basic biology. We are mainly concerned about the frequency of their acorn mast. In the areas we hunt, the main white oak subspecies are northern white oaks and bur oaks, which are one-year species, meaning that they are capable of producing acorns every year. They flower in the spring and produce acorns that fall. Though they can produce acorns every year, the time between good mast years is usually longer. One-year species produce a good acorn crop about once every two to three years. Yearly crop failure, due to late frost or insect parasites, is common in all oaks. To make acorn masts even more unpredictable, individual trees in a stand of oaks are not necessarily synchronous. And some trees simply produce more acorns than others. Use this to plan your hunting.

White oaks are easily identified. They have rough bark all the way up the tree and out their branches, and their leaves have rounded lobes. Red oaks have smooth bark farther up the tree and out their branches, and they have pointed lobes on their leaves. During our preseason speed tours we check the oaks for acorns. Oaks that have a good crop are put into our hunting plans.

Apple species also vary in a couple ways when it comes to hunting. Some apples ripen in the summer and drop all their fruit by late summer or early fall, and others carry their fruits well into the rut phases and even beyond. The trees that drop their fruit early are only good for hunting during the early part of the season because the apples will be gone well before the rut phases begin. Their apples are generally fully developed and yellow by mid-August and begin dropping around the same time frame. Most species of apples found where we hunt drop their apples in the fall and often throughout the main rut. These apples are usually green or red throughout the summer and are fully developed and dropping by our season opener. There are also differences in sweetness between apple species, and deer prefer the sweeter apples.

When postseason scouting, you can identify apple trees by their shorter height and mass of sprawling branches. When scouting in April, you can identify them by their blossoming buds, but we have never been able to tell what type of apples a particular tree will have. If an apple tree is in the right type of location, we set it up, and when we go back to do our preseason speed scouting tour, we check it out. Once we know what type of apples a specific tree produces, we note it on our maps for future reference.

Wherever fruit and mast trees are in limited supply, there will be competition for the food they drop. Finding a couple fruit trees or white oaks in an area otherwise devoid of them can be a shortcut to a nice buck. On evening hunts, if you allow several deer to pass undisturbed, a mature buck may arrive to feed beneath one of these trees during daylight.

Water is something, like food, that deer can't do without. As we inspect our aerial photos before scouting, we can usually tell if water is abundant in the area. The maps show ponds, creeks, rives, ditches, and low-lying swamps. When we scout an area with little water, we keep our eyes open for any water sources and pay extra attention to small waterholes, such as deep puddles or pools of water in an otherwise dry ditch or creek. Depending on the weather, an isolated water source in an area otherwise devoid of it can be an excellent hunting location at any time of day or any season. In a location like this, during unseasonably warm weather, deer will visit and drink water throughout the day. The majority of activity will take place either in the morning, as deer stop to get a drink on their way back to their bedding areas, or before heading out to feed in the evening. On hot days there will be midday traffic as well. If you can stand the heat, hot days call for all day sits. The morning and evening drinking routine will remain constant, but when it is really hot, a good isolated water hole will usually see some action during the hottest part of the day, usually between 2:00 and 4:00 p.m.

The sheer amount of activity at such waterholes means these spots transform into communication centers with several nearby scrapes and rubs. If the surrounding area has perimeter and transition cover, mature buck may signpost in the daytime. Some waterholes can be premier hunting spots, even in years with normal precipitation.

When you find isolated food sources or water you should select a nearby position. Once finished, mark it on your map. You will only know if these trees will be worth hunting next fall after your preseason tour to confirm mast, fruit, and water.

Interiors of bedding areas

Although bedding areas are third on our list, we spend more time per acre scouting them than any other type of terrain. During our springtime scouting, we walk through and inspect any and every possible bedding area on any new or old property we are scouting. Bedding areas can vary tremendously in makeup, but they are usually a bit thicker than the surrounding terrain, where the deer are least likely to be disturbed by hunters. There are several reasons hunters rarely scout and hunt in bedding areas. Gun hunters shy away from them because they can't see very far and they have a long-range weapon. Bedding areas are often very difficult to access and require waders or a canoe, which immediately eliminate 99 percent of hunters. Bedding areas usually have extremely dense ground cover that requires more work to scout and even more work to prepare a proper location and make an entry and exit route. The number one reason hunters stay out of bedding areas is that they like to leave them as safe buck sanctuaries.

Locating crossing points or transition areas in the interior of bedding areas must be done postseason or in the spring.

Right: Sometimes excellent hunting locations can be found by crossing rivers or other bodies of water.

We too used to stay out of bedding areas, but that has changed over the last decade. A bedding area, like a home, is usually a relatively small area when compared to the unlimited directions a deer could go and unlimited places it could be outside. The more confined the area, the more apt you are to encounter a buck. And mature bucks in pressured areas spend most, if not all, daylight hours in bedding areas during the early portion of the season, and a good portion of daylight hours in bedding areas during the rut phases pursuing does. Only if you have total control over a couple hundred acres, or are in a large, antler-restricted cooperative with neighboring property owners, should you leave a bedding area as a sanctuary. If you have either of those luxuries, you are not hunting pressured whitetails.

Bedding areas come in many forms: swamp grass interspersed with trees and brush, cedar swamps, timber with thick understudy, dense cover along rivers and creeks, and areas of autumn olive or brown brush with interspersed trees. Any of these bedding areas need to be thoroughly scouted for isolated mast or fruit trees, converging traffic areas, rub clusters, rub lines, and even primary scrape areas. Bedding area hunting locations can be incredible hunting spots, but only if you follow a very specific plan.

You should only hunt inside a bedding area when you can commit to hunting all day. You must be on stand at least an hour and a half before daybreak and only depart well after dark, so you don't spook deer with your coming and going. When hunting in any other time frame, the likelihood of spooking deer is very high. The goal is always to hunt without pushing deer from the area. The other part of that strategic plan is to only hunt interiors of bedding areas during the rut phases. This is when a mature buck may search the area for estrous does. A small bedding area should also never be overhunted, not more than two or three times per season. Hunting interiors of bedding areas like this will eventually pay dividends.

The interiors of some bedding areas—such as tall CRP weed fields, cattail marshes, and standing corn—generally require a natural, or pop-up, ground blind. Look for points of concentration such as converging runways inside such bedding areas, or small dry islands within a wet marsh. While weed fields and cornfields may receive some bird hunting pressure, or hunters walking through or around their perimeters, cattail marshes are about as free of human intrusion as the bottom of a lake, and big bucks know it. John took his second largest buck from an island, knee deep in water in a cattail marsh on public land. Any

Cattail marshes often provide secure cover for mature bucks, and they should be thoroughly scouted postseason for hunting possibilities in the fall.

locations prepared in CRP fields and cattail marshes will need to be revisited during preseason to cut new growth in the blind area and shooting lanes.

Deer will bed just about anywhere that provides security from disturbance. Over the years we have encountered many areas where deer bed that just didn't make sense to hunt. Since we concentrate so much of our seasonal efforts into the short rut phases, we pass on substandard bedding locations that don't have enough adequate sign to warrant a hunt.

Funnels

A classic funnel is a narrow neck of woods connecting two larger woods, but funnels can vary widely, anything from a saddle between two steep hills or ridges, a tall weed-filled ditch through an open field, or even a brush-filled gap between two houses. Some more subtle funnels can be as inconspicuous as a point of grass extending into a field, a narrow area of heavy undergrowth in otherwise open woods, or a farmer's grown-over two track through some thick brush. All funnels are in areas of transition cover where deer movement is bottlenecked or pinched to a narrower, more confining point. There will almost always be other, more exposed routes that deer can take, but the majority of deer movement going from point A to point B in a particular area passes through these more protected areas of transition cover. Funnels used by bucks will have

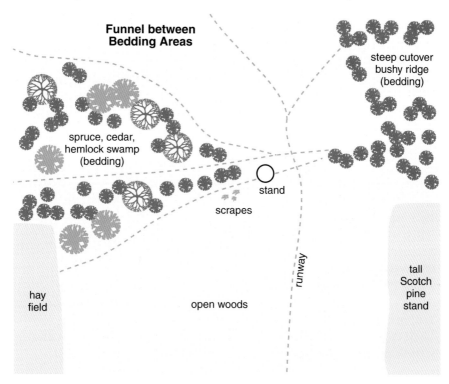

rubs and possibly an occasional scrape scattered throughout the length of the transition route.

Finding a good funnel for hunting is all about determining what is at each end of the travel route the funnel connects. In our scouting system, the most important type of funnel is a travel route between two bedding areas. This type of funnel will be less obvious than most typical food-to-bedding funnels. This is because travel along these routes is almost exclusively the domain of bucks during the prerut and rut. During the prerut and rut, bucks use funnels between bedding areas when scent-checking for estrous does. Hunting this type of pinch point during the rut periods can be paramount to success.

The next type of funnel we look for are funnels between bedding and feeding areas. These are along main corridors where both does and bucks travel. This is what most people think of as funnels and travel routes. All deer have to eat and do so every day. When scouting, each and every route between each and every feeding and bedding area should be identified and inspected to determine when deer use them. We pay particularly close attention to funnels in close proximity to bedding areas. Since bucks are generally the last to exit bedding areas in the evening and first to return in the morning, the closer you are to the bedding area, the better your chances for a mature buck. However, you must be able to get to this point undetected, so a balance must be met between proximity of your stand to the bedding area and entry and exit paths that allow you to get there and depart without spooking the deer.

We set up funnel locations for the early and late parts of the season depending on the types of food sources that are connected to the bedding areas. Our rut phase funnel locations are set up according to the bedding areas between them and if the transition zone connects to a primary scrape area.

Rut staging areas

A rut staging area is where a buck lays in wait for does to pass by and checks for receptivity during the rut phases only. Rut staging areas are sometimes difficult to identify because there may not be much tangible sign for a hunter to see. Generally, they will be within some form of cover, perhaps even an adjacent bedding area, that borders a more open area such as a short crop field or a stand of mature oaks with sparse undergrowth, with an open view for some distance in the direction that does may approach from. The cover could be as obvious as a tall-weed-lined and overgrown fencerow, a depth of woods, on the edge of a swamp, or even within the perimeter rows of a standing cornfield that borders another short crop field. The main components are back cover and a line of sight to approaching deer. Primary scrape areas located within the perimeter cover of a short crop field or stand of mature oaks are also often used for bucks to stage in. These are the easiest rut staging areas to identify.

John learned how bucks use rut staging areas in the late 1970s. Back then he followed a typical hunting routine: On morning hunts he would usually be on stand about 15 minutes before first light. He also overhunted his premium stands. During the prerut in a spot where a cedar swamp bordered an open stand of mature white oaks, he would always spook a buck bedded along the edge of the cedars with his entry. John knew it was a mature buck by the strong rutting odor left behind. The first two times it happened he was simply upset at a missed opportunity. When he bumped that buck on his third trip to that location he stopped in his tracks and the bells finally went off. That buck was bedded (staged) in a position where he could see or hear every deer that came through that stand of oaks after daybreak. From that day on we began calling that type of location and behavior rut staging areas.

A rut staging area is a spot that offers a buck the opportunity to intercept does either on their way back to their bedding area or on their evening routes from a bedding area, and remain in the safety of cover while doing so. If danger approaches, usually in the form of a hunter, the bucks just vanish into cover, most of the time completely unnoticed by the hunter. This is a movement pattern that causes many hunters to consider mature bucks totally nocturnal.

By staging this way, bucks are able to avoid danger and save energy. They avoid danger by being in the security of cover before daylight, and if they do intercept a hot doe, they are already within some form of security cover and will attempt to guide her into thicker cover during the chase. They save energy by letting the does pass by them, instead of chasing them all over the countryside.

Staging is what a buck might do before daylight when returning from a night of pursuing does. We have also seen and taken bucks that had staged in the early afternoon in hopes of intercepting evening doe traffic. Whenever a staged buck intercepts an estrous doe, he will take up chase. The most common times mature bucks stage are before daylight until late in the morning. If nothing catches their interest, they will rise and scent-check their core areas. The midday movement patterns of mature bucks during the prerut and rut are often followed by staging in a secure afternoon location that overlooks evening doe traffic. Obviously these locations are nearly impossible to access without spooking the bedded buck. John took one of his all-time favorite bucks at an afternoon staging area in which the buck was bedded a mere 40 yards from the tree he set up in. Winds over 30 mph that day masked John's entry, and when the buck John had been pursuing for four seasons stood up to leave the area, John about fell out of his tree in shock.

Mature bucks tend to display rut staging behavior more in heavily pressured areas than in lightly hunted ones, and more in farm country than in big woods areas. Any buck that reaches maturity in a heavily hunted area will have already learned to use a solid strategy for survival; otherwise he would not have lived that long in the first place. In less pressured areas, there are more mature bucks, making the competition for does more intense. This means bucks will be on their feet and in pursuit more, and in less pressured areas, bucks are less likely to be targeted at a young age and don't necessarily experience the dire consequences of encounters with hunters.

Rut staging takes place more often in a landscape that has defined feeding and bedding areas, as most agricultural areas do. Staging in big woods where deer density is lower and bedding and feeding areas are less defined is less effective for the bucks that spend more time on their feet cruising for receptive does. While big woods bucks will stage, their core areas are generally several times larger than those of bucks in agricultural areas, and the areas in which they may stage are even less definable than in agricultural areas. If they stage, it will be in a general transition zone or at a location overlooking a preferred feeding area such as a stand of oaks.

Rut staging areas should not be confused with what most hunting literature generally refers to as staging areas. The difference between a rut staging area and common staging areas is in their purposes and possibly locations. Common staging areas are locations where bucks move before dark and hang back before entering the nearby exposed feeding area later in the evening or after dark. This is generally an early season behavior; bucks are concentrating more on feeding than on rutting activity. Unfortunately for those hunting in pressured areas, mature bucks simply do not make any more vulnerable movements than absolutely necessary, and their previous experiences have taught them that stepping outside the security of their bedding area before dark can be extremely hazardous to their well-being, so they stay within the confines of their bedding area until after dark before moving to any exposed feeding areas. So in pressured areas feeding staging areas are almost nonexistent.

Rut staging areas are similar in design to the more-written-about feeding staging areas, but their appeal is strictly based on breeding, and their seasonal and daily timing is totally different. When scouting, be aware of how these areas work and keep an eye out for such areas, because the buck sign, other than maybe a few rubs, will not be noticeable during postseason. We have often discovered these subtle areas during season when spooking bedded bucks with our entries, and when we do we make a mental note to set up a location after season for future seasons.

Scrape and rub lines

A scrape line and or rub line is a travel route with intermittent singular scrapes or several rubs along its path. We have never seen a scrape line without accompanying rubs, but it is common for a rub line not to have accompanying scrapes. We can only assume through our observations that scrape and rub lines are social as well as territorial markers and that they are occasionally made

John inspects some scrapes. Scrape and rub lines are types of sign that give you a lot of information about the bucks you are hunting.

strictly out of frustration due to high levels of testosterone and lack of breeding opportunities.

When spring scouting, we often travel through the woods on deer runways; after all, runways are sign, they are the easiest routes to follow, and we don't care if we spook deer or leave any odor. We walk down runways in both directions to see where they go, and we note any rub lines or scrape lines that were made and left along the routes bucks transitioned down during season.

We look for a combination of sign to justify a hunting site, and most of the time a rub line or scrape line will lead through a funnel to a primary scrape area, a staging area, between bedding areas, or most commonly between a bedding area and a food source. You may also find them along runways that parallel a preferred crop field's edge just inside the bordering cover. Just like any other sign we find, we attempt to decipher what portion or portions of the season the routes were used, whether the route or area offers enough security cover for a mature buck to move through during daylight hours, and if that particular buck was taken last season.

If a line of signposting leads to a food source, that source is an indicator of when a buck was using it. If it led to a crop field, find out what was in the field, whether soybeans, corn, alfalfa, wheat stubble, or something else. For instance, deer primarily feed on soybeans throughout the summer and early fall before they dry and turn brown. A scrape or rub line that leads to a beanfield was probably made prior to or early in the season. On the other hand, a scrape or rub line between two bedding areas was probably used during the rut phases, when a buck was pursuing does throughout his core area. Understanding when deer eat what and when bucks abandon their early season bedding-to-feeding-area routines will give you an idea of when or if you should set up along that line. There is no sense waiting until the rut to hunt an early season rub line or hunting a rut phase rub line early in the season. Movement patterns by mature bucks will vary over the course of the fall.

Sometimes a mature buck will have his own early-season route that is seldom, if ever, used by other deer. Scrape or rub lines may be the only indication of these unique travel routes. Always be on the lookout for these lesser-used, sign-laden trails because they could be excellent to hunt early through the October lull, if the area they transition through offers adequate cover. Unlike destination areas, such as isolated food sources and primary scrape areas that attract many bucks from the local population, an individual buck's rub or scrape line may not be used by another buck once that buck dies.

You can read a little into the buck's behavior and size by inspecting his rubs. A rub line between a bedding and feeding area with all the rubs facing the bedding area was probably made in the afternoon, evening, or after dark as the buck was leaving his bedding area to feed. It would also indicate that it was used early in the season when he was constantly moving from bedding to feeding. Rubs mainly facing the feeding area were more likely made in the morning as the buck was returning to bed down. It is quite common for bucks to take a circuitous route, alternating between morning and evening movement corridors. This explains one-way rub lines and should help you decide if a line is worth hunting and when. A rub line with rubs facing both directions, however, indicates both morning and evening or after dark travel. Rub or scrape lines found between bedding areas or going to a primary scrape area were likely made during the rut phases, and if the security cover is adequate, they could be used at any time of day.

Rubs themselves can give some indications about the size of the buck that made them. As bucks age, they grow taller, their antlers extend higher off their head, and they grow taller tines, all of which make their rubs higher off the ground than that of subordinate bucks. Young bucks generally rub an area from 14 to 30 inches up the tree, whereas older bucks' rubs reach as high as 48 inches.

The rub itself can also give clues to antler size and characteristics. Young bucks generally have narrow spreads and short tines and tend to pick on saplings and trees with diameters of 6 inches or less. Young buck rubs are also typically rather smooth, as if someone rubbed a pipe up and down the trunk. Large-racked bucks generally rub on trees with larger diameters and occasionally shred bushes. Large-antlered bucks will rub on smaller trees and bushes as well if that's all that's

A rub tells you something about the buck you will be hunting. A rub like this is a good indication of a mature buck.

Right: A rub like this one on a fencepost usually indicates a really good buck or two.

available in the immediate area, but they will rub larger trees within their core area too. Mature bucks that only rub on small-diameter trees usually have an antler form that doesn't allow them to rub larger trees, such as main beams that are close together at the tips. When a rub is seriously frayed—strips of hanging bark and deep gouges in the trunk—it was likely made by a mature buck with heavy pearling around its bases and or very short points. Further markings to look for that verify mature bucks are extra tine signatures well above or to the side of the rub, tine scratches on trees or offshoots that share the main rub's base, and rubs on horizontal branches above the main rub.

None of these things will tell you exactly what a buck's antlers look like; they are just general tendencies, and indeed several bucks may rub on the same tree. Some larger rubs are even perennial, meaning they get rubbed every season and by many bucks, and these are most often found in good hunting locations with combinations of other sign, such as at a primary scrape area, in a tight pinch point, or at an isolated mast or fruit tree. During an evening hunt in 2008, John witnessed four different subordinate bucks come to an isolated apple tree and rub on the same small nearby sapling.

In pressured areas, a mature buck that develops and follows a unique travel route will stick to it from year to year as long as feeding areas and hunting areas remain the same. Mature bucks have survived when using them so there is no reason to change. If that buck is not around anymore, the route may not be lost; other mature bucks in the area, either those that move in or those in the area that grew to maturity, know that route was abandoned.

Our best results from hunting scrape or rub lines have been during the first few days of season when bucks may be caught off-guard in their daytime summer routines moving from bedding to feeding areas. In pressured areas, rubs and scrapes made by mature bucks between the first few days of season and the rut phases will be primarily made during the security of darkness. Once the rut phases begin and mature bucks start moving during daylight hours, we may hunt rub or scrape lines, but we will always reconfirm that they are being used before hunting them.

When we locate a scrape or rub line, we first analyze it to see whether it is worth hunting, and if so, we mark it on the map.

Other sign combinations

There are numerous other sign combinations that we look for such as brush- or weed-lined fencerows between crop fields, fingers of security cover that reach out into fields, low spots, holes or gaps in fences, and swale holes.

Fences and ditches

In some agricultural areas, overgrown fencerows and ditches are sometimes the only cover between fields and woods. Since bucks will use the best available cover to their advantage, in areas where these are the only available transition cover, you should inspect them. In one area Chris hunted, a wide, brushy, deep ditch connected two squares of woods about a half-mile apart. During most falls, the ditch was dry. Even though the ditch took a more circuitous route out along the edge of a cow pasture and through a picked beanfield, there was a small runway along the bottom of the ditch, and every year it was lined with buck rubs. Bucks in the area would cruise from woods to woods during the prerut and rut, staying completely out of sight.

We always inspect fences that separate areas of cover for holes, gaps underneath, downed or low spots, or obvious crossing points. Although they are not natural, these are a form of funnel. We have watched deer walk over a hundred yards out of their way to walk through a downed area of fence or a gap with a chain across it instead of having to jump over it elsewhere. For several years throughout the mid-1980s, John hunted a spot where the property own-

Ditches and fencerows are often used as travel routes. This runway along a deep overgrown ditch is a good example.

ers on either side had left a gap in a 4¹/₂-foot-tall wire fence wide enough for a tractor to drive through. The property on one side was a tall open stand of Scotch pines, and on the other consisted of open woods with tall undergrowth. There was a sprawling beech tree 20 yards from the gap, and the deer would walk well out of their way to avoid having to jump the fence.

When we discover a crossing point with enough cover for daytime activity, we select a location and possibly even alter the fence to our benefit. This may mean propping areas of fences back up, or blocking a hole, either of which would entice deer to our spot. Be creative and you can funnel deer closer to your stand just by giving a length of the fence in both directions a little attention. We may prop a portion back up with tall forked sticks or fill in holes with sticks and branches, but we never do anything without first getting permission from the property owner.

Grassy buffer and fencerows

Other points of scouting interest are grassy buffers and fencerows that divide cornfields. These buffers can become well-used travel routes. They provide excellent security cover and are easier to walk along than the dense corn or sorghum, especially when the buffers connect to woods or other crop fields. Setting up a pop-up blind or natural ground blind made of corn stalks a few yards into one of the fields is a good option along these buffers for a couple different reasons. The first is that mature bucks tend to take up daytime residency in them and will sometimes travel these buffers during daylight, even during the October lull, when they normally only leave the corn under the cover of darkness. The second is that if these fields are still standing during the prerut and rut, bucks will cruise these buffers both to scent-check for estrous does that crossed from field to field and to use them as funnels between bedding areas. Setting up these types of locations is described in detail in chapter 23 on corn.

Fingers and points

Narrow fingers of tall vegetation, overgrown brush, trees, or any combination of these that extend into fields are terrain types where we have had some success over the years. These fingers usually form a sort of interface between the woods and the surrounding farm country. Deer naturally gravitate to edges and points. They serve as both travel routes and communication centers. Since most deer in a population will pass through these areas, it is common to find them being used as both primary scrape areas and staging areas, even if they happen to be some distance from the nearest woods or natural bedding areas. This is especially true during years they are surrounded by corn.

One area we hunted for nearly ten years was a narrow draw filled with trees and brush that extended half a mile into crop fields. The draw ended in the field and adjoined a large woods at the other end. There were never less than fifteen scrapes and countless rubs there every year. This spot was always good but par-

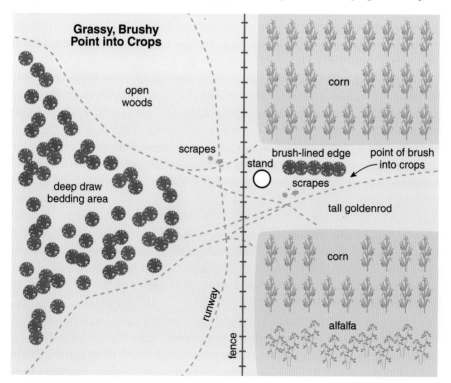

ticularly productive in years that the fields were in corn. During the fall when corn was present, much of the local deer population bedded in the corn. In season, bucks would heavily mark the draws' edges because it was the only place there were trees and bushes at an interface. When draws, or sometimes ridges, extend into crop fields and are wide enough and provide security cover, bucks may use them during daylight. Anywhere we find points extending into crops, or even CRP fields, we inspect the area as a potential hunting location.

Swales

Swales are small, low, wet spots in fields, points that are most of the time too wet to farm. Sometimes they contain thick brush and tall weeds that offer excellent cover. A swale can be a small safe haven for deer because people rarely walk through them, and hunters overlook them because oftentimes they are out in the middle of open country. Also small swales are sometimes impossible to hunt because you can't get close to them without spooking any deer inside, especially when the surrounding crops are short. The only years swales can be successfully hunted is when the field surrounding them is in corn. We suggest you scout any swales on your hunting property, and if they look promising, set up a location for the years the surrounding crops are in corn.

If you find a swale where a buck is bedding and it is impossible to get close, there is another option. In the late 1980s, John was hunting a location that had a small swale in the middle of a large weed field and a buck bedding in it. There was absolutely no way to hunt in, or even close to, the swale. John's solution was to walk through the swale from time to time just before season and during the first couple weeks. His goal was to force the buck to a nearby wooded area where he hunted. The first three times John walked through the swale, the buck burst out the other side. By the fourth and fifth times, the buck was gone. John ended up taking that nice seven-point buck later in the season. Sometimes you just have to be creative and think outside the box.

Single oaks and fruit trees

Occasionally you will find a single white oak or a fruit tree in the middle of a field. These trees should be hunted as you would a swale. The difference is that you can only hunt these trees when they bear mast or fruit and are surrounded by standing corn. If you find such a tree, prepare to hunt it when conditions are right. During seasons when corn is growing there, always make a late summer trip to check the trees for fruit. If fruit is present, quickly prep the location for later hunting.

Every bit of sign counts

Just because a parcel of land may not contain a primary scrape area, isolated apple tree, or good bedding area doesn't necessarily mean it isn't worth hunting.

We have taken mature bucks from land that many other hunters would scoff at because it lacked features and sign. On the other hand, we have scouted a few pieces of property where we just threw our arms up and thought, nothing on this property warrants a hunt. But typically, if deer are using a piece of property, there is some way to hunt them. It usually boils down to correct seasonal and daily timing and how frequently you hunt there. In order to be successful, you might have to hunt in an unorthodox manner, such as hunting only the early season, only when temperatures are high, or only as long as the corn is standing. You may have to wait out the early season and only hunt during the rut, or wait even longer and hunt after the rut is over and the deep snow and cold has set in. In most pressured areas, you'll have permission to hunt on small parcels that rarely offer as many options as larger parcels do. On sub-par properties, you need to scout and take into consideration every sign combination possible. There is no patent way to bowhunt, so try to be as adaptable as possible, be patient, and have a strategy that best suits what you have to hunt.

Other hunting and human activity

Nothing affects deer movement more than consequential hunting pressure and general human presence. On every property we have to hunt in Michigan, there are other bowhunters, with even more on surrounding properties. Depending on the property, there may also be pressure from small-game hunters, upland bird hunters, and perhaps even duck hunters. Public lands and some private prop-

Sign left behind by other hunters is just as important as sign left behind by deer. In this case a gun blind is very obvious.

erties may have other non-hunting activity such as walkers, bicyclers, kids on quads, and even property owners in golf carts. All these activities are out of your control, but they affect deer movement patterns. Therefore, it is critical while scouting to note any human activity on any parcel of land.

As we scour a property for deer sign we are looking at the same time for any sign of other hunters and human activity. We follow any marked or obvious trails used by hunters. Any cut sapling stumps or other sign of cut vegetation will immediately catch our attention. When we find another hunter's location, we inspect it and try to decipher the ability of the unknown hunter. How high is his stand? Is it in a good location? How far is it from a parking spot? Does he have adequate shooting lanes cleared? Was he using bait? We glean as much information as we can from the stand and stand location itself. The main questions you want to answer are: Why is this guy hunting where he is? What effect will he have on the deer movement in this area? And how can I react to, or benefit from, his presence?

Most of the time you will encounter bowhunters with average or less knowledge, ability, and time. This means the hunter will have just a couple stands. His hunting will take place primarily the first couple days of the season, then afternoons on the weekends, and perhaps a few more days of intense hunting around the rut. In most situations, an incomplete scent control system will be an issue, as is overhunting stands, and most of the mature bucks will simply turn nocturnal prior to or shortly after the beginning of the season due to his presence. In this situation, you need to find out how the deer avoid that hunter and hunt accordingly by selecting other areas to hunt during the rut phases.

How other hunters hunt and what they do on the property is out of your control. We have encountered the complete spectrum of hunting ability and occasionally some downright unusual hunting tactics. The most common situation is hunters heading to and from their stands at prime time, at the crack of daylight and a half hour before dark. Another common mistake these days is driving a quad basically to a stand. We have often encountered still-hunting bowhunters who think a walk through the woods in perfectly still conditions is still hunting. You never know what type of hunter you may run into in the deer woods, so be creative and make an attempt to adapt to their hunting if your land options are limited.

It also doesn't hurt to ask the landowner when the other guys hunt. He will usually have some idea when, and how often, any hunter on his land hunts. For instance, if another guy only hunts weekends, then adjust your schedule during the rut to hunt on Thursdays and Fridays. If he hunts only evenings, hunt mornings. In most cases the other guy isn't a real threat to the mature bucks in the area, and if he impedes your hunting a couple times, just laugh it off and adjust.

Knowing the amount and intensity of gun hunting pressure will help you make decisions about bowhunting. The amount of gun hunting pressure on the

John scouts the edge of a field that was planted in corn last fall. Crop rotation is always a major consideration while planning hunting strategy for the upcoming season.

land you hunt and surrounding properties will help you decide when and how to hunt. If a piece of land gets heavy gun pressure, you can expect more hunters a week or two before the gun season opener, as they scout and prepare the land. You may have to alter your hunting plan for that area, choosing to hunt within that sanctuary bedding area on the property during that period, for example. The most noticeable result of really heavy gun hunting pressure is the near elimination of mature bucks. In much of Michigan, somewhere between 80 and 90 percent of bucks are killed within the first few days of gun season. This means that you must capitalize on any opportunity at a mature buck before the guns start blazing.

Small game and duck hunting are other human activities to consider while scouting. We always ask property owners if there are any pheasant, squirrel, quail, or partridge hunters who hunt the property. Pheasants and quail are usually hunted in the same CRP weed fields and standing cornfields that deer often bed in, and when hunted with any regularity, the deer will quit bedding in them. A mature buck may tolerate being pushed out of a bedding area once or twice but usually not more than that before taking on a new bedding area. Duck hunters sometimes have the same effect, though they concentrate on marshes and bedding areas around water.

You need to know where the deer go after these disturbances begin. Generally after a few days of bird hunting, any deer that had bedded in the fields were pushed into places more easily bowhunted from trees and less attractive to bird hunters. Bird dogs will assure that any deer that happens to be bedded will depart. These alterations in movements may turn out to be a good thing during the rut.

Some hunters have capitalized on openers of bird and squirrel seasons by knowing where the deer escape routes are and setting up on them before the small game hunters set out. This, however, is not something you can tell by scouting but rather through a season or two of hunting and observation. Once you learn the escape routes, you can also set up in the same locations when farmers pick the corn.

Non-hunting activity

Walking trails and other recreational activities are normally constant in areas where they take place, and the deer in those areas become habituated to them. This type of human encroachment effects deer movement in a couple different ways. One thing we have found in areas with well-used walking trails is that the deer movement avoids the human trails during daylight and will often parallel it through better cover. The deer know full well where the humans are supposed to be and will accept their presence from the security of cover, often standing still allowing people to walk by. One example is a property we once hunted that bordered a large grassy field, on the other side of which was a well-used feeding area. The neighbor walked her dog on a trail around the edge of the grass field every morning just after eight o'clock. The deer, in that particular spot, crossed back to the woods every morning just before she started her walk.

Another area Chris hunted was in a suburban area that was laced with walking trails. The deer on that property had developed a system of trails that paralleled the walking trails, mostly keeping 40 or 50 yards away from them. The deer seemed to know the locals who walked those trails, and their dogs. When people were on the trails, the deer would simply freeze, allow the walkers to pass, and then continue on with their routine. The mature bucks in that area used the areas with the most cover and were far less likely to be on their feet during daylight than the does and fawns. Interestingly, in this area there was heavy deer activity as long as the foliage was still up, but as soon as the leaves dropped, the deer almost completely abandoned the area for larger woodlands in a neighboring section.

Mark all human activity areas and other hunter's stands and blinds on your map. Sometimes patterns will become obvious that reveal deer safe areas and even perhaps a funnel induced by human activity that wasn't apparent by terrain features alone. On some larger properties where we have marked such things, it becomes instantly apparent that most people, hunters included, will not walk more than a quarter mile from a road or trail. Gaps may become apparent, and you will know where to concentrate your subsequent scouting and hunting.

Access routes

The best hunting location in the world is worthless if you don't have a way in and a way out. You must plan your entry and departure routes for each location so you don't spook deer. This seems obvious, but judging from the stands we find as we scout, the concept hasn't hit home for some bowhunters. We would rather walk an extra mile and have a chance at a mature buck than walk a short distance and potentially spook the deer we intend to hunt.

It's not simply about long walks, though. Whenever you find a spot you want to hunt, you should ask yourself, What time of season will a mature buck be attracted to and pass this point? What arrival time does this location require to intercept a mature buck? Where may the buck be when I approach my stand? How do I get here without spooking deer? How can I depart without being detected? If you can't answer these questions, you have more work to do, and if there is no way to get to, or out of, a spot undetected, you might consider finding another location, or developing a tactical plan knowing full well that you will spook deer.

Access routes for hunting morning stands must be such that you avoid the area where the deer spend their nights. This means you cannot cross the fields that you expect the deer to be chasing or feeding in. Look for terrain features that provide some cover, along edges of head crops, such as corn and milo, that allow you to slip behind the lines, or a shallow creek bed, ditch, or gulley you can walk through.

For evening hunts, you can walk across the center of the very short crop field the deer will be coming out into to feed; however you have to be able to retreat by another route with good cover. Spooking deer when you leave can be as detrimental as spooking them when you arrive, and many hunters pay no mind to it because it just doesn't affect that particular hunt. Do this a couple times and the afternoon deer movement by mature does and bucks may completely dry up in that field, not to mention pushing any mature buck with any sense into a more nocturnal routine. Many bowhunters simply climb out of their stands just after dark with no concern for spooking the deer that just walked past them. Bad hunter exits have saved the lives of countless mature bucks.

A proper entry and exit route usually means a huge amount of extra work. We often spend as much or more time creating and marking a viable access route to a tree as actually prepping the location itself. We try to keep entry and exit trails as inconspicuous as possible, while creating a good path that we can follow well before sunrise or after dark. We always try to keep our stand locations as invisible to other hunters as possible. In pressured areas, and especially on public lands, other hunters may find, disturb, or even hunt known spots. We attempt to avoid any conflict by remaining as invisible as possible. A route to a stand might mean creating a long trail through an entire swamp or long woods with dense undergrowth.

We attempt to create routes that we can follow without leaving any sign that they are trails. When we scout or hunt, we always look for paths created by other hunters. Our natural instinct is to follow them to see where they lead, and we assume other hunters do the same. Use natural terrain features as a guide for your route, if you can. There is no sense marking the entire edge of a wood line with reflective tacks, if it is so obvious that you can walk along it in the dark. Oftentimes hunters go overboard with their trail markers, making them far too frequent and obvious. If you have to cut or mark a trail make it as inconspicuous as possible, and if you can, use existing game trails. We incorporate existing deer trails into our own trails whenever possible because they often do not require reflective markers. Deer will also incorporate portions of our trails into their transition routes just as we do theirs.

Reflective tacks and ties are important pieces of equipment, but use them sparingly. You should be able to follow your own tack line, but make it almost impossible for someone else to follow. Unless you hunt your own property that has no other hunters, the last thing you want to do is put a white reflective tack at eye level every couple of yards all the way to your stand. You'll be asking someone to follow your trail to your stands. When you use reflective markers in areas where you are concerned about other hunters finding your locations, use dark brown tacks, which are far more difficult to see against dark bark in the daytime than white tacks (see chapter 3). Also, place your tacks well above the normal line of sight, above the normal beam of light hunters shine on the ground on their way in. If you put them too low, the new growth of summer may obscure them when you go back during season. Use two tacks in a tree to signal a turn.

When you finish your entry and exit routes, draw the route as precisely as possible on your hunting maps. Be careful to mark any turns or landmarks that you will use to get both in and out of an area. If an access route is tricky, note the more difficult portions either on the map or in a notebook and add a reference on the map. Before hunting that spot, refer to your notes and maps to refresh your memory. See chapter 5 for more on preparing entry and exit routes.

Scouting and Map Logbook

In our notebooks, we number and list all the hunting spots and make a few quick notes about the best seasonal time to hunt the area; best seasonal and daily time to hunt each spot; amount of cover; species of tree so we know when it loses foliage; reason we chose it, such as nearby mast, fruit, or scrape area; how many steps we need to ascend; if it is a morning, midday, or evening spot; whether we need hip boots or waders; the best wind direction; and any other information that might be of interest. We hope to begin each season with several hunting properties and a notebook full of specific hunting locations with detailed notes for each. After we do our preseason speed tours, we browse through our maps and notebooks to create a specific plan and review our notebooks to remember exactly what we have to do when hunting each location.

On a separate page at the back of the notebook we list the trees we plan to hunt for each portion of the season. We try to prepare for each portion of the season, listing the four or five best trees for the early season, the five best for the October lull, prerut, rut, and so on. Of course, hunting strategy can literally change with the wind, but having a solid plan for the entire season helps to follow a solid rotation and builds confidence because we know we have something ready for most eventualities.

Summertime Scouting

After postseason scouting, we turn our attention to more general scouting, which means concentrating a bit more on land access acquisition. There isn't much to do in the summer unless you happen into new hunting property, in which case you can follow the same routine as in the spring, but avoid the inside of bedding areas. There is still enough time to do general scouting, as long as you finish in a day or two, to allow the deer to resume normal movement patterns before hunting season begins. The best plan for the summer on already-scouted properties is to leave them and the deer alone, shoot your bow, go fishing, get in shape for fall, and enjoy the nice weather.

5

PREPARING TREE SADDLES AND STANDS

After you have thoroughly scouted a property, you have pinpointed trees that need to be prepared for hunting. Return to the best spots first, and work in reverse order until you have all your stand locations completed. This work is the most physically demanding portion of bowhunting. Much hunting literature says it takes only a couple minutes to prepare trees to hunt from. What could be easier than walking into the woods and running a tree stand up a tree? Everyone should be able to get this done in a matter of minutes, right? This simply isn't so, if you want to do a thorough job that will allow you to get shots at mature bucks when they pass within range.

Most of the trees and locations we prepare to hunt from take us hours of work to get just right. On an average, we take around three hours of work per location, but working with a partner can cut that time by more than half, and in a full day of prepping trees, we can get about three trees ready. Between scouting and tree prep, we take several weekends in the spring to get a piece of property just right.

Why a Tree Saddle

Deer movement is never static, and over time deer evolve habits to find new ways of eluding predators, including hunters. In the pressured areas we hunt in Michigan, mature deer actually scan the trees looking for hunters. We are not talking about a deer picking you out because they notice your silhouette, or because you are sitting too low in a tree—these deer continually look 20 to 30 feet up in trees for hunters. You've got to see it to believe it. As hunters, we need to adjust our hunting styles to deer's ever-changing defenses and movement patterns if we want to achieve regular success. The absolute best tool we use for achieving this is a tree harness hunting system, the tree saddle. We do the vast majority of our whitetail bowhunting from a tree saddle. Here are our reasons.

A tree saddle and a climbing stand side by side: The small size, comfort, and expanded opportunites the tree saddle provides make it our hunting stand of choice.

Ambush Tree Saddle benefits

1. **Cost.** With a single $200 saddle, the number of trees you can set up and hunt from is limitless. If you had the time and the hunting land, you could have a thousand trees ready to hunt before season, without incurring added costs.
2. **Weight.** The Ambush tree saddle weighs a mere $2^1/2$ pounds compared to between 7 and 23 pounds for a conventional stand.
3. **Bulk.** The Ambush saddle is made of quiet nylon fabric, so you can roll it up and put it in your backpack or wear it around your waist. This makes it easier to get to your hunting spots and change locations.
4. **Few tree limitations.** Unlike conventional stands that are limited to specific tree diameters, a saddle allows you to set up in trees from about five inches in diameter to several feet. While some stands will adjust to trees that lean, the saddle can be used in trees leaning as much as twenty degrees. Basically, you find a good location and make a nearby tree work.
5. **Branches.** Unlike most climbers where the tree trunk must be free of branches in order to ascend, you can adjust your climbing strap around the branches with a tree saddle.
6. **Setup noise.** While most modern hang-on stands have nylon straps instead of noisy adjustment chains, their large frames still have to be carried or pulled up into position and hung, which can make noise. It's also

The hunter is set up and ready to hunt. He can easily swing around the tree so his body profile is hidden from deer entering from any direction.

difficult to be quiet while ascending a tree with a climber. Saddle setups are quiet, and that is a big deal when hunting close to bedded deer.

7. **Safety.** When it comes to safety, the saddle is unique in that it comes with its own safety climbing harness system so that you are safely tethered to the tree from the moment you leave the ground until the hunt is over and you step back to earth. It is almost impossible to fall out of, even if you happen to briefly fall asleep.

   The tree saddle is probably the safest stand hunting system on the market. Since the inception of commercial tree stands, and safety straps used in conjunction with them, many hunters have fallen and been severely injured or killed. Many models of stands over the years were poorly designed or improperly manufactured. Most of the old tree-stand safety harnesses also had design flaws when it came to safely distributing and supporting the weight of a fallen hunter. When hunters were injured because of faulty product design, they sued the manufacturer, and in several cases these lawsuits put the company out of business. Lawsuits became so prevalent that responsible stand manufacturers banded together to form the Treestand Manufacturers Association (TMA). TMA now inspects tree stands, safety harness systems, and hunting harness systems and essentially dictates what is allowed into the marketplace. TMA is so important in today's hunting marketplace that very few stores, due to liability insurance issues, will carry any stand that isn't TMA certified. (Trophyline tree saddles are TMA approved.)

8. **Fear of heights.** Once you get used to sitting in a saddle (and there is a learning curve), you will gain a sense of security because the tree trunk is right in front of you. When sitting or standing on a conventional stand, you are facing a wide open freefall, and if you are afraid of heights, this can be intimidating. The security of knowing that you are always tethered to the tree and that the tree is in front of you at all times will help eliminate your fear of heights. In areas where mature deer look for hunters in trees, setting up higher in the tree will put you farther above a deer's peripheral vision and likely provide more shot opportunities.

9. **Hunting locations.** With a saddle you can prepare as many trees as you want and hunt them all with a single saddle. It is common for deer activity to change during season, and you can adjust to the changing activity with a saddle. Rotating hunting sites increases the element of surprise, which is critical when pursuing mature animals.

10. **Hiding.** In pressured areas, most mature buck opportunities occur after the foliage has dropped. Deer seeing hunter silhouettes against an open sky is big problem for conventional stand hunters. With a saddle you can quietly move around the tree and use the trunk to hide behind. We do this to allow deer we are not targeting to pass. For shooting purposes, you can remain mostly hidden until you make the shot.

11. **Noise while hunting.** Unlike metal stands, a saddle doesn't have a creaky seat or platform that squeaks when you shift your weight during a shot opportunity. In cold weather, you don't have to be concerned with noise from crunchy snow or ice on a metal platform.

12. **Shooting mobility.** While hunting from conventional stands, there is a zone behind you where it is impossible to shoot. This no-shot zone varies in size between 45 degrees and 180 degrees, depending on the setup. Mature bucks don't always conveniently come where they are supposed to, especially during the rut phases when bucks are pursuing estrous females on unpredictable routes. In heavily pressured areas, your odds of getting a second opportunity at a mature buck during the entire season are extremely low. Being able to shoot a full 360 degrees around a tree is a notable advantage.

13. **Comfort.** Many hunters who consider purchasing a tree saddle are concerned with comfort. They cannot imagine that hanging from a harness could be as comfortable as sitting in a conventional tree stand or ladder stand. On the contrary, we find our tree saddles to be far more comfortable than any tree stand or ladder stand we have ever hunted from for several reasons. The first is that you sit in a position sort of like leaning forward in a slanted easy chair. Your knees are slightly bent and either slightly straddling or against the trunk of the tree. The second reason is that you are facing the trunk of the tree and can rest your head on the lead strap in front of you. And third, without the confinement of a platform or solid seat, you can adjust your sitting position, which keeps your muscles active and limber, as opposed to trying to remain perfectly upright and motionless in a tree stand, which can cause muscle fatigue and cramps.

14. **Theft.** On every property we hunt in Michigan, public or private, treestand theft is an issue. Most hunters who don't own land can relate to this. It is a major letdown when you get to your tree only to discover your stand has been stolen. Because you always carry your tree saddle with you, you don't need to worry about theft.

15. **Shooting.** Shooting from a saddle is much easier than from a conventional stand. When you correctly move into a position for a shot, you will be in a somewhat standing position. Both of your feet should be securely resting on steps and your body securely braced, with the lead strap, to the tree. When properly set up, it is more comfortable to shoot from a saddle than from the ground. We feel we can shoot more accurately as well, because our upper body is braced. No matter what type of weapon you shoot, the more parts of your body that are braced, the more accurate you will shoot. In a standing position, only your feet are braced.

A saddle will change the way you hunt and increase opportunities.

Chris's 2008 Michigan Cruising Buck

Some hunting stories just aren't that long. It was the first week of November 2008 and I had just unexpectedly returned early from a successful hunting excursion in the suburbs of the Twin Cities. Since I had some extra time, I decided to hunt a spot that I hadn't hunted in two years. It wasn't that the tree wasn't good, it was just that it wasn't exceptional, more of a public land secondary spot, where anything could happen, and about a mile walk. My tree was along a marsh that was a mix of brush and cattails with small patches of poplars, basically a midday cruising route for rutting bucks. There were a few lightly used runways that paralleled the bedding area. Though I had hunted this spot occasionally over the course of about six years, I had never even seen a buck there, just a few does. The area, though, looked too good to give up on, and I knew that eventually something good would happen there.

To get to the tree two hours before daylight I had to get up at 3:00 a.m. The long walk woke me up and I slid up the single straight trunk to about 30 feet. The trunk was nestled into the branches of a pine, which provided good background cover. It was cold and still and in the twenties. I tucked myself into my saddle and dozed through daybreak, and typical to my prior experience at this spot, nothing happened, at least as far as deer activity is concerned. There were plenty of squirrels and birds to watch throughout the morning. The hours slipped by slowly as the temperature rose. Just after 11:00 a.m. I looked at my watch and decided to give it another hour.

No sooner had I decided this I looked up and saw a tall rack floating though the brush, along the runway that paralleled the bedding area, and moving steady. Immediately I took my eye off the buck and grabbed my bow. Returning my focus to

Location Preparation and Tree Saddle Setup

Selecting a tree

You'll have several trees to choose from at most prospective hunting locations. One tree will always be better than the others, because the sign will be most concentrated there. Unlike a conventional tree stand, which limits the trees you can hunt from, a saddle allows you to select a good general hunting location and usually allows you to hunt from the best tree. You do not have to settle for a tree that is somewhat out of position because your stand wouldn't fit on the best tree. A better position means more shot opportunities.

Although the saddle allows you to shoot in every direction, you still need to take several minutes to select a tree. The most important variables are the loca-

Chris killed this buck as it cruised for does late in the morning.

the buck, I noticed the doe he was following about 20 yards ahead of him. Only seconds later the doe walked quickly straight down the runway and crossed through an opening at 23 yards. The buck would be there shortly. Before I knew it I drew my bow and was about to blat to make the buck stop when he stopped on his own. The arrow was on its way immediately. At arrow impact the buck just flinched a little and didn't even seem to notice that an arrow just passed through his chest. With one eye on the buck, I reached for another arrow as he stood there, still looking at the doe. The arrow was just about knocked when the buck sort of crouched, hunched his back, and shuffled about 30 yards before dropping. The long-tined eight-pointer didn't even know what hit him. Some spots simply take time. 🦌

tion, size, and type of tree. Beyond that, consider what time of season the tree loses its foliage, what time of season you plan on hunting it, the height you need to be at in that specific location pertaining to seasonal timing and available cover, background cover from other trees, the amount of lane clearing it will require, and whether the slant of the trunk is best suited for right-handed shooting. Initially we walk every runway in a potential hunting spot while inspecting every potential tree. The best tree is the one where you can get the most shots to the most runways. If there is more than one suitable tree, choose the one that provides the best cover.

There are a few more things to consider when selecting a tree. When a location is good, but the tree doesn't provide much cover, go a bit higher. Use the

A tree saddle allows you to shoot a full 360 degrees around your tree. Shots straight behind you are no problem.

trunk as cover when deer approach. In small-diameter trees in transition areas, if the immediate situation calls for it, stand upright on the steps and hug the tree so that you can't be silhouetted. This is handy to allow deer you aren't targeting to pass through. Sometimes the margin between remaining undetected and getting a shot is thin.

Do not set up in trees with small-diameter trunks at destination points where non-targeted deer typically linger for long periods. This would only serve to further educate the local deer and lead to frustrating hunts. Because we are right-handed, we also look for trees where our most likely shot opportunities will be to our left. We try to set up for a shot distance of between 15 to 20 yards. Although you can shoot a full 360 degrees from a saddle, the best shots are the ones where you don't have to maneuver at all.

The lean of the trunk is also critical when selecting a tree to hunt from. Just about every tree in the woods will lean in one direction or the other. Set up on the upper side of the lean similar to being on a ladder. This way you can sit in a comfortable, relaxed position, leaning your upper body forward. If your saddle setup is on the bottom side of the lean, due to gravity, you will be essentially hanging directly below the trunk, which will become very uncomfortable very quickly. The straight down lead strap will not allow you to comfortably lean forward. In this position it is also very difficult to move around the tree because gravity is working against you.

This tree is set up for a tree saddle. (The exact spot is the second trunk from the left.) This tree provides fantastic cover but would be difficult to hunt out of with a conventional tree stand, so the saddle is the ideal solution.

After selecting a tree, walk each runway again and mentally note where the shooting lanes must be. A single shooting lane should cross more than one runway. The goal is to have as few shooting lanes as possible yet have a shot to every runway or destination point. If you have more than one shooting lane option to the same runway or runways, choose the lane that requires the least amount of clearing so as not to alter the area any more than necessary. Before you begin cutting the lanes, however, clear the actual tree. The only way to know exactly where your shooting lanes need to be is from the exact position you will be shooting.

Tree preparation

After selecting the location in the tree, start out just as you would to set up any conventional stand. First, don your safety climbing system with an adjustable strap for differing tree diameters when preparing trees so that you have both hands free for placing steps, cutting branches, and scraping bark. Every saddle comes with a TMA-approved, 9,600-pound-test adjustable climbing safety strap for the sole purpose of having both hands free while preparing trees, ascending, hooking-up at the top, and descending during a hunt.

Place your steps at the base of the tree, beginning on the right side at knee height. Placing your foot on the first step, use your knee to measure for the next step on the left side. Continue until you arrive at the height you intend to hunt. Unless we are in a tree with an exceptional amount of cover, we normally hunt at least 25 feet off the ground and most of the time around 30 feet. Depending on how tall you are, elevations of 20 to 30 feet require somewhere between twelve and twenty steps.

When you reach your desired height, place steps around the entire trunk about 6 to 8 inches apart for standing on and maneuvering. Four to seven steps is usually sufficient. In trees with large-diameter trunks, the three or four steps on the front side (where you will be hanging from) will all be parallel to the ground, and as the steps progress to the back of the tree they will need to be placed $1^1/2$ inches or more higher per step. The front side steps are both footrests and

John preps a tree for a tree saddle by sawing off branches that may impede a shot, scraping loose bark from the shooting area, and placing steps.

leverage for maneuvering around the tree. The steps on the back side of the tree are placed higher to compensate for the lead strap shortening as you move around the tree. In areas where screw-in steps aren't allowed, you can place several strap-on steps around the top and overlap their straps.

After the top steps are in place, stand on the two steps you will rest your feet on and attach the lead strap. While the instructional DVD that comes with each saddle suggests you tie off the lead strap at arm's length, we prefer a shorter lead. We tie off a bit higher on larger trees so that there is enough lead strap to allow us to move around the tree, but we never tie off at arm's reach. Two important criteria are met with this lower lead strap tie-off. As opposed to hanging nearly straight down with the lead in your face, you will be leaning back into the seat with your upper body leaning forward toward the now more severely angled lead strap. When you lean back into your seat, you will have much less side pressure on your hips and it will be much easier to adjust your weight and drape, all of which add to the overall comfort during a long hunt. Second, with the angled lead, when you straighten your legs to take a shot your body will automatically rise and the lead will be at even more of an angle and totally out of the way for shots to your immediate left (if you are right-handed). During the drawing process your elbow will not even come close to hitting the lead strap.

Once you have tied off the lead strap, feed the opposite end of it (from below) under both cinch straps (straps connecting the front two corners of the saddle) and connect the V portion of the adjustment buckle on the lead strap to the hook at the end of the tied-off lead (the hook should be hanging below the tied-off knot). Then loosen the cinch strap all the way out and adjust the lead with the adjustment buckle until you are in a comfortable sitting position. During the entire time you are preparing the tree, make sure you are securely fastened to the tree with the safety belt. After attaching the lead, feeding its opposite end under both cinch straps, attaching the V side of the lead strap's adjustment buckle to the hook end of the lead strap (below the tied-off knot), loosening the cinch straps all the way out, and then adjusting the lead strap so that you are in a comfortable position, somewhat seated, you can remove the climbing safety belt and continue preparing the tree. This is the exact same position you will hunt from.

Decide on a position to hang your pack (ours is usually on the right side, somewhat to the back side of the trunk). Screw in a bow holder there and leave it upside down so that the top loop strap on the pack fits in the slot between the tree and the holder. By placing your backpack farther around to the right side (past 90 degrees), you keep it out of the way if you need to swing to the right for a shot opportunity, yet it is still within easy reach.

Select a place to hang your bow while hunting. We always place ours on the left side of the trunk with the grip about waist level so we can easily reach it with as little movement as possible. We never hold onto our bows while hunting from a tree saddle. We also place another bow holder at the same height but farther

John shoots from a tree saddle set up in a group of Scotch pines.

around to the left, toward the back of the tree. While hunting, if a shot opportunity appears to be coming farther around the tree to our left, we will lift the bow off its hanger and reach around and place it on the hanger farther around the tree. Now we can move into position with both hands free and still not have to hold onto the bow while waiting for the shot to present itself. It is better to rest comfortably with your hands tucked into your pockets or a muff and grab your bow when you need it, instead of holding onto it all the time. Holding a bow for any period of time isn't really practical from a tree saddle.

With the lead strap securely fastened, move around the tree, look for and cut (with your handsaw) any branches that may interfere with a shot opportunity. You might need an extension saw. The last thing to do at the top is to cut or scrape bark. Many trees have ragged and loose bark that needs to be removed to guarantee you do not make any noise when moving around the tree for 360-degree shot opportunities. Some conifers have thin, scaly, paperlike bark that is easily scraped off with the back side of a handsaw. Thoroughly remove any bark that could make noise, concentrating your efforts on the areas around the steps and at knee level, where you are in constant contact with the tree. Now you can turn your attention back to your shooting lanes.

Shooting lanes

You have already begun to plan your shooting lanes from the ground. Now you should double-check and make your shooting lane decisions. You can only be certain of the exact location of a shooting lane from the exact point from which you will be shooting.

Return to the ground to begin clearing. When clearing your shooting lanes, cut all forbs, saplings, brush, and trees level to the ground. Then cover all their stumps to make them disappear. Cover sapling and brush stumps with leaves or moss, and on stumps 2 inches in diameter or larger, rub dirt into their exposed white surfaces and then cover them with debris such as dead branches, bark from old deadfalls, or chunks of old stumps. The objective is to make the shooting lanes inconspicuous and not easy for other hunters to recognize. When you do this preparation in the spring, new summer growth will make your shooting lanes look completely natural by the time most other hunters start scouting.

The width of the shooting lanes depends on the hunting location. If you are setting up in a small destination point where deer will loiter, such as at an active scrape area, staging area, or at a mast or fruit tree, you don't need to make shooting lanes any wider than 4 feet. If you are in a transition area where deer have no reason to stop, make the shooting lanes 6 to 8 feet wide to assure you have the space to stop them for the shot. Once the shooting lanes are finished, there won't be any runways within shooting range that you cannot shoot to. Remove every branch, stick, weed, or anything else that could possibly deflect an arrow. If you leave a branch, thinking you will be able to shoot around it, it will come back to haunt you.

This shooting lane points to a convergence of runways in thick cover.

Make sure you block runways that are out of bow range. By doing this in the spring, the deer will adjust their movement closer to your tree by fall.

The width of your shooting lanes also depends on how often you intend to hunt a particular spot and how much cover you have from the tree. Any location that will be hunted more than three times per season should have narrower, more subtle shooting lanes. You also need narrower lanes when hunting from a tree with little background cover.

While clearing shooting lanes, you might need to go up and down the tree several times to make sure every lane is perfect. When you are completely satisfied, remove the bottom six steps from the tree. By removing the bottom six steps, you keep them out of sight for other hunters, and the remaining steps are hard to steal. The work, however, isn't over yet.

Next you need to inspect and possibly alter runways. Whenever a runway that feeds your location passes through heavy cover, walk it for at least 50 yards in either direction to open it up. A clear, wider runway may cause deer to select that route as opposed to a more congested one. Bucks with wide spreads also tend to prefer more open routes, if there is a choice.

Alter runways that are out of your comfortable shooting range. Block them with deadfalls or other brush and debris. Then widen an existing alternative, or create a new path that brings the deer closer. On occasion we have also cut completely new narrow trails through thickets and small bedding areas in hopes of creating runways to our location. Deer are creatures of habit, and if given a choice, they will take the path of least resistance, as long as it is through what they feel is a secure area. Altering or creating new runways in the spring gives the deer time to adjust and incorporate the new route into their daily routine by fall. If you do this preseason, you warn the deer of the approaching hunting season and most likely push any mature buck into a premature nocturnal routine.

Next carry or drag every sapling, branch, or bush from the hunting location to an out-of-the-way spot. Make sure that it all disappears from sight, even if that means dragging cuttings as far as a hundred yards. You can tuck them under low-hanging brush, stand individual cut saplings into nearby sapling thickets so they look natural, or toss them in gullies. This usually requires cutting larger stuff into manageable lengths before dragging it away. The idea of moving everything away from the hunting area is the same as cutting stumps as close to the ground as possible—you must remain inconspicuous, especially in pressured areas, even if you have sole permission for a property. Unless you are there to regularly patrol the place, people will walk through.

A final inspection of the spot should reveal an area that looks a little disheveled but natural enough that with a little summer growth it will be difficult to identify as a hunting spot.

Lastly, when the location is ready to hunt, choose the best entry and exit routes, and if necessary, mark them with reflective markers. Always try to complete the preparation work, rather than leaving it for a later date.

6

Scent Control

S cent control awareness and scent reduction technology are probably the most important developments in bowhunting over the past twenty-five years. If all other factors remain the same, strict attention to scent control will have a hugely positive effect on your hunting success rate. If you are not taking advantage of a full range of scent elimination technology in controlling your human odor, you are unwittingly missing opportunities at mature deer.

It is impossible to totally eliminate your scent, but with a thorough scent control system you can reduce your scent signature to such a low level that it becomes nearly impossible for deer, or any other game animal for that matter, to detect you. Our opportunities at mature bucks, and deer sightings in general, have increased tremendously since we began seriously implementing scent control products in the early nineties, despite hunting in nearly the same manner as before. Over the course of a couple decades we have become totally committed to a strict scent control regimen. Serious attention to scent control has become a cornerstone of our hunting system and has provided us with some incredible bowhunting moments that otherwise never would have taken place.

Just Play the Wind?

Before scent-reducing and scent-eliminating products hit the market, "just play-ing the wind" was the only number in town. And even today we hear countless hunters claim there is no other option, meaning they believe scent control is useless and that there is no way to fool a deer's nose. To put it bluntly, that is sim-ply not true. You can fool a deer's nose. We do it almost every time we hunt. But let's step back and start at the beginning, with a normal hunt in the days before we implemented a strict scent control routine.

Stepping out the door of our house, we would check wind direction, or if we were driving, we would look at a flag. Having a host of trees ready for the sea-son, we would then select an area or spot that was good for that particular wind. Hopefully the wind would remain constant and not change direction or swirl. It

78

was common that some trees we saved for the rut phases would never get hunted because the wind direction necessary for those locations never occurred during that short time frame or during the time we had available to hunt.

When we selected and prepared trees, we would occasionally have to ignore the best tree and pick a secondary tree better suited for the prevailing or swirling winds. Secondary tree choices usually put some of the runways or signposts that would have been within shooting range of the best tree out of range. Swirling winds are always a factor when there are undulating terrain features such as saddles, hills, and ridges. And before the leaves fall, a line of trees can act like a brick wall, and even a constant wind will not totally penetrate the wall of foliage made by the line of trees. A portion of the wind will turn when it hits the wall and follow its edge, and if that edge changes direction, as it does in the corners of fields and in small openings within timber, the wind will swirl. Knowledge of terrain features and foliage walls that naturally created swirling wind helped us decide which trees to set up in, and oftentimes we would even get winded in our secondary trees and have to totally abandon the location. To state that wind dictated where we could hunt more than deer activity did would be an understatement.

We tried to take routes to our stands that didn't cross any runways that we expected deer to use on their approaches. Although we took a page out of the trapper's manual and even then wore knee-high rubber boots, we left a line of scent along our entire path to our stand. This faint ribbon of scent was the first point that alerted deer to our presence. Anyone who has ever hunted bear, or even deer during the rut, knows that you can easily smell when a bear, or rutting buck, has recently walked through an area. Imagine what we must smell like to animals with a sense of smell hundreds of times more sensitive than our own. Basically, a thin blanket of human scent covered the entire area downwind of our entry trail. Any deer approaching from downwind of the scent line would, at a minimum, be on higher alert than normal, and we are certain that many deer simply smelled us and didn't appear.

Climbing into our tree, we hoped the wind would remain constant, so then we would know there was only one downwind direction that a mature deer would not come in from. If the wind switched directions or swirled, as it often did, our chances of seeing a mature buck basically evaporated. It was not uncommon, especially when the foliage was on, to suddenly hear snorting from downwind without a sighting. When non-targeted deer appeared from upwind and passed within shooting range, or even far out of range, they often crossed at some point into our wind, or crossed the path we took to our stand, and spooked. Once they stomped their hooves or snorted and spooked, we rarely had a deer we wanted to take come within bow range during that hunt. On occasion, a doe that was being pursued by a buck would spook, and that hunt was abruptly over as well.

Of course, sometimes hunts worked out perfectly, and we arrowed a mature buck, but having deer spook was part of the routine. After hunting an area, or a single location, a couple times, the number of deer sightings would decline to almost nothing. The spot would be contaminated with our scent, which the mature does and bucks were able to distinguish well after we departed, mostly after dark, and naturally they avoided the area during daylight. Our hunting spots almost always went sour, despite tactical hunting and always attempting to use the wind to our advantage. Relying totally on the fickle wind to hunt mature whitetails is sort of like relying on slot machines to fund your retirement plan. You may get lucky sometimes, but why rely solely on luck when you can use skill, hard work, and science to make success happen?

A Scent-Controlled Hunt

Now let's describe the difference in hunting while implementing scent control. Stepping out the door, we check the wind direction, more out of interest in current weather conditions and how the deer will react to them than to determine which way the wind is blowing. We are so confident in our ability to control our scent that the wind direction has little influence on the trees we will hunt. Current deer movement, not the wind, is the determining factor for the stands we select. This may seem a bold statement, but the proof is in the pudding. After being winded almost daily for decades, we have deer directly downwind almost every hunt without having them spook.

If you do not implement strict scent control, you leave a long scent ribbon along the way to your stand every time to walk to it.

Though we still take care to approach stands in the least obtrusive manner possible, we don't worry about spooking deer because they cross our path or are downwind of our entry route. The scent ribbon we leave behind is so minimal that it appears to be undetectable to most deer and doesn't seem to present a threat to deer that may occasionally stop to investigate. Deer routinely follow our exact footsteps to within bow range.

Climbing into our tree, we are not concerned with the wind changing direction or swirling because our scent is reduced to such a level that the behavior of approaching deer is completely different than when we just played the wind. When the first deer of the evening steps out and passes through, completely unaware of us lurking in the branches, more deer follow. The sound of an unseen deer snorting from somewhere downwind and out of sight has become a thing of the past. It is no secret that big mature bucks are often the last deer to show themselves, and by allowing deer to pass unalarmed, the chances of that elusive buck presenting an opportunity become much better. We see more deer, and more bucks, than we ever did just playing the wind.

On rare occasions deer will sometimes catch a mild wisp of our scent. Usually they stop, lift their heads, and double-check for the source of the scent while scanning the area with both their eyes and ears, and then with an "everything is alright" flip of the tail, go on about their business. The scent we emit is so faint that they do not react as if we are an immediate, or close, threat. There is a big difference in reaction between a deer thinking, "Okay, there is something there, but it is a mile away," or, "A person must have walked through here yesterday," compared to, "There is a predator 20 yards away!" Almost everywhere in the whitetail's range, there is some residual human scent in the woods. This baseline of human scent makes scent control products even more effective. The very few times we have been winded in the last fifteen years have been from occasional lapses in our system through small oversights, such as when John rattled in a buck by tying his rattle bag on the end of his bow rope and rattling it on the ground. He forgot to pull the rope and bag back up in the tree, and the buck winded it and spooked. Or the time Chris got winded because he used a new bow rope that he hadn't yet washed in scent-eliminating detergent, or the time he forgot about the cloth band on his watch that he wore everyday and got winded two days in a row because of it. Paying attention to detail is paramount.

An excellent example of an overly obvious scent-controlled hunt took place in 1999. Wearing full Scent-Lok, John was perched about 18 feet up a small, acorn-laden white oak. At one point, three mature does and two fawns came sauntering in to feed, and the lead doe visually picked John off. At the time they were all upwind of him, but the curious yet cautious doe let the others know that something was out of place by stomping the ground. Within a few seconds the other does were also looking up at him as he sat motionless. They all circled wide to get downwind of the tree and John, and as they were moving their noses were working in overdrive. When dead downwind of John, they were stretching their necks with their noses straight up in the air trying to pick up any foreign scent. After about five minutes they gave up, wagged tails, and came under the tree to feed. They kept an eye on John as they fed, and he would have had a very difficult time trying to make a move and kill one, but they never winded him even though they tried.

The advantage to hunting deer behavior over hunting the wind is that you can concentrate your hunting efforts on the spots where the deer activity is right now. You can plan your hunts and the entire season based on seasonal deer patterns and anticipated changes in deer behavior to an extent that was impossible by just playing the wind. You can also hunt areas many more times before they turn sour, or are contaminated by consistent leftover scent and entry and exit noises until the deer avoid the area. Depending on the layout of an area, when you hunt very carefully you can hunt areas (not individual locations) for an entire season without notable deer behavior disturbance. The principle difference in the hunting experience while implementing full scent control compared to just playing the wind is that you see more deer and more mature bucks than before. The difference is amazing and worth every bit of the effort. We now are able to observe more natural behavior from a very close range and have shot opportunities that never would have happened in the past.

A Solid Scent Control Routine

Hopefully we have convinced you of the benefits of scent control. In order for scent control to work as we have described you must follow a full routine and pay attention to every detail. Being successful at implementing a scent control routine is a matter of degree, the more effort you put into it, and the more you concentrate on details, the more you will get out of it. A little scent control may perhaps help a little, but it won't give you the really positive results you seek. Leaving out any important element of a scent control routine can potentially make your other efforts useless. Here is a simple analogy: A car won't drive at its peak performance level if it has a flat tire, even though there are three more. Scent control is similar; your routine won't work to its peak performance level if you miss one aspect of it yet do everything else right. If you take a stinky backpack into the woods, your scent control routine is missing a tire. A solid scent control routine takes into account your clothing, your gear, and your body.

Clothing
It may seem counterintuitive to begin with clothing in our scent control routine instead of the primary source of odor, our bodies, but we have reasons for this. The absolute most important part of a scent control system is activated carbon clothing. Activated carbon clothing is sort of a catchall product that is the final

barrier to prevent scent dispersal, even in situations where it is difficult to reduce your body odor, such as on freelance or bivy hunts. Activated carbon clothing will often cover other scent control lapses and is the only scent control
product that adsorbs every type of scent. Before Scent-Lok appeared on the market, we experimented with various scent control products available in the early
nineties and found them mostly ineffective in stand-alone situations. After we
tested activated carbon clothing in hunting situations, we were quite shocked
and very satisfied with the results, and we relied almost solely on Scent-Lok
clothing for scent control for several years.

Other manifestations of scent control have made great strides in technology recently, but if you are not taking advantage of activated carbon technology
in your bowhunting clothing, you are missing opportunities at mature bucks.
Since we began using Scent-Lok brand clothing in the early nineties, our hunting experience has been transformed; sightings and success have increased dramatically. Anyone who claims activated carbon doesn't work either has ulterior
motives, has fallen for the false arguments of people with ulterior motives, or has
not used the product correctly. Scent-Lok activated carbon clothing can reduce
your scent so much that you become undetectable to the deer you are hunting.

Activated carbon is a universal filter material used in a host of applications,
commonly in air filtration systems. Some areas outside of hunting where you
will find activated carbon air filters are in industrial kitchens, garbage-burning
power plants, airplane air filters, museum air-filtering systems, and dry-cleaning
facilities, among many others. Applied to clothing, activated carbon functions
basically as an air filter that covers your entire body. Activated carbon is used
worldwide by militaries, and large industries, in chemical protection suits. For the
U.S. military, activated carbon suits are produced under the brand name of
Saratoga. The company behind this brand claims to have sold more than eight
million activated carbon suits to militaries around the world. We have a hard
time believing that there would be worldwide use of this activated carbon clothing by militaries if the technology didn't work. Although chemical suits function
as a protection by filtering molecules from outside, and therefore keeping the
person inside the suit safe, activated carbon in hunting suits functions in the
same manner, but in the opposite direction. Scent molecules emitted from the
body are highly reactive, which is the reason we can smell them, and are easily
adsorbed in the activated carbon, and are therefore kept from entering the surrounding environment. (For details on the science of activated carbon, please
see the sidebar Scent Control Science.)

Scent-Lok clothing is a tool. Like any other tool, for the best results you
have to follow basic directions and use it correctly. Try buying a hand drill, never
recharging the battery, and see how much work you can get done effectively.
This basic analogy applies to Scent-Lok activated carbon clothing as well. Scent-
Lok clothing is not a magic bullet, like some hunters mistakenly think. Buy a
Scent-Lok suit and hang it in the closet over your dog's bed for half the year and

you will certainly find it quite useless for scent control purposes. If you don't use it according to basic directions it will not work, at least not for very long. You also need to wear a complete suit, with headcover (including facemask) and gloves. If you don't wear the headcover, the suit is not complete, and your odds of getting winded will be excellent. You should also keep your mouth and nose covered with the headcover drop-down facemask, and when an opportunity arises, pull the facemask down under your chin so as not to hamper your anchor point and release.

You should consider wearing activated carbon clothing an all or nothing proposition because the more gaps you leave in your scent control armor, the more likely you are to get winded and then falsely blame getting winded on the suit.

The following are some basic care and handling procedures for Scent-Lok clothing:

1. New activated carbon garments should be regenerated before use. To regenerate, put carbon garments in a household or commercial dryer for 30 to 40 minutes on high heat. Always regenerate carbon clothing separately; never dry other hunting clothing in the same cycle. We regenerate our suits every four to six hunts. Due to the extreme amount of odor coming out of your hair follicles, mouth, nose, and hands, head covers and gloves should be regenerated more frequently than the jacket and pants. The low-temperature thermal de-adsorption (the scientific term for regeneration or reactivation) of activated carbon particles begins at around 45 degrees Celsius, but the recommended temperature for best results is 60 degrees Celsius (approximately 150 degrees Fahrenheit).

2. All carbon garments should go directly from the dryer into an airtight storage container. Never place scent wafers, pine boughs, dirt, or any foreign items in the container with your suit. Foreign odor molecules will load up the carbon, requiring more frequent reactivations and shortening the effective life of the suit.

3. Keep carbon-lined garments in the container until you wear them in the field. Do not wear carbon garments anywhere other than while hunting.

4. Any non-carbon exterior layers must be washed in unscented detergent and stored in an airtight storage container.

5. Scent-Lok garments can be washed periodically (once or twice per season) to rid them of any dirt or blood. Wash them in a washing machine using a small amount of carbon specific scent-free detergent. Suits should be air-dried in the dryer first to make sure they don't shrink (some suits have several different fabric layers). Once air-dried, regenerate them as described in step 1.

6. You don't need scent-eliminating sprays over your suit, and do not spray cover scents on your suit.

7. If possible, shower and shampoo with unscented soap, and use a scent-free antiperspirant prior to each hunt.
8. Always wear clean rubber boots (rubber up to the knees) in conjunction with your suit, and wear your pant legs outside the boots instead of tucking them in. Every time you take a step, the air you displace when your foot moves comes out of your boots; the carbon in your pant legs will adsorb it.
9. Keep your fanny pack or backpack scent-free just as you would your clothing by frequently washing it, and keep it in a separate airtight container as well. Wear carbon gloves whenever reloading or reorganizing your pack for the next hunt.

Points four, eight, and nine bring us to the next step in a complete scent control routine. All of the other clothing you wear both under and over your Scent-Lok should be washed with scent-free, or scent-eliminating, detergent. (You should only wear clothing over your Scent-Lok suit during foul weather.) Your Scent-Lok won't do much good if you use a flowery-smelling detergent to wash a jacket you wear over it during foul weather.

Be aware of the odors existing in the washing machine or dryer you use. Leftover, or residual, scent from ultra-scented detergents or scented dryer sheets can cause big problems. One time Chris was hunting with a friend and had to wash his outer Rivers West jacket. He washed it with scent-free detergent in his friend's washing machine, but it came out smelling like a flower garden because of leftover detergent and fabric softener residues in the dispensers. It took about six more wash cycles and airing out outdoors for about a week to finally get the smell out of that jacket. Anytime you use a washing machine, run a load of other clothes or towels with scent-free detergent before washing hunting clothing.

Chris only allows scent-free detergent in his household washing machine. The same goes for his dryer; no perfumed dryer sheets allowed. John would love to do the same, but his wife will not cave in to his requests, so he has to wash a load of towels and washcloths in scent-free detergent before he washes and dries or reactivates his hunting clothing. We always use scent-free towels after a scent-free shower anyway, so we need to frequently wash a load of towels anyway.

Whether regenerating your carbon lined clothing or drying your other hunting clothes, as soon as the dryer cycle stops immediately put them in their appropriate airtight bags or containers so they do not pick up any odors. We keep all our exterior suits (Rivers West foul weather and Scent-Lok carbon suits) in their own carbon-lined storage bags to keep them scent-free. We use airtight, ScenTote containers and label each according to its contents.

We stack our containers neatly in the back of our minivans for quick access. Just as with our Scent-Lok suits, we leave everything in the containers until we park, step into the back of our minivans, change, and go hunting.

Gear

We handle our gear much the same way as our clothing. The best activated carbon scent control routine is useless if your gear stinks and alerts every deer that approaches of your presence. We go to great efforts to make everything as scent-free as possible. This means washing everything that is washable in scent-eliminating detergent and using our LOG 6 ozone generators on specific items to kill bacteria.

We wash our backpacks in scent-eliminating detergent and store them the same way as our clothing. It is amazing how many hunters who practice a scent-free regimen never wash their backpacks, yet before or after each hunt they reload or reorganize them with their bare hands. A backpack can quickly turn into a large human scent wick. We alternate our backpacks and wash them when we feel one is on the verge of scent contamination. Also every item in our pack or that we carry with us that is washable, we either toss in the washing machine or wash by hand. Examples are ropes, saddles, rattle bag covers, fabric covers for quivers, pop-up blinds, 3-D blind material—basically anything made of washable fabric.

Every item that perhaps shouldn't be submersed in water we frequently wipe down with scent-eliminating spray. This is especially important for items that we handle with our hands, such as our rangefinders, binoculars, bleat cans, calls, release aid, folding saw, water bottles, and even our pee bottles. A lot of hunters shoot the same release year-round and forget that it has absorbed a fair amount of their sweat. We wipe or spray our bows down as well, especially the grip area. And we now use a Log 6 ozone generator for these items as well. We store our loaded backpacks along with our saddles in ScenTotes and drilled a hole for our LOG 6 ozone generator tube. When we get to an electrical outlet, we insert the tube and set the ozone generator timer to 30 minutes. This kills bacteria that may have formed on and in our backpacks and saddles and other equipment.

Another item we carry with us is two sizes of Ziploc freezer bags (quart and gallon and a half). Anything that picks up scent on our way to our stands, such as a sweaty undershirt from a long hike to a stand location, we take off, place in the large Ziploc bag, and seal. We keep our used air-activated warmers in the quart-sized Ziplocs. We carry scent-eliminating wipes for our faces in case we perspire, and store them in a quart bag.

We are also very scent-conscious in our vehicles. We keep the inside as clean and scent-free as possible by regularly spraying any fabric with scent-eliminating spray and wiping hard surfaces with scent-free wipes. We also do not allow any smoking inside vehicles any time of the year. It is a good idea to avoid using any perfume scented mirror hangers because their odor is designed to be penetrating and is nearly impossible to remove. Chris uses seat covers during hunting season and regularly washes them in scent-eliminating detergent. John uses a 1-inch deep, ventilated, folding seat cover whenever he drives to a hunting location and keeps it scent-free by leaving it outside when not in use. This keeps him from touching any portion of the van's seat covers that he sits on during the rest of the year. Keeping your vehicle clean is just another step that can keep you from picking up scent as you drive to your hunting location.

We also have a heavy-duty rubber mat in the back of our vans to change our clothing on. We can wipe up any water or dirt left in our changing area after a hunt; otherwise the carpet would get wet.

Seasoned trappers use elbow-length or longer rubber gloves and wear knee-high rubber boots because their human odor can't pass through them and contaminate their sets. Like trappers, we wear knee-high rubber boots so that we don't contaminate our entry and exit routes with human odor. Leather and Cordura boots breathe, allowing foot odor to escape. Leather also leaves a foreign odor, especially when damp or wet, and foreign odors can spook deer or cause them to be more aware.

We have several pairs of rubber knee-high boots for different weather conditions and store them inside our deer sleds in the back of our minivans during season. During the off-season we keep them in an outside garage or storage area. We never wear them for anything other than hunting. When hunting boots are used for non-hunting purposes, they can collect foreign substances in their soles such as oils, gas, manure, and grease, and while these are not human odors, they are still foreign in deer habitat and can alarm deer and cause them to spook or simply pay closer attention to their immediate surroundings, either of which could cause a lost opportunity.

Body

Now that we have covered clothing and gear it is time to think about the main source of stink, our body odors. Our bodies are constantly producing and emitting odor, caused by bacteria, sloughing off skin cells, gases, and so on. Your odor is constantly being released into the surrounding environment. Because you are not hermetically sealed in your activated carbon suits, there are a few gaps where scent can potentially be released, such as between your pants and jacket and around your wrists. Although there is overlap in the activated carbon and this scent release is minimal, it is a good idea to keep your bodily scent to an absolute minimum.

The first line of scent elimination before hunting is keeping your body clean and reducing its scent by showering with scent-reducing soap, shampoos, or body wash, and then using a scent-eliminating antiperspirant. Chris follows this up by spraying his body down with Vanishing Hunter scent-eliminating spray designed for use on your skin. Then use a baking soda–based toothpaste to reduce breath odor. We recommend doing this before every hunt, if it is possible. Reducing your baseline scent before hunting helps the effectiveness and longevity of scent controlling, activated carbon clothing.

Beyond showering and reducing your scent before hunting, several other factors contribute to your ability to control your scent effectively. One is hair. Your hair acts like a scent wick, both absorbing and holding scent and emitting it by harboring scent-producing bacteria. Ever notice by the end of the day how oily your hair becomes; your hair follicles become saturated with moisture and body oils emitted from your head, and they contain human odor. During hunting season, we cut our hair shorter than normal, and we always shave our armpits. Facial hair such as a heavy beard is another source of strong odors.

Another issue is the food you eat. You can naturally control the intensity of odor emitted from your body during season by avoiding garlic, onions, hot peppers, spicy chili, and other pungent foods that cause body odor and bad breath. Another food that causes anxiety, increased perspiration, and body odor, and stimulates the need to use a bathroom, is coffee. We like coffee but give it up on days we hunt. Be aware of foods that cause stronger than normal breath and body odor, and eliminate them from your diet.

Some people even stop eating meat for a few weeks before hunting season, claiming that avoiding meat makes them smell less like a predator. Unlike some of the previously mentioned foods that we can actually smell emitting from our body, we have never had any problems with meat; it could be possible, but we have a hard time giving up venison, especially during season when it's fresh.

Scent Control Routine

The best way to learn anything is by example, so we will describe our typical scent control routine. Follow these steps and you will be able to hunt without much regard to the wind. Well before hunting we launder all of our non-carbon-lined hunting clothing in scent-eliminating detergent and store them in their appropriate ScenTote container. We regenerate all of our carbon-lined Scent-Lok clothing and store it in its ScenTote container as well. Our backpacks, complete with all the contents for hunting, are also in their own tote. All of our labeled ScenTote containers, boots, and bows are neatly arranged in the back of our minivans before the next step.

We keep our gear scent-free by storing it in ScenTotes in our vehicles.

Next we jump in the shower, shampooing and washing with scent-eliminating soap and follow up by using scent-free antiperspirant and scent-eliminating toothpaste. We then pull on scent-free street clothes that were washed in scent-free detergent to wear while driving. While Chris has already washed his car seat cover, John places his ventilated folding cover over his seat. Now that we are about as scent-reduced as we can be, we jump in our van, wipe the steering wheel with a scent-free wipe, and drive to our hunting spots.

Arriving at our hunting spots, we open the side door or back hatch and immediately spray down our hands with scent-eliminating spray. It is only then that we pull on our hunting clothes. If we are in an area with traffic or homes nearby, we will step inside our vans to change, but if we are able to change outside, we do. Either

Strict scent control means dressing for your hunt at your vehicle.

way, we undress completely and redress in our hunting clothing. It is important to exercise discretion in this situation. During rainy or cold weather, we step between the front seats and into the back and change on our rubber mat.

Weather conditions and how far our entry walks are dictate how we dress our upper bodies. We always underdress as opposed to overdress in an attempt to keep from overheating and sweating. We fully dress our lower bodies (pants and garments under them) because we can't add clothing there once in our tree saddle. We store extra upper body layering garments in our backpacks.

Some hunters pack in their exterior carbon suit and put it on once they are on stand, but we always wear the Scent-Lok suit we are going to hunt in as our exterior layer during entries and exits. Odor molecules pass through non-carbon-lined permeable clothing at a rapid rate, and if a mature deer that sniffs everything along its path happens down or crosses your entry path, it will identify your faint body odors and likely spook.

Once in our Scent-Lok suit, we put on our rubber boots and drape our pant legs over them, pull on our Scent-Lok gloves, put on our backpack, grab our bow and spray it with Scent Killer, and head out. Our carbon suits and packs are already scent-free and do not require spray.

On the way to our stands we try to set a pace that keeps us from perspiring. Also, as a precautionary measure, we make a conscious effort not to touch or brush against any vegetation that we could perhaps leave scent on. If we do touch something and are relatively close to our tree, we will cut or break it off and toss it well off to the side (with our Scent-Lok gloves on). This may not be really necessary, but old habits die hard.

Once at the base of the tree, we tie our rope to the top of the bow, remove our saddle from our pack, put it on, attach the safety climbing belt around the tree, and begin our ascent. We put in the bottom steps as we go. Once we are at the top and securely hooked up, we hang our pack, pull up the bow, and make it ready before hanging it on its hook. Once we are in a comfortable, hunting-ready position, if needed, we redress our upper body. To redress, we remove our Scent-Lok jacket, drape it over a branch, put on the extra layering garments we preloaded in our pack, and then put the Scent-Lok jacket back on. We always load our layering garments in our packs in sequence so that in the dark we just put them on as we take them out.

If we overheat and sweat from a long walk in, we take off our damp bottom layer, place it in the gallon-and-a-half Ziploc bag, seal it shut, and put it in the bottom of our pack. We then wipe the perspiration off our face and upper bodies with scent-free wipes and seal the wipes in a quart Ziploc bag. Once our upper body cools down and dries off, we put on the extra bottom layer we always carry and continue redressing.

Lastly we put on our Spand-O-Flage facemask and our Scent-Lok headcover over it. We are now ready to hunt. After the hunt, we reverse the procedure and try to sneak out of the woods undetected.

Once back at the vehicle with our carbon gloves still on, we put our backpack back in its ScenTote, put all Scent-Lok clothing back in its totes, and the layering garments in their tote. We generally use our layering garments on a few hunts before washing them again, depending on whether we feel they are contaminated to the extent that washing them is required. We are not as concerned about our exterior Scent-Lok suit being able to adsorb an already-worn layering garment's odors as we are about putting the used layering garments in our packs and contaminating the pack (we do not use Scent-Lok backpacks) and everything in it. We always carry two large plastic bags in our vans and use them as laundry bags for our contaminated items. If we feel any of our carbon-lined clothing requires reactivation, it goes in one of the bags, and if any non-carbon-lined garments require washing, they go into the other. We never put clothing that we feel is too contaminated to rewear back in the totes.

This routine may seem like a lot of work, but it isn't really. It is merely a matter of adapting your way of thinking about hunting. The most important advantage game animals have over hunters is their amazing sense of smell. The steps above can help you overcome game animals' number one defense, and these steps become routine quickly. It is merely a matter of becoming as scent-aware as possible and staying dedicated to the routine.

Scent Control Science

The scent-eliminating market is booming with products claiming to cover, kill, absorb, adsorb, and mask human scent, so how do you choose? Most product claims have some legitimacy, but some are indeed better than others. Here is our take on the science of scent control, based on our own attempts to understand the science behind the products, and our own anecdotal testing.

Ozone Generators

Ozone generators produce ozone, which kills bacteria and microorganisms. Given enough time, an Eco Outdoors Log 6 ozone generator will kill all bacteria in a small space. Ozone cleaning technology is widely used in sanitary cleaning of hospital equipment and other industries and has now found its place among hunters as a scent controlling technology. We recently experimented with this technology and found that it works quite well to eliminate the scent on items that are difficult to wash, and it's a quick, practical solution to control scent on the fly and some distance from home or a Laundromat.

Detergents

Many companies make similar scent-free detergents that remove odors from your clothing. One of the most basic ingredients in many of these detergents is sodium bicarbonate, or baking soda. There are also detergents by Scent-Lok and Scent Blocker specifically formulated for washing carbon-lined clothing. While some scent-eliminating detergents on the market work a bit better than others, just about all of them do what they are supposed to.

When you select a detergent, check the label to make sure it is free of UV brighteners. Clothing (especially cotton) washed in detergents with UV brighteners will glow under certain lighting conditions.

Laundering your clothes to make them scent-free is a basic tenet of scent control; however, most hunting clothing is permeable, allowing human odor to pass through. So in essence you are only eliminating old odors left on the clothing but doing nothing to stop your bodily scent dispersal the next time you wear it; scent will simply flow through the clothes once you put them on. Washing your garments is only the first step and alone will never make you scent-free. If you stop with this step, you will get winded. After washing and drying any hunting clothing, remember to store it in airtight scent-free containers; otherwise it will pick up surrounding odors. Never place commercial cover scent products, or natural items, with any hunting clothes.

Soaps and shampoos

Showering with a scent-free wash and shampoo before each hunt is an important step in any scent control routine. The active ingredients in scent-eliminating soaps are much the same as in laundry detergent. We prefer to use soaps that contain glycerin. Glycerin is oil-based and penetrates deeper into the skin, allowing its scent-reducing qualities to work a little longer than other products. The science of soap is fairly straightforward. By scrubbing your scalp and body with shampoo and soap, you remove old skin particles, remove or kill odor-causing bacteria, and bind some of the odor molecules in a film of sodium bicarbonate.

Follow up your shower with scent-eliminating antiperspirant, and brush your teeth with scent-eliminating baking soda–based toothpaste. Your hair and mouth are two main sources of scent, so it is vital to give them a lot of attention.

Scent-eliminating sprays

Scent-eliminating sprays are huge sellers in the hunting marketplace, and like anything else some sprays perform better than others. A lot of hunters don't really understand how these sprays work, though. We have often witnessed hunters spraying the outside of their hunting garments before hunting and calling it good. This practice is basically useless. Generally, scent-eliminating sprays actually have to come in contact with the source of the scent to do any good.

Many scent controlling sprays for clothing and gear contain sodium bicarbonate and water. Sodium bicarbonate will for a short period of time absorb human scent molecules. This works best when it is used directly on the source of the scent, your skin. When you spray it on the outside of your garments you are several layers away from the source of the scent and unlikely to lessen the amount of scent you emit into the environment. It would be like having an exterminator spray around the outside of your home for bugs inside it.

Scent-reducing sprays containing carbon particles will adsorb scent molecules, but since the particles in the sprays don't bond with the skin, they do not stay uniformly in place but slough off, rendering them useful for only a very short period of time. When you use carbon sprays on your outer layer of clothing, the particles will adsorb some odor molecules, but once the moisture from the spray dries, most of the particles will slough off. Unlike carbon-lined clothing, which has carbon sandwiched between two layers of fabric, the loose black carbon particles are also messy, leave a black residue in the washer and dryer, and stain clothing.

Several companies offer scent-reducing sprays containing silver, which we also doubt is useful when sprayed on your outer layer. While silver is a superior antimicrobial agent that has been used by the military for years in socks and undergarments to kill bacteria, it only kills bacteria that it comes in direct contact with, which is why the military uses it only in undergarments. When you spray it on exterior clothing, the silver has little effect on killing the bacteria on your skin.

Scent-reducing sprays containing living enzyme organisms also have questionable effectiveness. Similar to silver sprays, they are designed to spray on your outer clothing and therefore rarely come in direct contact with your bacteria.

Another scent-eliminating technology that was developed in the United Kingdom and is used in a variety of applications to control odors in hospitals, the food industry, and the pet industry is called Byotrol, and it is exclusively used in the hunting marketplace by Tink's in several odor-eliminating products.

The best scent-eliminating spray we have found is designed to be used directly on your body and does three things: First, it kills bacteria that causes odor. Second, it creates a film of sodium bicarbonate on your skin that absorbs odor by binding with gases as they are formed. And third, through another chemical agent, it neutralizes the lactic acid that is produced by your skin cells. Predators produce notably more lactic acid in their skin cells because they eat meat. Neutralizing this acid makes hunters smell less like predators. After showering, Chris sprays his entire body with Buck Fever Synthetics Vanishing Hunter. This helps keep his scent production to a minimum at the main source. Other than that we only use sprays for spot scent elimination, such as on boots, bows, or areas where we inadvertently perhaps picked up scent.

Whenever you select a scent-eliminating spray, make sure that it is safe for use on or against your body. Some contain other agents that are potentially harmful, for instance some antimicrobials and other scent-eliminating chemicals that are used as surface cleaning agents. Make sure to read the label to find out whether the product can be used on bare skin.

Waterproof clothing

Waterproof garments were not designed to control scent, but they do to a degree. Although garments made with polyurethane and Teflon membranes are often labeled waterproof / breathable, their breathability capabilities are extremely limited from either side of the garment. Due to the lack of airflow (breathability) through these membranes, the clothing suppresses odors. Odors will, however, escape from neck, wrist, waist, and ankle openings.

Due to their lack of permeability, waterproof clothing will cause you to sweat more than normal and not allow that sweat to evaporate, with the end result being damp undergarments. We only wear waterproof garments when it is raining or extremely cold and windy to block the wind from penetrating through our permeable clothing. We never wear them as a scent control garment.

Activated carbon clothing

Activated carbon is produced from carbonaceous materials like nutshells, wood, coal, and more recently, polymer. The production process involves heating the carbon material to 800 degrees Celsius under pressure. The activated carbon particles have a porous structure that has an overall enormous surface area compared to its size. It has a very high degree of microporosity, which means its surface area is distributed over primary, secondary, and tertiary pores. The surface area varies, but a single gram of activated carbon particles can have a surface area, if you could spread out all the pore surfaces, of between 1,200 and 1,400 square meters. This large surface area combined with characteristics gained by the heating process give activated carbon its adsorption qualities.

Adsorption is both a physical and chemical process. The physical aspect of adsorption is easiest to visualize as a simple mechanical filter. Scent molecules are relatively large molecules in a gaseous state. The large molecules enter the activated carbon and become trapped in its crevices, as it moves from larger sized pores to smaller pores. Adsorption, however, is much more than merely a physical process. The physiochemical adsorption process is more important. Through the heating process during manufacture, the surface area of the activated carbon becomes charged, or it has free electrons that readily interact with the surrounding environment. Scent molecules are also charged and unstable, which means they too react readily with charged components. As a scent molecule nears activated carbon it is actually drawn into the carbon and held in place with light covalent bond. This bond is known as Van der Waals bond, and it keeps scent from dispersing into the environment. The large surface area of activated carbon allows it to adsorb very large amounts of scent molecules. With the highest quality activated carbon fabric, studies have shown that 1 square meter of fabric containing 80 grams of activated carbon can adsorb the scent equivalent of 1,300 liters of human sweat in clinical conditions. That is a lot of scent.

When activated carbon is applied to clothing, it is basically nothing more than an air filter that covers your entire body. Like every other kind of filter, eventually it will fill up. Fortunately, you can reactivate your activated carbon clothing to extend its life. There is a lot of confusion, misinformation, and purposely spread malevolent claims about reactivating activated carbon clothing. The misinformation stems largely from the fact that reactivation is the wrong scientific term for what happens. Reactivation actually means creating new carbon, which cannot be done except under the conditions described above. What can be done is better termed regeneration, or even better yet, low-temperature thermal de-adsorption. Low-temperature thermal de-adsorption simply means that by heating your activated carbon clothing you can remove some of the trapped scent molecules to free up space for further use. Heating gaseous molecules causes them to move faster than they do at lower temperatures. Heat also causes solids to expand. Heating activated carbon causes the micropores within the carbon to expand and scent molecules to move more, allowing a portion of them to break free of the Van der Waals bond. This process begins at temperatures as low as 45 degrees Celsius. For best results, you should heat your suit in a clothes dryer for 40 minutes at around 60 degrees Celsius, which can be easily done in a household dryer. You can never completely remove all the trapped scent molecules from an activated carbon suit, but you can free up enough space for another 40 to 100 hours of use before de-adsorption is again required.

In order to visualize the de-adsorption process, we like to use a sponge as an example in relation to activated carbon suits. Although a sponge clearly absorbs instead of adsorbs, it can help you understand how your suit works. A dry sponge will soak up liquid until it reaches full capacity. When a full sponge is squeezed with enough pressure, most of the absorbed liquid will leave the sponge, yet no matter how much pressure is used the sponge will remain damp. Activated carbon is similar in that it adsorbs scent molecules and the heat in the clothes dryer will cause the release of scent molecules, but activated carbon also retains some molecules as well. Not all the scent molecules will be removed. As any carbon-lined garment is used and de-adsorbed, more and more molecules remain bonded to the carbon. This is why carbon clothing has a lifespan. When properly used and cared for, a Scent-Lok suit has an effective lifespan of approximately 8 years with average use. Nothing lasts forever.

There are plenty of armchair scientists and conspiracy theorists who claim this technology doesn't work, but we're convinced that it does. Use carbon clothing correctly and you will be amazed at the results.

7

EXERCISE, CONDITIONING, AND DIET

Hunting season can be grueling and takes its toll both physically and mentally. In order to combat stress, we attempt to prepare both our bodies and minds for the test that hunting season provides. Your body and mind are two variables of the hunt over which you have the most control; like every other aspect of hunting, proper preparation can only help make you more successful.

Physical Fitness

Imagine getting up several hours before daylight, walking half a mile or farther in a state game area to your stand, sitting relatively motionless in the cold for six hours or so, walking back out, grabbing a quick bite for lunch, walking back in another half a mile or more to a different location, climbing up another tree, and sitting for another five hours or so, climbing down, walking back out, and after a short night, rising again to follow a similar routine the next day. Now imagine taking some vacation time and doing this for a week straight while maybe throwing in a couple long bike-in hunts, one or two canoe or wade-in hunts, and a couple all-day hunts. Bowhunting can be an extreme sport. In most states, bow season stretches for at least three months, with most bowhunters hitting the field at least two days per week, so you can see just how exhausting bowhunting can be. The higher your fitness level, the better you will be able to cope with the mental and physical stress.

You don't have to be able to run ultra-marathons to be successful at bowhunting. However, we recommend that serious bowhunters implement a 7- to 8-month off-season training routine that allows you to reach a level of fitness that keeps you healthy and ready for the challenges of a long hunting season. Hunting spans the gamut from large public lands where extreme physical measures are required to access the hunting sites, to small private parcels within an hour's drive of large cities where our walk-ins are less than 200 yards. For our type of hunting, our fitness routine should put us in the proper shape to be able to walk a mile through hilly wooded terrain, hunt for several hours, walk back out, and do it again for an evening hunt. If you feel as though you can do that without any difficulties, your fitness level is probably such that you are ready for the season. If, however, you get worn out and have to take breaks when walking long distances, or doing mild physical work, you need to start or increase your fitness training.

Training program

Though we try generally to remain as physically fit as possible, our fitness program is specifically designed and implemented with bowhunting in mind. Since we walk quite a bit during season, cardiovascular training is an important aspect of our training routine. A fair level of cardiovascular fitness can be achieved by raising your pulse for 20 minutes at least three times a week. How you do this is irrelevant; just do it. John likes to run on his treadmill. Chris rides his bike, runs, swims, and walks steep hills. Even just taking long walks will do the job.

A second aspect of training that we consider important is light weight training. To keep our muscles toned, we do some form of weight training several times a week. This is not bodybuilding, but simply keeping ourselves in shape. A set of light dumbbells is enough to work your entire upper body, and you can complete the workout in half an hour. John also regularly uses a pull-up bar to simulate pulling up his body weight while climbing trees. There are countless books and sources of information about specific exercises to do for weight training. Simply develop a routine and stick to it.

The third aspect of our training is stretching. Stretching is something a lot of guys just don't think of doing, but keeping your muscles flexible increases your range of motion, which is particularly important while reaching and climbing trees. Just like cardiovascular and weight training, we do not overdo it but simply make it a priority to follow a stretching routine a couple times a week to keep our flexibility and range of motion as wide as possible.

After each hunting season ends, we take a brief recovery phase and restart our training routines in mid-January. As we gain strength, we continue to increase our training until we reach our highest level sometime in late August. From that point we reduce our training time, and other than continuing our stretching exercises, we stop training a couple weeks before the season opener. We continue stretching throughout the season to reduce the chance of injury. Our last-minute preseason scouting ventures don't quite replace the pace of our fitness programs, but allowing our bodies to rest a bit before the long season ahead feels pretty good. We both have family obligations, and the time freed up by not working out is used to get our hunting gear ready.

During season, the bodily stresses of hunting are more than enough to keep us in shape. In fact, though we are always as fit as possible coming into the fall, in a typical season we tend to lose five to ten pounds off our already light frames. Some of that weight loss is due to a loss of muscle, and the rest is from walking so much in full gear and not eating as properly as we did prior to season. If you are serious about bowhunting, you should take the time to achieve a level of fitness that keeps you physically in the game.

Diet

Controlling your diet is important to your fitness. A fitness regimen won't be as effective if you are a fast food junky. The beautiful thing about the combination of diet and bowhunting is that as the primary reward for your efforts you receive some of the finest, leanest, most delicious meat on the planet. You can keep yourself a bit healthier by consuming wild meat as frequently as possible. Though we are by no means experts in this field, the mantra of "eat like a caveman," makes sense. Combine your meat with fresh vegetables, greens, and fruit. Simply refraining from eating too much deep fried and greasy food will help you remain fairly healthy. We back up our healthy eating with diet supplements and vitamins. Though healthy eating should provide all the essentials, we want to make sure our bodies have everything necessary to function properly. Vitamins are a form of insurance that we get all of the vitamins, minerals, and nutrients we need.

Diet concerns during hunting season are another matter. As much as we hunt, it is sometimes very difficult to keep up a healthy diet during the fall. In fact, the problem for us becomes not too much, but too little. Since you spend a lot of time out in the cold, your body requires a calorie spike just to maintain itself. As concentrated as we are on hunting, we almost have to force ourselves to consume enough calories. This means sometimes switching to a high energy, higher fat diet during the intense portions of the season. We also use diet supplements during the fall, including multivitamins, liquid diet supplement drinks, and energy bars, while hunting. Wilderness Athlete products are designed with the hunter in mind and can keep you going when proper eating habits falter.

Archery

For at least the six weeks prior to season, every bowhunter should regularly practice shooting his bow. Volumes have been written about how to choose a bow and shoot correctly, and our DVD *Archery Mechanics* spells it out pretty clearly. Our main interest in this book is simply preparing for hunting season, so we will not delve into those subjects. Our main concern is to be ready when the time to hunt arrives.

After hunting season we usually put our bows down for a couple weeks as part of our recovery. Sometime in late winter we start shooting again, a couple training sessions a week with the main goal to keep our muscles in shape and our shooting form up to snuff. We concentrate far more on form, release, and follow-through than on where the arrows actually go, but when those three

You should practice with your bow throughout the year. Here, John practices in his yard.

things are working smoothly, arrows tend to go where you want them. Our shooting is as low stress as it gets, and most of the time even serves as a way to relax in the evening. Too many bowhunters create far too much stress for themselves by constantly emphasizing competitive shooting. We know hunters who get upset with a single poor shot at their backyard target, and many, John included, have been stricken with target panic because of competitive archery. Being competitive is alright, but to us the only shot that means anything is the one at a live deer in the fall. So when you shoot in the summer, just relax, concentrate on the basics, and don't worry too much about errant shots.

Continue to shoot throughout the summer, practicing more and more the closer it gets to hunting season and by late summer, your shooting muscles and form will be on target. At this point it is critical to begin shooting like you would in a hunting situation. Since the majority of our hunting takes place from a tree saddle, most of our shooting practice is from elevations close to those that we hunt. Practicing archery from our rooftops is an Eberhart family tradition. Many hunters spend the entire summer practicing with their feet firmly planted on the ground and then take their setup out hunting from a treestand. They are setting themselves up for disaster. From an elevated position, these guys will invariably shoot high.

Beyond sighting in our bows from the height at which we do most of our hunting, we also practice shooting from our tree saddles. In the saddle, you can take shots in any direction. In order to eliminate surprises, practice all the angles

Most whitetail bowhunters hunt from an elevated position. It is critical to practice from heights similar to those you will be hunting.

and all the distances. Also practice from inside your pop-up blind from the ground with your bow sighted in for elevated shooting. If your bow is sighted in to be right on from 25 feet, you will shoot a little low from the ground. Also practice shooting from your knees, crouched, and from a chair while twisting your torso in the other direction and even straight in front. By practicing all these various shot possibilities, you'll ready yourself for any hunting situation. Any shot can arise, and it is better to have practiced than to rely simply on theory or hope.

Though we keep our bows generally in good shape and know a good bit about archery equipment, about a month before the opener we have an expert inspect both our main bow and our backup bows. We always have at least two bows set up identically going into the bow season. Usually the inspection brings nothing major to light, but by having it done early, if there is a problem, we have time to alleviate it well before the opener.

One area of archery practice that gets far too little attention is shooting during season. It is absolutely critical to shoot a couple times a week throughout the entire bow season. Many bowhunters, for the most part, stop practicing during the course of the hunting season. Shooting during the season has a different purpose than preseason practice. Preseason shooting is effectively a form of exercise. In-season shooting is more of a control mechanism. We generally keep these sessions short, shooting sometimes as few as a handful of arrows. We constantly check our equipment and shooting for any changes. A lot can happen as you carry a bow through the woods and pull it up into a tree. By shooting once or twice a week, you can both be certain that your equipment is functioning properly and that your shooting form hasn't changed. How many times have you heard of a hunter chasing a mature buck the entire season only to miss the shot because of some kind of equipment failure? Regular in-season shooting practice can keep this from happening.

Mental Preparation

Mental preparation for bowhunting goes hand in hand with physical preparation. If you've done the physical training, you are probably on the right path to being mentally ready for the season. Mental preparation tends to be vague and therefore little talked about in hunting. However, the mental edge is often the main difference between successful and less successful hunters.

The first step is confidence. When you know that your body is in good shape, you gain confidence. Knowing your equipment is functioning perfectly and that you have all the right gear to combat any situation, including weather conditions that may occur during season, will also add to your confidence. Having a solid hunting plan for the entire season is another important component. Simply having done everything possible to prepare for all aspects of the hunt will make you mentally ready.

Buck fever is caused by anxiety and is something that every bowhunter, including us, has at some level. When the time comes that our heart rate doesn't go up when a mature buck is coming within range, it will be time to consider taking up another activity. There is no doubt that a hunter's previous kills dictate his anxiety level. An entry-level hunter will likely get excited when any deer approaches, whereas a hunter who has taken many deer may only have an adrenaline surge when a mature buck that he wants to kill approaches. The best way to combat this anxiety is to get some kills under your belt before stepping up and attempting to concentrate on mature bucks. It is also a good idea to practice putting yourself in similar types of stress situations, say by hunting other species. Whether with gun or bow, hunting and taking other species, such as turkey, bear, predators, and even small game, will help in overcoming hunting fever. The more game animals you kill, the better your nerves will be while making the shot. We wish we could come up with a cure for buck fever, but unfortunately the only way to reduce anxiety is through experience.

Your expectations should also fit the area in which you are hunting. For example, holding out for a 150-inch buck may be an option in many of the lightly populated Midwestern states such as Kansas or Iowa, but you might hunt a lifetime in most areas in densely populated states such as West Virginia, Pennsylvania, New York, and Michigan and never even see a buck of those proportions. The hunting media is such these days that no one even blinks an eye at a deer if it gross scores under 140. Sadly, this creates false expectations, particularly for young hunters. Even though we have killed some very large bucks, we adjust our hunting expectations to the area we are hunting. In a pressured area in

Michigan a 100-inch buck is far more seldom and much more difficult to get close to than a 140-incher in Kansas. When we hunt that area in Michigan, any 100-incher is our target, and we are just as, if not more, proud of these bucks as our 140-inchers from elsewhere. In fact, we have gone entire seasons without even seeing a 100-inch buck in Michigan.

Do not set your goals higher than is possible for your hunting area. We rarely mention antler scores, because our goal is mature bucks. Most mature bucks where we hunt at home never make it into the stratosphere of the scoring realm. The top end of some mature bucks that reach $4^1/2$ years old might not even be the Pope & Young minimum. One of John's most prized bucks is a $5^1/2$-year-old buck from an extremely heavily hunted area in Michigan that scores in the mid-120s. It took him three years of serious effort to finally get a shot at this buck.

Good bowhunting requires extreme patience, endurance, and mental fortitude. Though even more difficult to quantify than physical fitness, these characteristics make the difference between the most successful bowhunters and average bowhunters. You must be mentally ready to put yourself on the deer's time, and deer are generally in no hurry. In this age of instant gratification, constant media barrage, and private electronic devices that keep us entertained and occupied 24 hours a day, sitting still for several hours has become anachronistic. You must be mentally ready to spend hours or maybe even a few full days on stand without success. Only when you are ready and aware that this type of commitment is what bowhunting takes will you become comfortable enough to hang for hours on end in order to be a consistently successful hunter. Eventually, you will reach a flat state of mind while bowhunting that is akin to meditation and allows hours to pass seemingly within minutes.

Dealing with Setbacks

Nothing ever stays the same. In bowhunting, setbacks are part of the game. Accept them as part of the learning process and move beyond them. Bowhunting is a defining character attribute, a way of life that we never want to do without. It can be really frustrating when you lose an excellent piece of property, have a terrible season, or when unforeseen events cast a shadow over the season you prepared for all year. Expect a little adversity in your hunting, because if you hunt long enough, setbacks will occur.

If bowhunting is your passion, you will find ways to get through the low points. As bowhunters, we should never expect success, but we should always prepare for it.

8

PRESEASON SPEED TOURING AND SCOUTING

Many hunters unknowingly ruin their chance at an early season buck by doing too much preseason scouting and new location preparation. By traipsing through the woods, busting through brush, hanging stands, clearing shooting lanes, and marking entry and exit routes shortly before deer season, hunters unknowingly alert mature deer that have survived through a couple hunting seasons that hunting season is fast approaching. Mature bucks in pressured areas are highly sensitive to any influx of human intrusions into their core areas; after all, unless turkey hunters were in the area in the spring, deer have been left to themselves for the previous six to nine months. And who hasn't heard or experienced that big mature buck that was sighted evening after evening all summer long only to vanish a couple weeks before the opener? Hunters themselves are usually to blame.

If there are any mature bucks in the area, they have likely suffered consequences from previous hunter encounters. Because of this, they don't distinguish between someone trying to kill them or simply walking through. They view our intrusions as an immediate threat to their survival and assume a more nocturnal routine. The negative impact of preseason disturbance on mature buck movements are not big; they are huge. Even something as seemingly benign as hanging a game camera within a buck's home area can have negative results for bowhunters.

Speed Touring

Despite the concern about the effects on mature bucks, you still have some preseason work to do. About three weeks before the season opener, we take speed tours of some of our hunting locations. Our timing is meant to coincide with when mature bucks in Michigan have shed their velvet. This usually happens during the first week of September and allows us to identify any fresh buck activity. If your season opener is before that, or you hunt in a southern region where bucks rub much later, adjust your tour accordingly.

John puts the final touches on one of his trees while on a speed-scouting tour.

Speed touring mainly involves checking some existing locations for current buck activity. The locations we tour are only those that we feel may have suitable activity during the first few days of the season. Since deer activity at that time moves between bedding and feeding areas in a relatively consistent way, our focus is on points in between or feeding destination locations. We do not speed-tour spots that we know won't be active until the rut phases. The main idea now is to have as little impact as possible, so obviously it is time to begin taking scent control seriously. It is nearly impossible to totally mask the noise of a physical intrusion, but by practicing a careful scent control routine your tour will be as scent-free as possible.

The arsenal of scouting tools we take on these tours is trimmed down to an absolute minimum so we can easily move through cover and still do any work necessary. We take an extension saw, sheathed handsaw, compass, and six tree steps (most of our trees had the bottom five or six removed after preparation). We wear our climbing harness, and depending on how well we know the property, take our maps. We wait until later in the morning, after most deer have bedded, before taking our tours, and try to leave the area before they begin moving again in the evening. Touring your locations during the hottest part of the day may make you uncomfortable, but not spooking the deer you will soon be hunting can be crucial to regular success. We also always take the least invasive route to our sites so as not to alarm any more deer than necessary. This usually means taking different entry and exit routes than what we had previously marked when setting up the locations.

We focus our attention on small destination sites such as feeding destination sites, primary scrape area sites, narrow pinch point sites between bedding and large preferred feeding areas, travel routes into standing corn, and waterhole sites. Here is exactly what we are looking for.

Feeding sites

As we check our small destination feeding sites we are looking for actual food first, and if there is food both in the tree and on the ground, we then look for confirmed buck sign. Where John lives the primary food sources at his secluded food sites are apples and white oak acorns. If a fruit or mast tree is producing and dropping food, it will likely have buck sign in the form of rubs, scrapes, or large identifiable tracks nearby.

While preseason speed scouting, you should always check oaks for acorns like on this white oak.

Scrape areas

In pressured areas where few bucks survive to reach maturity, active primary scrape areas will rarely be active before season. When you come across an active primary scrape area at this time of year, it is a pretty good indication that a mature buck is in the area. It is not that uncommon to find several scrapes opened up under a low-hanging apple or white oak branch before season. Of course the only time you will ever see this is when the tree is dropping food. If one of our secluded apple or white oak sites has active scrape activity, it moves near the top of our list of places to hunt immediately.

Funnels to food sources

During our tours, we check the funnels between bedding areas and preferred food sources, such as crop fields and large stands of mast or fruit trees, for fresh rubs and well-used runways. We also check any travel routes where they enter standing cornfields. If there is an abundance of fresh rubs, or a rub line, that appear to be made by a large buck, or well-used runways with what looks to be large tracks, the location will be put on the to-hunt list.

Secluded waterholes

Because water is so abundant in Michigan, we only have a few sites at secluded waterholes that are the only water sources within a half mile. During unseasonably warm weather, these locations become very important. Under special conditions these spots will see an exceptional amount of deer traffic.

Keep an eye out for isolated waterholes, like this one, while preseason scouting. When conditions are right these turn into good spots to waylay a mature buck.

Whenever there is ample buck sign that might warrant an early season hunt at any location, we cut any new growth from our shooting lanes, climb the tree to cut branch sprouts and loose bark, remove any recent deadfalls that may have blocked a runways, and note the amount of sign for further review after all our listed sites have been toured. We immediately move on and check any other sites on the property and leave immediately after checking the last site. We do not scout for new locations at this time. Once all our locations have been toured, we evaluate our notes, and if there are a few suitable locations, we create a plan of attack for the first few days of season. The next time we visit any of the sites we take a kill tag and a bow with us.

Preseason Scouting and Tree Preparation

We had a couple worst-case scenario years when none of our existing locations had enough buck sign to warrant hunting them. The reasons for lack of sign at our existing locations were poor mast and fruit yields, and local crop rotations that altered where the preferred nighttime food source was, which in turn changed general deer travel routes. When this occurs, there is no option but to scout new locations.

Scout new areas just as you would in the spring (see chapter 4), but implement a full scent control routine while doing it because you may hunt there within a few weeks. Also, try to wait until a rainy day or extremely windy day to scout. Even with the best scent-free regimen, you cannot prepare a tree, cut shooting lanes, move cut brush and trees, and mark entry and exit routes during hot weather without leaving human odor. A hard rain or wind will aid in masking your tree and shooting lane preparation noise and will dissipate odors more rapidly.

Whenever we have to scout and prepare locations preseason, we find that on average our mature deer sightings at those locations are lower than when we hunt our preset locations that we only speed-toured. The reason for this is simple: Speed touring is far less noisy, leaves less human scent behind, and doesn't noticeably alter the deer's surroundings. Only scout in the late summer if you happen to gain access to a totally new piece of property or you absolutely have to.

Scouting Cameras

Game cameras, or scouting cameras as they are sometimes called, are huge sellers in the hunting industry. Most bowhunters own one or more. We have all seen and heard the media-hyped success stories, and clever marketing, of killing giant mature bucks because of them, bucks that no one would otherwise have known were even around. The fact is, however, that these cameras save the lives of far more mature bucks. This is particularly true in areas with heavy consequential hunting pressure. Year after year hunters show us scouting camera photos of mature bucks taken in the summer and preseason. They may have a couple daytime pictures of a mature buck from prior to season, but by the time season begins any photos of the same buck are taken in the middle of the night. What happened?

Likely, the hunter went out to hang his stand a few weeks before season, and while he was doing that, he also placed a scouting camera near his best spot. The buck moved through during the first day or two and was alerted to the hunters presence by both leftover scent and the sound and possibly the infrared flash of the camera. We have seen enough photos of bucks looking directly into infrared cameras that we believe they can either hear the camera take the shot or even see its infrared flash. The hunter then returned at least once a week to check the camera and left more scent or even spooked deer walking in and reinforced this buck's decision to avoid the area or turn nocturnal. The hunter got those couple of photos, but the quality of his location has been compromised.

Those of you hunting pressured areas must consider this outcome and resist the urge to set up cameras at or near your hunting locations. Every return visit is detrimental to that location's potential. If you want to use a camera, place it in an area that you know the deer use after dark and that can be easily accessed with minimal consequences. This way, you may be able to get a good idea of the quantity and quality of the bucks in an area. If a particular buck is using the nearby feeding area and moves during daylight, there is a good chance that

Game cameras can be used to locate nice bucks, like this one, but you must be careful using them.

you will see him while hunting. If, however, you tromp into a hunting spot with a camera, that same buck might avoid that location.

In exclusive and other lightly hunted areas where mature bucks either have little contact with hunters or are conditioned to having no negative consequences with hunter interactions, scouting cameras can work quite well, and you may get hundreds of photos of mature bucks. One thing is certain, any hunter who consistently takes motion-camera pictures of mature bucks at his hunting locations and then kills those bucks there is definitely not hunting in a pressured area.

Trail camera pictures are nice, but the best pictures of bucks are those with your hands firmly wrapped around the base of their antlers.

9

Yearly, Seasonal, and Daily Timing

We cannot emphasize enough how critical your yearly, seasonal, and daily timing is to becoming a consistently successful bowhunter. Unless you hunt an unbelievable chunk of property laden with mature bucks, you will never reach your full bowhunting potential without understanding the seasonal and daily habits of deer and melding that understanding into your year-round hunting game plan.

It has taken us decades to get our seasonal timing right, decades to learn how a whitetail's reaction to hunting pressure affects its daily timing and movements, and decades to figure out a yearly plan of how to attack these timing issues. And we are still trying to learn and adjust. Understanding the natural seasonal changes in whitetail behavior and how hunting pressure affects their movements is extremely important. If you implement our yearly plan, you'll cut years off your bowhunting learning curve and put yourself in a better position to regularly kill good bucks for your area.

Yearly Deer Behavior

We are not biologists, nor have we ever studied enclosure deer that never see hunters. Like other whitetail enthusiasts, we enjoy reading studies about the social interactions and habits of captive deer. But we are also realists and know that there is a big difference between captive deer and their brethren in areas of heavy pressure. We are hunters and our observations are based on time spent afield observing deer that get hunted and either learn to react to pressure or die.

Throughout this chapter we are primarily discussing seasonal patterns and daily timing of mature bucks, because they are our primary target. A side effect of becoming fairly proficient at getting close to mature bucks is that in doing so your opportunity to observe younger bucks, does, and fawns increases exponentially. Astute observation of all deer, in order to learn as much as possible, should be a natural condition for all hunters.

Yearly, seasonal, and daily habits may be slightly different from state to state and even from area to area within states depending on terrain, habitat, and most importantly, hunting pressure. The patterns we describe in this section are typical in Michigan. Keep in mind that Michigan has a five-day gun doe season in mid-September, a two-day either-sex youth season in late September, an October 1 bow and crossbow season opener, a sixteen-day gun season starting on November 15, a nine-day muzzleloader season in early December, followed by another bow and crossbow season until early January.

January through March

There is normally snow on the ground during these months. The deer will have grouped up by early January. Even during winters with little snowfall, deer will gather in small groups. They shift their range close to the best food source in the area, and will bed as close to that food source as possible.

In large timber areas, where there is no agriculture for many miles, the deer gravitate to cutover areas and low-lying cedar swamps to yard. Deer commonly migrate 5 to 10 miles to yard. In cutovers they feed on young saplings and left-over tops, and in cedar swamps they primarily feed on cedar boughs. The low-lying, dense cedar swamps also protect deer from the frigid winds. In many northern regions of the state that receive heavy snow, the DNR will occasionally clear cut areas of timber just so the deer will have food to survive the winter. By late February and March, depending on the amount of deer and the carrying capacity of where they are yarded, they will be eating browse that has little nutrition. During severe winters there are always deer that starve.

In agricultural areas, deer will also group up, but they usually don't make long migrations. There are usually sufficient food sources close by. Depending on the depth of snow, deer will primarily feed in alfalfa, corn, soybean, and wheat stubble fields. These deer round out their diet with natural browse and seek out low, out-of-the-wind, protected areas in which to bed.

During winter months with deep snow, you can walk through areas that had held many deer just a few weeks earlier and find no sign whatsoever, not even a single track in the snow. Many areas simply do not have enough food to sustain deer through a long winter, or the landscape makes them too vulnerable to strong winter winds. Consequently the deer make short migrations. This happens in many areas we hunt in Michigan.

April and May

As soon as the snow melts, the deer that left their core areas move back to them. The new growth of spring offers an abundance of food. They shed their heavy winter coats and break back up into matriarchal doe groups and bachelor groups. As fawn-bearing does near their birthing cycle, they force last year's offspring to keep their distance. Last year's buck fawns will often move off and relocate.

Sometime in May or early June the does drop their fawns and bucks begin growing their new set of antlers.

June through August

It's still all about food during hot months. Deer become lazy and take on a regimented routine that is totally focused on food options. A typical day goes something like this: They bed in the morning, get up periodically throughout the day to browse, in the evening they slowly work their way to their first preferred late evening/nighttime feeding area, move into that area before dark to feed, move to other preferred feeding locations throughout the night, and slowly browse back to where they bed in the morning. By late July and throughout August, you commonly see the area's biggest bucks in full velvet feeding in short crop fields in the late evenings. Get a good look now because in pressured areas these habits will change very soon.

There is also so much cover during summer that deer bed just about anywhere. It is common to jump deer bedded in places you would never find them during season. Few humans intrude into their core areas during this period, so they don't seek the deep security of thick bedding areas.

September and October

The lazy days of summer gorging continue as deer put on layers of fat that will help them survive the winter months. But the influx of hunter intrusions by a five-day September doe season, a two-day either-sex youth season, and a wave

John waited until the timing was perfect to hunt this big Michigan buck. It took only a single hunt in late October.

of preseason scouting by bowhunters will usually cause mature bucks to adjust their summer movement time frames before bow season opens. Oaks and fruit trees also begin dropping food during these months, which immediately alters deer movements.

In early September mature bucks shed their velvet and begin sparring and establishing hierarchy. In pressured areas, the bucks that survived the previous hunting season while sporting legal antlers will seem to vanish into thin air. By mid-September nearly all bucks shed their velvet. Rubs appear throughout their core areas.

By late September and throughout October the foliage turns color and drops, and ferns and tall weeds wither. This is a severe change in the whitetails surroundings. The sudden loss of cover combined with hunting activity causes mature deer to abandon their summer patterns and bed deep within dense bedding areas or in smaller secure areas.

By the bow season opener, the older bucks have abandoned bachelor groups. They begin fighting for the dominant breeding position in the herd and aggressively signpost their territory with scrapes and rubs. Most will become totally nocturnal outside their secure bedding areas. This behavior remains about the same until the rut phases begin. We believe there is no such thing as a completely nocturnal buck, but we do believe that in pressured areas, until the rut phases begin, whatever daytime movements they make are within a short distance of where they bed. Nearly all the mature buck sign you locate just prior to and during the early part of the season was made after dark.

By late October, testosterone levels in mature bucks rise to a point that somewhat overrides their normal state of caution. They begin to take chances and move some during daylight, seeking early estrous does. In pressured areas, the older bucks still maintain a rather nocturnal pattern. Most of these bucks' daytime activity takes place at midday. This is the beginning of the rut phases. We call this period the prerut. During the prerut, signposting by mature bucks reaches its peak.

November

In early November the percentage of does entering estrus continues to rise. By the end of the first week, the prerut becomes the main rut, when the majority of does enter their estrous cycle. This closely coincides with the beginning of our gun season on November 15. With the majority of does in estrus, the mature bucks are in breeding mode. As does get close to their cycle, they remain relatively true to their core areas and run their fawns off.

Feeding and signposting by mature bucks now take a backseat to tending and breeding. During the chase, mature bucks may leave their core areas and expand their range. Core areas overlap, and after a buck tends a doe through her estrous cycle, he will take up chase on the very next estrous doe he crosses paths with. If that doe is on the edge of her core area, she will likely lead him back within hers and out of his. This process continues throughout the entire rut.

Typical mature buck behavior in a pressured area during the rut phases is to enter into the security cover of the bedding area before daylight. Transitioning back to a bedding area before daylight doesn't make a buck nocturnal, it only means the buck moves within the safe confines of his bedding area during the day. Bucks that move around within security cover after daylight are simply reacting to a negative history of hunter encounters in exposed areas. This one small safety precaution saves the lives of more bucks than just about anything else.

Mature bucks are the first to return to security cover before daylight. They may also move into the perimeter cover surrounding isolated mast or fruit food sources or primary scrape areas to stage. They stage in these secure yet high traffic locations and wait to intercept does returning from their nightly routines. By doing this the buck can scent-check several does in a population without expending too much energy or exposing himself to danger out in the open. If danger does happen to approach in the form of a hunter, the buck hears it and quietly departs, leaving the hunter with no clue the buck was ever there. If there are no intrusions and he encounters an estrous doe, he will follow her directly into cover, where most of the daylight breeding activity takes place.

When bucks stage and no does of interest pass through, they rise later in the morning and cruise the edges or interiors of the bedding areas within their core area to scent-check and look for estrous does. They use the best available cover when traveling between bedding areas and any other secure areas such as active scrape areas and isolated food sources. What this means from a bowhunter's perspective is that if the bowhunter is there first, he is putting himself in a position to intercept this movement. Normally mature bucks will pass through to their bedding area or staging area before daylight, and if they remain undisturbed, there is a good chance that they will still be on their feet and moving just after daylight. If they bed, they get up later in the morning and possibly move by you when they search for does. The mythical nocturnal buck is not so mythical after all; he just deprives some hunters of extra sleep.

During this period, most mature bucks everywhere have a natural pattern of midday movement, usually sometime between the hours of 11:00 a.m. and 3:00 p.m. After bedding or staging through the early morning hours, bucks get up and cruise through the secure confines of their core area in search of estrous does. What is so interesting about their midday movements is their intensity. When mature bucks move through their core area, they are on a mission; they move rapidly and steadily. They know they are moving through secure areas and seem to be oblivious of hunters, probably because they have never ever encountered any at that time of day before.

In pressured areas it is also common to have high deer populations and many more mature does and fewer mature bucks. In these areas the dominant bucks are less likely to travel outside their core areas to breed because they have no competition. If they cross a hot doe's route and she is with another buck, they just force him away and take over. In severely unbalanced deer herds it is also quite common for matriarch does to actually pursue the dominant bucks as they get close to their estrous cycle, thus making it less likely that he will leave his core area.

Older bucks everywhere also attempt to hold estrous does in cover and keep them there during their entire cycle. The cover makes their movements less visible to other bucks and to hunters. The less an estrous doe travels, the less likely it is that another buck will cross her path and present competition. In 2004 John took a great 10-point in Missouri while he was attempting to push a doe back into the standing cornfield he had just ran her out of. Unfortunately for the buck, his circle took him a bit too close to John's tree.

In our travels to lightly hunted states, where it seems there are as many bucks as does in every age bracket, we have found that mature bucks often travel several miles during the rut because of the breeding competition. We once witnessed three monster bucks closely pursuing one hot doe, and they were constantly swinging their antlers at each other during the pursuit. She was definitely queen for the day.

Our gun season opens on the 15th, at which time we like to leave to hunt elsewhere. During gun season, the hunter numbers more than double. After the first several hours of the season, the vast majority of deer are just searching for places to hide themselves until the shooting stops. The rut and breeding process continues through gun season, but the vast majority of breeding takes place after dark. Following the peak rut is the late rut, which in pressured areas is akin to the prerut. Most of the does have been bred, and the competition for the late does becomes intense. Bucks resume signposting and searching for does. This late rut is largely theoretical in Michigan because most of the bucks will have been killed during gun season. The remaining bucks indeed get the job done, but almost exclusively after dark.

December
The postrut continues with bucks searching for late estrous does and early-born doe fawns that come into heat for the first time. There is a brief week or so of gun silence followed by a nine-day either-sex muzzleloader season. Due to the accuracy of modern in-line muzzleloaders, this season has become as popular as the regular gun season, and many hunters hold onto their doe permits specifically for this season. In areas that get pounded with gun hunting pressure, most antlered buck activity and nearly all mature buck activity takes place during the security of darkness. In areas where lots of doe permits are available, even mature does are active primarily after dark.

In lightly hunted regions of the country, a high percentage of mature bucks will survive through the gun seasons and continue searching for late receptive does during daylight hours. In many of these areas, the postrut is often the premier hunting period of the entire season. Bucks in these lightly hunted regions have been pursuing does in the daytime for several weeks on unpredictable routes, and by now the majority of does have been bred. Bucks go back to their core areas and to their prerut routines in search of late estrous does. They have become very comfortable moving during daylight, and they are now following a somewhat regular, more predictable routine that makes them more vulnerable to hunters.

By December, mature bucks have lost a lot of weight from pursuing does so aggressively during the rut and not eating much. They will now begin feeding on a regular basis to replenish their weight loss, and the odds of catching a mature buck on a feeding route are now as good as on a postrut routine. During years when there is deep snow in December, the deer will alter their routes to the easiest accessible food source and in big timber areas will start to migrate to other wintering areas with more abundant food sources.

Hunting Timing

Yearly timing

As we have shown, you should have a yearly hunting plan. This means doing the majority of your scouting in the spring and then staying out of your hunting areas until a short round of scouting preseason, followed by actual hunting.

Seasonal timing

Seasonal timing simply means having enough hunting locations prepared to be able to capitalize on deer movement throughout the entire season. It is possible to waylay a big buck anytime, if you know what the deer are doing and when. You certainly don't have to wait until the prerut and rut to tag a big buck, though this is naturally the best time. In fact, by waiting and only hunting prime time, you could potentially be less successful than otherwise, depending on the characteristics of your hunting territory.

Have trees ready for every portion of the season and give thought to why things happen the way they do in the deer woods. The biggest mistake hunters make in seasonal timing is simply hunting their premier stands too early and too often. It is very tempting to run out to that primary scrape area first thing and then hunt there every couple of days. The problem is that the buck making the scrapes might be primarily nocturnal early in the season and is gauging your activity under the cover of darkness, which may be enough to cause him to avoid that particular spot or remain mostly nocturnal in that area throughout the rut.

The second mistake hunters make is overlooking spots that are seasonally and situationally important, such as lone fruit-bearing trees early in the season or travel routes only used by bucks as long as the leaves are still up. Hunt each spot at the right time of year, when the bucks are actively using it.

Daily timing

You have to be at the right spot well before the deer arrive there. In order to do this you have be able to read the terrain and decipher how the mature bucks will use that terrain, and, most importantly, when. The best way to understand daily timing is to illustrate the movements of a so-called nocturnal buck. We believe there is no such thing as a completely nocturnal buck, though mature bucks in pressured areas tend to move more nocturnally than bucks in lower pressured areas. And as bucks age, they become more and more nocturnal in their patterns. However, every deer moves during daylight, even if it is within the confines of its own secure bedding area. Sometimes that is the only place to hunt them. The question becomes whether or not you can be where that deer will be during daylight. Granted this is not always possible because you may only have access to a small portion of the property a buck uses, and because a buck only uses the hunting area available to you after dark, but that buck does move during daylight. There are spots where every buck is vulnerable, if you can position yourself there.

The most common time for hunters to enter the woods on a morning hunt is right at daybreak or just before. This common hunter entry period plays well for the mature bucks. Typically, mature bucks enter the cover of the woods just before daylight. Normally mature bucks are the first to seek out cover after a night of feeding or rutting activity. Moving back to the woods before daylight doesn't make a buck nocturnal, it only means the buck moves within the safe confines of cover during the day. What happens most of the time is that hunters entering the woods just before daybreak simply push the buck in more secure cover with their approach. The buck that would normally move around for a while after daylight is simply reacting to the intrusion of a predator.

This one small aspect of mature buck behavior saves the lives of more bucks than just about anything else. The logical answer to this behavior is for hunters to be on stand before the bucks return. In most cases this means being on stand and set up at least an hour and a half to two hours before dawn. You must have a route to your stands that does not spook the deer you intend to hunt. An early arrival will prove useless if you simply march across the fields that contain the deer that are your target animals for the day. Sitting in the dark for a couple hours before shooting light might seem like a long waste of time, until you understand how the bucks move normally.

Chris killed this buck by hunting over a waterhole during a hot spell early in the season.

Jon executed perfect planning and timing to kill this nice Michigan buck.

John's 2006 Michigan Midday Rain Buck

As much as I had prepared for this Michigan season, it wasn't going very well. During the first five weeks of season I saw only one buck that would surpass the 100-inch mark. Hunting seasons can go from dismal to fantastic in mere seconds however, so it's best just to keep on hunting. On November 7, Election Day, my plans were to hunt near home in the morning, vote, and then drive a couple hours south to hunt midday through evening.

Shortly after first light that morning I caught sight of a doe running into a nearby fallow weed field with a beautiful young six-point buck closely in pursuit. Even though the doe wanted nothing to do with him, he kept up the chase until it seemed they covered every inch of the small field. The six-point didn't seem to care that the doe was unwilling to stop. He was a young buck doing what they do best, chasing every doe within sight. After several minutes another doe stepped into view, and the little buck gave up on the first doe and took off after her. Despite the constant action, I was true to my plan—left early, voted, and headed downstate. The fact that the odds of taking a larger antlered buck in southern Michigan are much greater than in northern Michigan had a lot to do with that decision.

The southern Michigan location was on a 40-acre parcel with the property owner's home and yard in the center. There were three other bowhunters on this tract, but they hunted mostly weekends, strictly mornings or evenings, never midday. A unique feature on this land was dense transition cover between the road and owner's home. Earlier that spring while scouting the property I scouted that cover and found a primary scrape area in its center. The transition cover paralleled the road and ran the full length of the property. It extended beyond the property line in both directions. The front edge of the travel corridor was a mere 15 yards from the road. This was probably the reason the other hunters never hunted there. In fact, one of the other hunters later told me that he never even considered scouting that close to the road.

Mature bucks are the first to return to the cover of the forest before daylight. When they are not disturbed, they often spend much of the morning around the edge of their bedding areas, making a great deal of lateral movement. During the early season, they are most often feeding, signposting, and lingering before bedding for a couple hours. Later during the rut stages, a buck will bed at the edge of cover in staging areas or near primary scrape areas and wait for does returning from their night of feeding. This way, the buck can scent-check numerous

John used careful midday timing in combination with a tarsal drag to bring down this great Michigan buck.

Shortly after noon I reached my tree, ascended it to my perch, attached the lead strap of my Ambush saddle, and began setting up for the hunt. Setting up usually takes me about fifteen minutes, but due to the light drizzle it was going a bit slower. No sooner had I pulled on my Rivers West rain jacket I noticed a buck coming toward me. The buck was moving rapidly, as they often do during midday. As he closed the distance I hurriedly pulled on my armguard and tab. On the way to the tree I had dragged a tarsal gland across all the approaching runways and hung it in a tree about 12 yards away. If the buck remained on the runway he was on, he would cross directly under my tree, giving me nearly a straight down shot, which is a very poor shot angle. Fortunately, when he hit the dragline he stopped immediately, put his nose to the ground, and started to search out the right direction to follow it, turning him perfectly broadside. As soon as his head turned away from me I came to full draw and released my arrow. The shot was true and I watched as he bolted 50 yards, stopped, and tipped over. 🦌

does in a population without expending too much energy or exposing himself to danger out in the open. If danger does happen to approach, the buck is only steps away from cover. Also if he encounters an estrous doe, he can follow her directly into cover, where most of the daylight breeding activity takes place. When bucks stage and no does of interest pass through, they will rise and either cruise the edge of the bedding area to scent-check other possible entry routes or will use funnels between bedding areas to get to other areas that might hold estrous does.

What this means for the bowhunter is that if he is there first, he puts himself in a position to intercept this lateral movement. Mature bucks often pass through before daylight, but if they remain undisturbed, they may still be on their feet moving just after daylight. The mythical nocturnal buck is not so mythical after all.

The second aspect of mature buck behavior is movement a little later in the morning. Most mature bucks have a natural pattern of movement later in the morning, usually sometime after 11:00 a.m. and before 3:00 p.m. After bedding or staging for a couple hours, bucks get up and move. This pattern often stays within the confines of a secure bedding area but sometimes includes lateral movement along the edge of bedding areas, and from one bedding area to another, particularly in the rut stages. Early in the season, there is a lot of midday activity around isolated food sources, such as lone apples trees or mast-bearing oaks close to bedding areas or in cover.

For the hunter this means trying to be on stand during this portion of the day. You can either get in early and sit through this period or you can target this period directly, if you can get to your stand locations undetected later in the morning, usually sometime after 9:00 a.m.

Our hunting style focuses heavily on morning and midday hunting. Though we hunt afternoons as well, mornings and middays present a far better opportunity at mature bucks, and the majority of our mature bucks have been killed on morning and midday hunts. We key on this morning return behavior and midday lateral movement pattern because it provides an opening where mature bucks are most vulnerable.

Afternoon hunting is a bit different: Though you certainly can kill mature bucks in the evening, you must be positioned far enough away from the bedding areas so you don't alert the deer of your approach. You must be on stand as early as possible. We like to be set up on afternoon hunts just after the midday buck movement period, or just after 2:00 p.m. This allows us to move in during a natural lull in activity, and hopefully allows time for the dust to settle on any disturbance we may have caused. Mature bucks are usually the last animals to leave the bedding area, a lot of times right at the cusp of darkness, or just after. This presents a situation much like the normal entry time for most bowhunters, but instead of pushing deer ahead to you into the bedding area, bucks will encounter you on your way out, just as they too are heading out to feed or breed for the night. Encountering hunters departing reinforces more nocturnal movement patterns and can actually cause more morning and midday movement. Wait for the right moment to depart the woods. If there are deer moving past your tree, don't climb down and walk out of the woods. Try to wait until the deer have passed through before departing. You might have to wait for an hour or so after dark, but at least you will be able to get out undetected and be able to hunt that location again, assuming you have an exit route that avoids alerting deer to your presence.

Making Time to Hunt

Many of our previous readers have been confused over the amount of time we actually put into hunting. Many of them think we put all the effort we outline in our books into every year. This is simply not the case. Though we are clearly invested into our hunting, we do have some other interests. If you really put an effort into scouting and preparing trees for a few years, then you will have a solid base to work from. In the past we have claimed to have as many as eighty trees ready to go during some seasons, and that is true. However, those eighty trees weren't new trees we scouted out and prepared from scratch that year. We have trees that we have hunted from for more than a decade, and these remain in the rotation until something happens and they are no longer viable hunting spots. After you prep a single piece of property it will generally remain more or less constant over a long period of time, barring any major changes to the landscape, and require only minor annual adjustments as the years pass.

We put in about the same number of hunting hours as most avid bowhunters do, although our seasonal hunting schedules are probably different. One of the main tenants of our hunting system is tactical hunting. Generally, a three- to five-day push at the beginning of the season is followed by a span of more sporadic hunts at secondary stands during midseason. This is followed by a couple weeks of intense hunting of our best locations during the prerut and rut phases. During the late season, we hunt as necessary.

10

HUNTING TOOLS

Although we don't consider ourselves total gear junkies, we always enter the woods as prepared as we can be for anything. For this chapter, we emptied our packs and made a list of all the things we carry into the woods. Every hunter is a bit different, so pick and choose from these items and select the ones that work best for you.

Backpack

We always wear a backpack. Chris uses a couple different Badlands packs. John prefers Kathy Kelly Design's 1600-cubic-inch Deluxe Daypacks when hunting. These packs are quiet, durable, and strong, and have quiet zippers and internal pockets. The fabric is deep-napped polyester fleece with a quiet yet strong, thin nylon inner liner and padded should straps and waist belt. They can also be washed many times. We each own a couple packs and always keep a clean one in one of our totes and alternate them when we feel they have picked up too much scent.

Inner fanny pack

John carries a small, three-pocket fanny pack within his backpack with all the gear he needs once hooked up to the tree. He hangs it on the same hook as his backpack. This pack contains his extra bow holders, tab, armguard, quiver holder, antihistamine, cough lozenges, Manzella Gobbler gloves, Spand-O-Flage face-mask, and Scent-Lok headcover. These are the next items he uses and this pack makes them more easily accessible. Once he has the gear in place, the fanny pack goes back inside the backpack.

Rangefinder

A compact laser rangefinder is an absolute must and is one of the first items we use once on stand. At daylight we measure distances to specific landmarks around our trees. Deer can pass through shooting lanes quickly, so knowing distances to certain landmarks in shooting lanes is a must.

122

Having the right gear with you for any situation leads to regular success. Here John shows the contents of his hunting pack.

Steps

We never know how many steps we need to take to any particular hunting location until we refer to our maps and notebooks. Since every property owner has different rules concerning steps in trees, we have to note after each location is finished how many steps we need to ascend that tree.

We prefer Gorilla's half-inch diameter Vortex steps. They screw in easily, they have heavy knurling for a better grip while climbing, and they are comfortable to stand on for long periods. Another favorite are Cranford's (EZY) single- and double-fold steps. We recommend these for hunting from trees with thick bark. You can screw their entire length of threads into the wood of the tree, between the creases of bark. With non-folding steps you can't get the threads buried all the way into the meat of the tree. Cranford and Climbpaws are the two types of strap-on steps we use.

Rope

We carry a 40-foot, $^3/_8$-inch diameter rope that is nylon to the core. This large-diameter rope does not tangle as easily as smaller diameter ropes and will not crimp-up over time as poly core rope does.

Tree saddle

We use Ambush saddles by Trophyline. Saddles roll up small enough to fit in our backpacks with all the rest of our gear.

Scent-eliminating spray
Chris carries a small bottle of Vanishing Hunter scent-eliminating spray for spraying down anything that may pick up scent along the way.

Ziploc bags
We carry a gallon- and several quart-sized Ziploc freezer bags. The gallon bag is for stowing scent-contaminated clothing from long walks, and the quart bags store Grabber warmers after hunting.

Grabber warmers
Grabber's adhesive body warmers are a great tool in cold weather. On a mid-December hunt in 2008 John had five adhesive body warmers strategically placed on his bottom layer, one in the center of his chest, one over each kidney, one on his lower back and one at the base of his neck. He also had one under his fleece headcover to keep his head warm. The temperature that evening was 7 degrees with 30-plus mph winds, making the wind chill minus 30 degrees. It was also snowing heavily. His bare face took a beating that evening, but the rest of his body was toasty warm.

Grabber's adhesive body warmers can be adhered to your bottom layer of long johns without burning your skin. They have very controlled heat release and do not get warmer than 145 degrees. Other styles of warmers can get extremely hot and burn you because the air hole size and patterns in their outer fabric provide less control. The more air they get, the hotter they become. At the end of a hunt, if our warmers are not spent, we seal them in freezer bags. Sealing the bags stops the oxygen-based chemical reaction. They can then be used again on following hunts. We carry extra hand, toe, and adhesive warmers in our packs.

Compass
Never go into the woods without a compass, even in areas where you think you do not need one. On countless occasions a compass has been invaluable after tracking a deer after dark. It is easy to get so involved in a blood trail that you end up not knowing where you are.

Saw
We carry a Gerber folding handsaw and also the extra pelvic saw blade that can be easily exchanged into it in the field without tools.

Water bottle
A 20-ounce plastic water bottle is always in our packs.

Pee bottle
We also carry 20-once wide-mouth plastic bottle to urinate in.

Food

We always carry some sort of high energy snacks or food, depending on how long the hunt will be. For single-session hunts, we take a chocolate bar, Wilderness Athlete bar, apple, or a couple granola bars. Many of the bars we take come in noisy wrappers, so before we go hunting we take them out of their wrappers and put them in a quart Ziploc bag. On all-day hunts we pack a bigger lunch.

Bow hangers/gear hooks

We take several Cranford (EZY) or HME bow hangers with us at all times. These two brands screw easily into even the hardest of trees, and we use them as gear holders and screw them in and leave them upside down for hanging the nylon loops of our backpacks on.

Screw-in quiver adaptor

We always have a quiver adaptor that screws into the tree. We always remove our quivers from our bows. Bow clearance can be tough in awkward shot positions, and having a quiver full of arrows is a disadvantage.

Antihistamine tablets and cough lozenges

We carry these for the times we need them. It is quite common for us to take an antihistamine tablet on cold mornings when we have colds to keep our noses from running so we don't sniffle and to keep our eyes from tearing up.

Rattle bag

We prefer to carry a rattle bag with wooden sticks rather than a set of large real or fake antlers. Rattle bags are user-friendly, quieter to carry around because they are compact, small enough to fit in an exterior backpack pocket, and they work fine in pressured areas where aggressive rattling tends to be detrimental to success.

Grunt calls

We carry a low-volume homemade inhale grunt call for close encounters and an older MAD-207 exhale grunt/wheeze combo for the times we need to reach out longer distances. Because our grunt calls are made of plastic and are kept in the same pocket with our saw and rattle bag, we cover them with foam stick-on material so they won't make noise hitting each other or the saw when we take them out or put them back.

Bleat-in-Heat can

We have called in and taken bucks as a direct result of using a Quaker Boy Bleat-in-Heat can. We have cold-called bucks in and called in bucks that were with does with this call, and it is simple to use.

Knife
We prefer a folding Buck knife with a non-serrated $3^1/2$-inch blade.

Gloves
We wear Scent-Lok gloves to and from our stands until we are tethered to the tree. While on stand we wear Manzella Gobbler gloves that have been washed in scent-free detergent. These gloves are like a second skin.

Extra release or tab
It is wise to carry an extra release or tab.

Toilet paper
We carry toilet paper in a Ziploc bag for all-day hunts. When the urge arises, we get down and go as far downwind of our location as possible, dig a hole, do our thing, and cover it up. In tight quarters (bedding areas), we will climb down, go to the base of the tree, go to the bathroom in a gallon Ziploc bag, wipe, and seal it shut. We leave the bag on the ground at the base of the tree and cover it with debris until we leave.

Binoculars
Whenever we hunt open areas, we carry a pair of 8 x 32 binoculars. In Michigan, we seldom use binoculars, because we are generally in such thick cover that we can't see very far anyway.

Flashlights/extra batteries/extra bulbs
We carry three flashlights. We use a two-cell AAA flashlight for entries and exits. In the dark we cup our hands over the head of the light just enough to see our tacks or the ground. Deer react to flashlights, so we do not use super-bright flashlights or headlamps for entries or exits in the dark. You can't control beams on your head, and others are simply too bright, invasive, and obvious. The other two flashlights we carry are two-cell AA Maglites for blood trailing. We also carry extra batteries and bulbs for each.

Reflective tacks and ties
We carry these for two reasons. The first is to replace missing tacks or markers along our entry or exit routes. The second is for marking a path to a downed buck, so we can find it again after dark to retrieve it with a cart or sled.

Extra clothing
Extra clothing and raingear is important. We put it in our packs in the order that we will put them on when we take them out. If the forecast calls for rain, we pack a Rivers West rain suit.

Everything in our packs is organized and goes in the same pockets and in the same order on every hunt. Keeping the same order means that we can reach for things in the pack without even looking. This sure helps when we need something as a mature buck is on the approach.

11

EARLY SEASON

Across the country the opener of bow season spans from sometime in late August through mid October. Depending on which state you hunt, the opener can bring different hunting conditions, from the bucks still being in velvet to the onset of the October lull. However, no matter where you hunt, the first few days of season can provide some excellent opportunities.

Do Not Disturb

We have discussed how proper scouting, preparation, and planning is critical to early season success. Most hunters have witnessed a big mature buck that appears like clockwork in a certain field all through the latter half of the summer, only to disappear between the time it sheds its velvet and the season opener. It is almost as though the deer magically sense the approaching season. And that is indeed what happens, though there is no magic involved.

The average hunter's routine, and mistakes, warn the buck that hunting season is about to begin. Most bowhunters start busting brush and setting up stands about the same time bucks start shedding their velvet. The vast majority of hunters do not practice any scent control. Mature bucks are extremely sensitive to intrusion into their core areas, especially after they were undisturbed all spring and summer. The sudden influx of human intrusion simply causes these bucks, especially the mature bucks, to enter a more nocturnal routine earlier than they otherwise would have naturally. Imagine a row of big blaze-orange danger signs suddenly showing up along the road you travel daily to your job. Certainly, your first reaction would be to slow down and try to size up what that danger might be. The signs are analogous to the intrusion signs most hunters leave behind. Mature bucks are reacting just as you would in a comparable situation, and in pressured areas they have likely been shot at before and know to turn back and avoid that area. The sudden hunter presence reinforces a nocturnal behavior tendency in mature bucks.

Often there is also a simple and natural shift in areas that bucks use at this time. We have some hunting locations where we rarely encounter any mature buck signposting prior to and early in the season, yet they show up later during the rut phases. As bachelor groups break up and food sources change, some bucks adjust their movements within their core areas. The buck may not even enter a nocturnal routine but instead move back into his bedding area, which local hunters leave as a sanctuary. This movement, though, is reinforced with the sudden influx of scouting and hunter activity. Remember from chapter 4 on scouting that the vast majority of your scouting should have been completed in the spring. You should have a number of trees set up specifically for the early portion of the season. Apart from a quick speed-tour, these spots should have been left completely alone since spring. By having your trees ready in the spring, you dramatically increase the element of surprise by appearing without any previous warning. This approach increases your chances of waylaying a mature buck before it either goes nocturnal or adjusts its movement patterns.

Do not disturb is the mantra to remember, and it is probably even more important for early season success than later during the rut phases when bucks tend to think with other parts of their body than their brains. There are a couple different ways we approach the early season.

Buck Core Areas

Before the rut stages begin, mature bucks are true to their core areas. During most years we enter the season without even finding an early season target buck. This is due partially to the changing nature of the landscape we hunt, which is more cut up into small tracts than it once was, allowing far fewer observation opportunities than previously, but also to heavy hunting pressure in the areas we hunt. Neighboring hunters' scouting activity is usually more than enough activity to push mature bucks off of feeding areas before dark.

Before the rut stages begin, bucks stay near their core areas, generally not venturing far until the sexual urges of the rut get them moving in late October or early November. These core areas almost always incorporate last season's primary scrape areas, staging areas, and main travel routes into bedding areas. Even though there may be some shift in a mature buck's core area from late summer to late fall, these types of locations are secure enough that they are always used. These are the locations where you have hopefully completely prepared trees from your spring scouting and confirmed activity during your speed scouting. During the first week of the season, we hunt a rotation of our best spots. We arrive at our stands at least an hour and a half before first light, and we remain on stand until at least noon.

Jon killed this Michigan buck during the early season in its core area on public land.

This early season buck fell to Chris's arrow as it moved from bedding area into a cornfield during midday.

John's 2007 Michigan Buck

It was the last Saturday in August when I received permission to hunt a farm in central Michigan. I met the property owner after a seminar at a local sports shop, and he asked if I would be interested in helping him scout his property. His following sentence really aroused my interest. He said that if I scouted the property, I could also hunt there. That was an offer I just couldn't refuse. After all, the property was only a half hour drive from home and would be the nearest property to home I would have to hunt. This new permission couldn't have come at a better time because earlier that summer I lost permission on a 40-acre parcel I had hunted for a decade. It was one of my best spots, lost because the owner's daughter married and her husband was a bowhunter. He was in, and I was out. I was bummed, but losing permission happens all the time in heavily hunted areas. If you don't own or lease property, you can lose permission fast.

To prepare, I printed an aerial photo of the new property, which had a large river running through it. The farm is cut in half by a major highway. There are about 50 acres of woods on each side of the roadway. The river meandered through the entire length of the woods, making what appeared on the map to be a great river bottom hunting area. After a couple phone conversations we set a date to scout. Two other bowhunters were already on the property, so I asked where their hunting locations were and how frequently they hunted. The opener was right around the corner and I didn't want to start out on the wrong foot with the other hunters. Setting foot in that river bottom was initially disappointing. Nearly the entire woods were devoid of undergrowth. There were only a couple patches of thicker cover.

As we began scouting, one of the first things I noticed was easy, and hidden, access to the timber from side roads, and the lack of no-trespassing signs along them. This property had easy access points for trespassers, and it wasn't posted. This meant that there almost certainly would be people hunting this land without permission. Situations like this are something you have to think about in Michigan.

That day we discovered one small primary scrape area. It was located next to the river where three different travel routes converged, and would require waders to access. Although it was already mid-September and none of the scrapes were being hit, there were a couple fresh rubs leading to the area. Unfortunately there was also other sign, in the form of cut branches and scarred bark, in a nearby tree. Some unknown hunter had been hunting there in recent years. We also found some other decent locations, but due to time constraints only set up a single tree near the scrapes and tacked a no-trespassing sign on the scarred tree. The landowner was a bit surprised to learn of the extent of the trespassing on his land.

John's 2007 Michigan Buck continued

I returned two more times to set up the trees in areas we found on our first scouting venture, to create access routes, and to hang posted signs at all the obvious access points to the property.

On opening morning I arrived at the scrape area tree an hour and a half before first light to find that my steps had been stolen. I do not carry enough steps to totally set a tree up, so my opening morning hunt was ruined. My initial concern about trespassers was confirmed, and I returned home. The next morning was like the first, and all my steps were gone again. This time, though, instead of going home I returned to my van and waited for daylight before walking the property. When I arrived at the scrape area I found a treestand. Not only did the guy steal my steps, the posted sign was gone, and he hung a stand. His stand was well hidden just above some branches in a huge white pine. I took the stand down, tacked up another sign, and placed steps back in my tree. This time, however, I removed the bottom six steps. Unless he had steps with him he would have had to shimmy up the tree about 14 feet to the first step. I scoured the property for hunters, footprints, stands, and scarred trees from climbers, but didn't find anything else. Later, one of the other bowhunters on the property did find another stand and removed it. I hunted the property a few more times in mid-October, mainly to check for trespassers. I didn't find any trespassers, but I did see a few yearlings and one very nice wide-racked buck.

In late October I loaded up my waders and headed back to the scrape area tree for an evening hunt, hoping my steps would be there. They were there, but the nearby scrapes were not yet being used. Instead, there were some new scrapes about 50 yards away and behind some brush. Most of the deer traffic that ended up at the new scrape area passed by my tree, so I ascended it for the evening hunt. Perched about 30 feet off the ground in my Ambush saddle I soon saw two button bucks walking toward me followed closely by a doe. They passed within 8 yards and continued on the runway that passed by the new scrapes. After they were out of sight I could hear them splashing into the river as they headed to a nearby picked cornfield. Within minutes a spike came from the same direction. He was followed by a 2$^{1}/_{2}$-year-old eight-point, and both used the same runway the doe and fawns had been on. They too passed by the scrapes and crossed the river. The next hour was uneventful. Facing in the direction of the scrape area I caught the movement of some branches. One of the licking branches over one of distant scrapes was moving.

I could not see the buck because it was standing behind the brush. Two thoughts were going through my mind: The first is that I would like to get a look

This Michigan buck fell to John's arrow in late October near a primary scrape area.

at the buck. And the second was I hoped the buck would come my way. The chances of him passing by me were slim because the other deer went toward the cornfield. No sooner had these thoughts passed through my mind that the buck stopped working the scrape and began walking straight to me. His rack was wide with short tines. He was soon on the runway the other deer had used, and presented an 8-yard shot opportunity. The shot was true and I watched as he dashed about 60 yards and collapsed. He sported an 18 inch inside spread and had nine points. I used my Radisson canoe to take him downriver and out. 🦌

We hunt these spots a time or two and then completely leave them alone until the prerut phases begin about a month later. If a mature buck doesn't appear, he is probably already in a nocturnal routine that he won't come out of until the prerut. By applying too much pressure, and leaving too much scent, you may cause that buck to alter his movements to avoid that particular spot, or even push him into an even more nocturnal routine, that can last deep into the rut or throughout the entire season in heavily pressured areas. A common mistake bowhunters make is overhunting their best spots early in the season. We admit this is very tempting when there is fresh visible sign, and we were guilty of this digression quite often as young hunters. These core areas will usually have a lot of deer activity, and more buck sign than surrounding terrain, and it is natural to want to hunt there. Being patient though, by allowing deer to be undisturbed, will pay off in the end.

Early Season Food Sources

We focused much of our spring scouting on locations at any isolated mast and fruit trees that offered security cover on the hope that they would produce food that fall. In our area we are talking mostly about white oak acorns, apples, and occasionally pears. Some other foods in this category, especially in big timber areas where there are no crops or apple trees are wild grapes, red oak acorns, and perhaps chokecherries. These foods are available for a short time only, and the deer feed on them on a first come, first served basis. You have to hunt these spots while the fruit, or mast, is on the ground.

Being able to distinguish the local varieties of oaks in your area is extremely helpful. There are numerous varieties of oaks, and in our area deer tend to prefer white oaks over red oaks. White oaks contain less tannin and are less bitter than red, but faced with eating more bitter red oak acorns versus not eating acorns at all, deer will swarm to red oak acorns. Keep in mind, however, that they will consume white oak acorns first, given the choice. But a red oak with acorns in good cover may get visited before a white oak out in the open. You can distinguish a white oak from a red oak by looking at the leaves: White oaks have rounded lobes on their leaves compared to pointed lobes on red oaks. Red oaks also have smooth bark, whereas white oaks have rough bark.

Distinguishing between white oaks (right) and red oaks (left) can be critical to early season success.

Another oak tree biology fact that can help a hunter is the bloom-to-mast cycle on the various species. White oaks bloom in the spring and bear mast in the fall of the same year. Red oaks bloom in the spring of one year and bear mast during the fall of the following year. This means a white oak can potentially bear acorns every fall, and red oaks only every other year. Other influences such as spring weather and insect infestation affect acorn crops, so rarely does an oak have a good crop of acorns at a steady interval. However, knowing which type of oak tree is on your hunting property will help you make your decision where to look for acorns and how and when to hunt.

As described in chapter 8, sometime during late summer we pay a quick visit to our prepared food source locations to see if they produced food. During our preseason tours, we sometimes find excellent sign near or under isolated fruit trees dropping food. If one of these potential spots is begging to be hunted—for instance, an apple tree along the edge of a bedding area that is drooping under the weight of its apples—we will plan on hunting that spot immediately at the beginning of season, and we might even hunt it all day if the buck sign warrants it. Even early in the season deer still have a midday movement routine, and fleeting preferred food sources available only for a short time and on a first come, first served basis might even lure a mature buck in for a midday visit. We will hunt these spots at regular intervals throughout the season until the food is gone.

Rub or Scrape Lines and Clusters

If you find a fresh rub line, active scrape line, or a fresh cluster of several large rubs within shooting distance of an existing tree and inside good cover during your preseason speed tour, put that spot on your list of trees to hunt early.

Inside Bedding Areas

Hunting inside bedding areas is another early season option. If you are in an area where you are certain that the mature bucks are on a nocturnal routine by the opener, you may want to hunt those locations the first two days. This is especially the case on heavily hunted public lands and places where fruit trees are within the bedding area. Plan on a very early arrival and plan to sit all day, which is always the standard routine for bedding area hunting.

A tactic that we like to use while hunting bedding areas in the early season is rattling. Rattling is almost a misnomer. The key to success at this time is to imitate very light sparring sequences. Once mature bucks enter the security of their bedding areas, they sometimes become curious about what goes on inside the cover and may be drawn to the sound of light sparring.

In 1978, 1992, 1999, and 2001, John rattled in mature bucks using subtle, early-season sparring tactics, and took all four of those bucks. On all of the occasions, the bucks came in out of curiosity. On three instances, John was settled

John rattled this nice Michigan ten-pointer to within bow range during the early season.

in to his hunting locations well before first light when he heard deer moving, or bucks sparring, in the distance. Judging from their location he knew the deer wouldn't pass close to him on their own. About an hour after daybreak, John grabbed his rattle bag and performed a very soft, fifteen-second sparring sequence. The bucks wandered in casually to see what was up. The fourth time, a buck came in to cold calling, a thirty-second sparring sequence. Making subtle, tine-tickling sounds is often all it takes to make a mature buck's curiosity get the best of him and want to investigate the situation. The key is that it has to be in an area where he feels secure.

Before you attempt early-season rattling, always give a bedding area spot time to work on its own. Deer are always easier to kill when they are naturally passing through, compared to when they are on alert because they are reacting to a call. Attempt two short fifteen- to thirty-second sequences about an hour apart, and then hang up your bag.

Taking Advantage of Pressure

If we hunt public land in Michigan during the first few days of bow season, we try to take advantage of the area's heavy hunting pressure. During our spring scouting forays, we pay nearly as much attention to sign from other hunters as we do to deer sign. When we find such concentrations of hunter activity we immediately search for safe areas, or transition routes from those areas. This often requires waders, a canoe, or boat to access. This is something we learned long ago through our experiences with the opening day of Michigan's gun season. When three quarters of a million hunters hit the woods, except on very exclusive tracts of land, normal deer behavior and movement patterns go out the window and the deer head toward the nastiest cover the area has to offer. Though the opening day of bowhunting isn't quite as extreme, there are some areas where nearly the same thing happens.

The best way for us to explain this is to describe an area where Chris hunted for a few years. Two tracts of public land were situated in large, irregularly shaped parcels of land, quite a bit larger than the usual square mile typical to Michigan. One tract was more than a square mile of mostly cattail marsh, with only a couple thin lines of actual woods, and was very difficult to get into because motorized vehicles were prohibited and the area lacked trails. The shortest walk he could expect to arrive at any trees was about a mile. The second tract of public land was a square eighty acres of nice woods, with variable and quality deer habitat. It had easy access with a couple parking spots. Due to the easy access and good habitat, there was practically a tree stand every hundred yards in those woods. Between the two public land tracts was a tract of private property that was hunted, posted, and so heavily patrolled that it too had extensive human presence. The entire outlying area was also private farmland, mixed with tracts of overgrown CRP and woods.

Two years in a row on opening morning, Chris hiked the mile through the cattails to hunt a thin line of oaks heading into the marsh on the public land just off the back of the strip of private property. He supposed that at daylight most of the public land stands would have hunters in them, and the private land hunters would also be active. Both seasons Chris had encounters with mature bucks late in the morning as they casually worked their way out into the safety of the marsh. A plan like this usually requires getting in front of the normal opening day onslaught of hunters and can be as simple as crossing a stream, canoeing across a small

Chris arrowed this buck far off the beaten path, on public ground in North Dakota over a mile walk from any road, where the deer were pushed by early season pressure.

lake, wading through a marsh, or just walking a mile. The key is to anticipate hunter behavior and know how any mature bucks in the area will react to the pressure. The spot Chris hunted was excellent only on opening day and was indeed set up just for that one morning hunt. After that, the deer in the area would alter their movement, sticking more to the private land and moving more nocturnally. He then considered this tree a secondary spot to be hunted randomly later in the season. Chris's spot was ruined when neighboring landowners made quad trail across their property and extended it illegally along an old railroad grade through the marsh right out to the thin line of oaks, giving them easy access. He returned the next year to find several stands and bait piles all in the thin strip of available public woods along the marsh, very close to his spot.

Hot Weather

Early season hunting can sometimes coincide with very hot and dry weather. While hot weather cuts down dramatically on the number of hunters who take to the field, it also dramatically reduces deer movement, but like all animals deer need to drink every day. During spring scouting, prepare for this eventuality whenever you locate an isolated water source, surrounded by security cover in an area otherwise devoid of many other sources.

During early season warm spells isolated waterholes surrounded by cover are premiere hunting locations.

When hunting season rolls around, wait for an unseasonably hot day, and be on stand at least an hour and a half before daylight. In hot weather this will often be many of the deer's last stop before heading toward the bedding area just as the day begins to warm up. If your waterhole spot is in good cover, try to stick it out through the hottest portion of the day, between 2:00 and 4:00 p.m. The dreaded fall heat wave that keeps a lot of hunters out of the woods can in some cases be a good opportunity. Isolated waterholes are premier locations any time of season that conditions are right.

The first few days of season can be absolutely excellent if you have the right plan in place and the mature bucks have not taken on nocturnal movement habits due to improper scouting by you and other hunters within their core areas. We have taken many bucks during this brief period.

12

OCTOBER LULL

Mid-October is perhaps the toughest time of the entire hunting season to kill a mature buck. The early season, late summer routine has come to an end with the onset of hunting pressure. The leaves begin to drop, leaving the woods far more open than just a week or two earlier. And the farmers have begun their harvesting, completely removing sources of both food and cover. The more intense rut phases and the coinciding buck activity and thus increased hunter opportunity have not quite arrived. The whitetail's world is in upheaval, but the hunting can be difficult. Fortunately, with a good plan and execution bowhunting success is certainly possible, even during the dreaded October lull.

What Lull?

To be able to understand the October lull, you have to understand typical deer behavior during this period. For years we experienced a dramatic drop in deer sighting during these few weeks, and other hunters we know also reported the same series of events. After an early season with many deer encounters and activity, it is as though someone flips a switch. Mature buck sightings drop to basically zero, though sign continues to appear and even increase.

Through years of observation, we have unraveled some of the mystery of the lull. There are a couple things going on with the deer at this time. The first is a natural response to a changing environment; many of the areas that offered security cover suddenly become barren. This normal phenomenon causes mature bucks to become naturally more nocturnal. The now-more-nocturnal buck will remain that way until the urges of the rut push him into a more vulnerable daytime routine.

The more hunting pressure an area receives, the more pronounced the October lull is. Sometimes it is as though the entire deer herd goes underground. This is a direct response to the heavy pressure, which coincides with natural seasonal behavior. The lull is even more pronounced when spells of hot weather occur in mid-October. The sudden drop in visible deer activity can be very frustrating. We say visible activity, because actual deer movement, and buck signposting, increases steadily throughout the month of October, but nocturnal activity dominates until the prerut kicks in. You have two options for this time of year: Either hang up your bow and wait for the prerut or create a feasible hunting plan specifically for this time of year. You probably guessed it: While we have not had tremendous success during this period, we certainly don't hang up our bows, and depending on your circumstances, neither should you.

Hunting the Lull

One of the main formulas of hunting the October lull is to remain patient. As more rubs and scrapes begin to appear during October, most hunters respond by hunting their best spots, assuming the signposting was daytime activity. Though this may be occasionally met with success, in most instances these hunters are only broadcasting their intentions and diminishing their chances later on at those specific locations.

Sometimes the October lull is a good time to try far-flung places. Chris killed this buck in mid-October on public ground in North Dakota.

Chris's 2005 Missouri Rain Buck

Ninety degrees and sunshine was the way it had been for weeks. The rivers and creeks were almost completely dry, except for a pool or two. It was downright hot and uncomfortable. During mid-October of 2005 I drove to Missouri to prescout and set up a farm that I had gained access to in the spring. Though I was hunting a little, my plan was to return later in the season. Despite abundant deer and buck sign my hunts had been far less than stellar. The deer just weren't moving in the heat. And my expectations were quite low, as all the corn was also up and it was the middle of the October lull.

The second day before I was set to depart conditions suddenly changed. At about noon thick black clouds pregnant with rain appeared on the western horizon. It was time to act. Immediately I grabbed my gear and began dressing for a hunt. By the time I pulled on my clothes the wind picked up and I could feel moisture. Although it was still warm I donned my Rivers West raingear, because it was clear that the precipitation would be here soon. As expediently as possible I hustled to my best tree that was accessible for an all day, midday, or afternoon hunt. The ancient white oak was in a fantastic spot that was a combination of many types of sign. The tree was at the base of an oak ridge where acorns were thick. Half of the ridge had been cut about five years previous, dividing the hill. The oak was in the corner of the cuts. At the bottom of the ridge was tall CRP, and a brush-lined creek that also served as a bedding area about a hundred yards away. In the corner where the creek, CRP, and cut all came together was also a primary scrape area. And the oak provided great cover between three trunks. The spot had just about everything you could hope for.

Almost the instant I attached my saddle the rain started. The downpour lasted several hours, steady thick rain. About an hour before dark the drops slowed to a drizzle. Immediately two fawns stepped out of the bedding area along the creek, crossed the CRP and passed by at about 20 yards. Soon they were followed by a big old long-nosed matriarch doe and her family group, a smaller doe and two fawns that I recognized from a previous sit. The doe crossed the CRP, as the fawns had done, right in front of me, but stopped near the scrapes and just looked up into the cut hillside. She then turned and crossed the CRP again in the other direction, stopping every 30 yards or so and peering up the ridge. Soon she was back where she started. It was getting dim, and I thought she was gone, but instead of departing for the crop fields across the road the doe suddenly turned and began working her way back in my direction. Just a few minutes before last shooting light the doe was again standing in front of me at about 20 yards staring into the bedding area. By now the precipitation had completely stopped. Suddenly she lifted her head

Rain changes everything. A good steady rain during the October lull had this buck up on its feet, and Chris connected.

and looked sharply behind. I followed her glance and there, standing exactly 40 yards away, was a good buck. He happened to be standing in a patch of taller grass that I had measured with my rangefinder as a reference point. The first thing I noticed was his extremely swollen neck and thick shoulders. Forty yards is a long shot, and I had never shot a deer at that distance before. Light was fading fast and I had to act. My bow was in my hands in an instant and I drew.

I aimed, took a breath, aimed again, took another breath, and let fly. The next thing I saw was a flash of white fletching about 10 yards behind the buck where my arrow met a patch of brush. The buck took two bounds and looked back at where he had been standing. I thought I missed. The buck then fell over. Apparently the shot was true. A bit later I would discover that my arrow had cut between ribs on both sides and cut the aorta just above the heart. After weeks of heat and sunshine a sudden heavy rain got the deer on their feet. It was October 17. 🦌

It is best to be patient and leave your premium hunting spots alone until they are absolutely ready to hunt. The prerut is the time for these. If you only have a few hunting spots, or access to a single small tract of land, you may indeed want to stay completely out of that area until the prerut begins. Deer can easily avoid a small piece of property, so think and hunt tactically. In many situations, hunting less and smarter is more effective than hunting more.

143

During your spring scouting forays, you should have cleared out several secondary locations. The secondary trees are locations that are good, but not spectacular. Most often our secondary stands are along travel routes between bedding and feeding areas. One key element to hunting the October lull is that your secondary locations must be in areas where your entries and exits do not interfere with your rut-phase locations. If they do, you tip off the deer to your presence and likely cause alterations to their movement patterns. Alterations of any deer patterns away from your rut-phase locations will affect their potential.

This is also time to go through a rotation of those unusual spots that you are always clearing out. For instance, hunting a single white oak or a fruit tree in a standing cornfield, or that tree on that tiny piece of property with only a fencerow between two unlikely looking swales where there wasn't much sign, or that tree in the middle of a big woods with a single runway along an ancient ditch. These unlikely spots keep you in the woods and put you in a position to kill a random mature buck while you are waiting for your best locations to heat up. We have killed several mature bucks in this fashion. Any location that is left alone may have a mature buck using it, and if that area isn't too disturbed, there is a possibility that particular buck will remain active during daylight throughout the lull. And a doe might come into estrus early, spurring a mature buck to break his nocturnal patterns to chase and breed her.

Take the opportunity to hunt with friends during the lull. When intense hunting phases are in gear, we hunt mostly alone, but the slow nature of the lull gives us the chance to connect with old hunting buddies. There are a few traditional group bowhunts that we take part in. The hunts are usually in decent areas, so apart from just relaxing and having fun, we have an outside chance of connecting with a good buck. Most of the time the properties have been over-hunted before we get there, but we have managed to take couple good bucks at friends' places over the years.

Lull tactics

Occasionally we will implement calling and scent tactics during the lull, but only under special circumstances. Tactic responses by mature bucks are rare during the lull, so be very conservative if you try them. What follows is an example of a special circumstance.

On October 19, 1999, John noticed an unusual amount of fresh mature buck activity on his way out of the woods after a morning hunt. The sign was not concentrated at a specific location, but strewn throughout open timber that contained numerous oaks. There were several fresh scrapes and many rubs. John could tell they were made by a buck he had been chasing that primarily bedded in a nearby overgrown CRP field. On the evening of the 20th, John dragged a real tarsal gland (he had shrink-wrapped and frozen it from a 1998 buck) along the grown-over lane that separated the fallow grassy field from the woods to his hunting location. He then hung the gland on a branch 15 yards from his tree. Later in the evening as it was nearing darkness, John performed a louder than normal thirty-second rattling sequence in an attempt to get the buck's attention. The rattling worked, and within a couple minutes the tall ten-pointer had his nose stuck to that scent trail. That buck was arrowed while his nose was touching the tarsal gland. This is a case where fresh activity dictated action, even during the lull. Perhaps a doe came into heat early and the buck was ready to defend his territory.

Jon killed this Michigan buck during mid-October when it stepped out of a bedding area to investigate the sound of two younger bucks sparring.

In pressured areas, tactics such as that are strictly a judgment call. We only perform tactics during the lull under special circumstances, and even then, the vast majority of the time, they don't work. During this period, we generally do not use scents or decoys. We rarely perform sparring or rattling sequences, do not cold call, and only use an estrous doe can or grunt call when we see a buck and try to entice him in.

13

PRERUT

This is the short period of the season we have been waiting for. Now is the time to shift gears, put in more time, and take advantage of all the hard work you put in throughout the year. The prerut lasts about ten days, beginning around Halloween and extending through the first week of November. It is the time just before the majority of actual breeding starts to take place. At this time, the buck's testosterone levels reach their peak, and mature bucks move more than they had been, searching for the first estrous does. As buck activity increases, most bucks start moving more during daylight. In areas where the gun season coincides with the main rut, the prerut is when your chances of arrowing a mature buck are best. It's now time to hunt your best spots.

Primary Scrape Areas

Learning to positively identify primary scrape areas and decipher how bucks used them was critical to the development of our hunting system. The prerut is the time to take advantage of active primary scrape areas. Other than perhaps a couple hunts during the first few days of season, if the scrapes were being used at that time, any primary scrape areas that are marked on your maps should have been left entirely alone until now. If you have any primary scrape areas on your hunting properties, check them now for activity. If they are active, hunt them first. We believe they are the best locations for intercepting mature bucks.

Scrape area hunting routine

Your first prerut visit to a primary scrape area should be on an afternoon hunt. Arrive very early, take utmost care controlling your scent, and sneak to your potentially best primary scrape area. Once at your spot, immediately inspect the scrapes. If they are active, climb up your tree and hunt. Hunt that evening, and if you don't get an opportunity at a target buck, come back again in the morning. We usually leave our bow hanging in the tree overnight so that we have one less thing to do in the morning, and it also guarantees us coming back. When we

146

All the work you did finding and setting up hunting locations at primary scrape areas should pay off during the prerut, which is the time to start hunting your best spots.

discover an active primary scrape area that is obviously getting pounded by a mature buck, we try to follow up the initial hunt with another day or two at the same spot. It will be obvious if the scrapes have been worked recently. Also inspect the licking branches. If there are a lot of branches at similar height and only one or two are being used, there may not be a lot of different deer using the scrape. However, many freshly marked licking branches indicate use by a lot of deer. Do not touch any licking branches, dirt in the scrape, nearby rubs, or anything else.

If the primary scrape area is not active at your initial visit, turn around and leave. You can return home, hunt an out of the way secondary spot, or try another piece of property. Return three or four days later and repeat the procedure again. If the scrapes are still not active and nothing interesting is happening at other locations, you can try to help the situation. Using a stick, open up the scrapes closest to your tree. Squirt some fresh estrous doe urine in them. It's hard to find doe urine that isn't spoiled, so Chris likes to use synthetic scent for this. Don't get carried away with the amount. If a buck happens by, he will smell the doctored scrape and perhaps start using it. Do not hunt the spot immediately after punching the scrape. Hopefully you have a backup tree in a nearby location. Return the following evening and check the scrapes again. If there isn't any fresh buck sign, refresh them again, and return to your backup location. Repeat this procedure a third time. If there is no activity after a third attempt, it's best to abandon the location. If you do not have many other good options, you may want to sporadically check for activity over a longer period. If there is activity, hunt immediately and follow up with the same routine outlined above.

Follow the same routine at each primary scrape location. Start with the scrape areas that have the most potential, based primarily on preferred food sources nearby, and proceed from best to worst. We never doctor up any scrape area with scents if the scrapes are being hit. Adding an improper amount of scent, or spoiled urine, could spook the deer already using the scrapes. Plan to be on stand through midday at active primary scrape areas. You can hunt morning and midday periods. We sometimes only hunt midday, which means we arrive on stand between 9:00 and 10:00 a.m. and depart around 3:00 p.m. Or we hunt midday and evening, arriving at between 9:00 and 10:00 a.m. and sitting until dark. Most of our all-day hunts also take place at primary scrape areas. We have hunted as many as four full days in a row at an active primary scrape area before encountering the buck we were after.

Bedding primary scrape area

Hunting primary scrape areas within bedding areas requires a different time frame. Wait until you know the prerut is in gear and head to these spots on a morning hunt. You should be settled into your stand at least two hours before first light. You will notice if the scrapes are active after the sun rises. Even if the scrapes aren't active, sit in that spot all day. Remember, you are hunting in the deer's bedroom, and in a destination area, simply walking out during the day can have negative consequences for any more hunting in that spot. If the scrapes aren't active, doctor them after dark before you leave the woods. Return a few days later for another morning attempt. Unless it is raining heavily, or is extremely windy, hunt all day. There is no way to enter a small, dense bedding area for an evening hunt, or depart after a morning hunt, without potentially spooking deer. Whenever you hunt bedding area primary scrapes, hunt all day.

Big timber primary scrape area

In big timber areas, the deer density is usually lower than in agricultural areas. During the rut phases, mature bucks travel much farther in search of estrous does than their brethren in more densely deer populated agricultural areas. This means that you may have to sit at a primary scrape area for several days before the buck you're after shows up. A friend of ours once went out to hunt a primary scrape area at 9:00 a.m. in a vast woodland area in Michigan's Upper Peninsula. When he got close to the primary scrape area he intended to hunt, he noticed a huge buck ghosting away. The buck had just worked the scrapes and was leaving the area. Though he hadn't spooked the buck, all our friend could do was stand and watch as the buck casually walked away. He hunted that scrape area for the next seven full days, and took the big ten-pointer on his seventh and last day of the hunt. That buck was covering such a large area that it took him a week to make his rounds.

Primary scrape hunting does not require a superhuman amount of endurance; actually the opposite is true. If you plan correctly, your best chance should be the first time or two you hunt. This is overall one of the very best opportunities of the entire season to kill a pressured mature buck. Basically, the entire season can come down to putting in a few long, hard days at a primary scrape area. A little more effort during the prerut can pay big.

Isolated Food Sources

Identifying preferred mast and fruit trees and other types of food sources during postseason scouting ventures is also critical. If an isolated tree has fruit during the prerut, it can double as both food source and primary scrape area. You should have noted this during your spring scouting and speed touring and set up accordingly. Every year such a tree drops food, it should have scrapes. These trees need to be hunted during the prerut. These are trees that you may have hunted several times during the early part of the season. However, as long as you didn't overhunt them, and left them alone during the lull, there should be plenty of general deer activity. During the prerut, you should hunt them again.

This buck fell during the prerut at an isolated food source as it approached to scent-check a doe feeding there.

If both red and white oaks grow in an area and are isolated food sources, hunt the whites first. The same goes for apples: If there is an option, deer select sweeter apples over more sour varieties. Hunt the trees that offer the best transition and perimeter cover, even if they don't have quite as much fresh sign. Apples are commonly consumed nearly as soon as they hit the ground. If there are a lot of apples in a tree, but none on the ground, climb up in the tree and shake some down. Only do this while wearing full scent control. This will generate more deer activity and increase the chances of a mature buck visit. If any isolated food source has active scrapes at it, do not doctor the scrapes because it's already an active destination area that doesn't need your help.

In many areas, or on small parcels, a primary scrape area may not exist and isolated food sources may present the best opportunity at connecting with a mature buck. Just as they do at primary scrape areas, bucks may check isolated food sources for doe activity, stage there, or simply stop in to eat a few apples. These locations can be hunted in the same manner and with the same daily timing as a primary scrape area.

Bedding Areas

We typically leave bedding areas alone until the full-blown rut. However, there are some exceptions when we hunt them during the prerut. The biggest exception is when the property is small and consists primarily of bedding area. If bedding is all the property has to offer, we may hunt in there a time or two during the first few days of season and then leave the area alone until the prerut. We only hunt them when we can hunt all day. There is always a chance of catching a mature buck scent-checking the interior of a bedding area for receptive does. If, however, the property also contains an active primary scrape area, or isolated food sources, we normally save our bedding area locations as last resorts. We then hunt them during the main rut. Bedding areas are security areas, and anytime you can get the job done without having to invade, you will be better off. The exception is standing corn, but we will get to that later.

Anytime you hunt a bedding area, you must implement a full scent control routine to perfection. Your entry and exit route and timing must also be perfectly thought through so you do not spook deer. Sloppy bedding area hunting can sour an entire area fast and ruin any chance you may have had at a mature buck.

Funnels between Bedding Areas

Tight pinch points along travel routes between doe bedding areas are great spots during prerut. When mature bucks travel during daylight in pressured areas, they use the best available cover to their advantage as they search for estrous does. Wherever that cover is narrowest is where you need to be. These locations were described in chapter 4, and if you have any set up, now is the time to take advantage of them.

Funnels like these can be hunted at any time. These are transition areas, not destination points, so you don't have to be concerned about mature bucks bedding, or staging, in them, as you do at primary scrape areas or an isolated food source. We have had great success hunting them on midday only hunts, arriving between 9:00 and 10:00 a.m. and hunting until 3:00 p.m. or dark. Hunting these locations can ease sleep deprivation following all-day hunts. Hunting these spots requires an entry route that allows you to remain a safe distance from either of the bedding areas that the route connects. These locations should also remain consistent year after year, no matter what the crop situation is, which mast or fruit trees have food, or which primary scrape areas are active. They are simply secure travel corridors that connect areas where does bed.

Rut Staging Areas

In pressured areas, rut staging areas must be hunted in the mornings only. To be effective you must be on stand at least two hours before the crack of daylight, and it is critical to remain still and quiet until it is light enough to see. On several occasions we have heard deer in the dark at staging areas only to have the sun rise to see a buck bedded nearby. On a couple occasions bucks bedded nearby and we never heard them because of the dew on the tall grass. When a doe comes through, the buck will rise and sometimes present an opportunity.

These areas are farther down the list because a stand-alone rut staging area will not receive the same amount of traffic from mature bucks as a rut staging area that is combined with other sign and therefore is a destination point. Most of the time, rut staging areas are found in combination with primary scrape areas, isolated food sources, or even an isolated water source during hot weather conditions. Rut staging areas that are also destination areas are categorized in our notebooks as destination areas and not purely as rut staging areas so they automatically take on higher importance.

You can hunt a stand-alone rut staging area several mornings in a row. The best time is well before daylight until noon. If a buck moved in and staged without you hearing him, by noon he should have risen to make his midday rounds, or at least to stretch, turn around, and bed again. Either way you should know what's around by noon. If you're not successful and the runways and sign warrant another hunt, come back in a few days and try.

Other Locations

It has been quite a few years since we hunted other types of locations during the prerut besides the ones mentioned. However, there were many years early

John killed this Michigan ten-pointer during the prerut at a primary scrape area in the middle of the day.

Holes under fences, like this one, make great funnels for deer, who go out of their way to cross at places like this.

on when we didn't have as many location options to choose. Many of you certainly face the same situation as we did. When your options are limited, or you only have a couple good spots, try not to burn them out. Improvise and hunt any reasonable location. This is a time of season you should be in the field as often as you can.

Other locations suitable for hunting are active rub and scrape lines, areas of clustered rubs, brush- or weed-lined fencerows or ditches between crop fields, and low spots, holes, or gaps in fences. We have found that during the rut phases bucks tend to abandon their previous bedding area to feeding area routes, switching their movements to travel corridors more suited for intercepting does. Previously well-traveled rub- and scrape-lined runways may not get the attention they had when the bucks were traveling them after dark. The same holds true for the other suitable locations as well. However, when there are few options, you have to hunt somewhere. Nothing is carved in stone when it comes to mature whitetail buck movements in pressured areas.

Tactics

Rattling

Primary scrape areas, isolated food sources, and isolated water sources all have one thing in common: They are small destination zones where deer are coming no matter what you do. In such areas we are very careful about when we perform a noise tactic. Our first hunt at each of these types of locations will usually remain tactic-free. On our second hunt, if we are hunting all day, we perform a couple subtle twenty-second sparring sequences at dawn, again at midday, and again half an hour before the end of shooting light. We make tine-tickling noises for five seconds, stop for three seconds, make another five-second sequence, stop for another three seconds, and then make our last five-second sequence. The two sequences are spaced about five minutes apart. During midday, we may get a bit more aggressive and loud because there is usually some wind and the sound needs to carry. If we are not hunting all day, we may perform the two sequences during whatever time frame we are there. Rattling is extremely effective when performed in moderation. The aggressiveness of your rattling will depend on the hunter pressure where you hunt. The higher the pressure is, the more subtle you have to be.

Doe bleat

During our second hunt at a location, we may also cold call every couple hours with a doe bleat can or a bleat mouth call. If we call, we call once and then again ten seconds later. We keep our bleats short and concise, not drawn out like a sheep. The first bleat may catch a wandering buck's attention and the second gives him a direction.

Chris's 2010 Minnesota Rain Buck

In the fall of 2010 I decided to spend the last week of October hunting in Minnesota. I hadn't been to my Minnesota spot since 2008, so I went through my usual short-term hunt scouting routine. The entire first day I spent scouring the property. It had changed somewhat since my last visit, and the landowner secured hunting permission for me on the neighbor's place as well, expanding the land I could hunt to 20 acres. Although I found a few good rubs, there was overall less deer sign than previously. The runs weren't as well worn and it seemed like simply not as many deer. A potential reason for this soon came to light: Some neighbors bordering the property began allowing several bowhunters on their land. A couple tree stands were hanging along the property line, perhaps cutting off the spot where I killed the buck on my last visit and perhaps changing the local deer's general routine. I had to adjust. The expanded access, however, turned out to be fortuitous. On the new property I was able to set up in a funnel that channeled deer from three directions, was close to a bedding area, and also functioned as a rut staging area, and most important the deer could use it without crossing through the newly hunted property. This spot along with my original stand in a spruce draw gave me two options. The stage was set for six days of hunting.

The conditions, however, were terrible. The temperatures were in the mid-60s, and to make matters worse, the skies were clear, and the moon full. It was so bright at night that a flashlight wasn't necessary, even several hours before daylight. A full moon and warm temperatures sure puts a damper on deer movement. Even though the prerut should have been kicking in, nothing was moving. I spent the entire first day sitting in the spruce draw and didn't see a deer. The second day I sat from well before daylight to dark only to see a single doe. The doe moved in an hour before daylight and bedded down about 40 yards away. She stood up at about 11:30 and cautiously snuck into the nearby bedding area. Having spent about 24 hours on stand it was time to make a decision. Clearly the weather was the problem.

The weather forecast always gets my full attention while I'm hunting. The prediction was for two more days of warm and clear weather followed by an abrupt change. Cloud cover and a couple days of solid rain was just a couple days away. I decided to stay out of my spots and bide my time looking for new areas until the change. This is really a tough call on a short-term hunt, but there is a fine line between hunting hard and hunting smart. Although I wanted to hunt my best spots, waiting for the right conditions is the smart thing to do when it is possible. So I gambled on the weather and for next two days explored some public ground nearby. Nothing really caught my attention, and I almost began doubting my decision, all the while rechecking the forecast about every hour.

A weather change had this buck on his feet during the prerut.

On the third morning I awoke to the wonderful music of raindrops on the roof. The forecast was right on. I could hardly wait to get to my funnel tree. Tossing on my River's West raingear, I made it to my tree a couple hours before daylight and hunkered in. The cloud cover made it a much darker night. For the next three and a half hours the light rain pitter-pattered on the bill of my hat. Everything was wet and a faint breath of wind kept the drops angling slightly from the west, perfect hunting weather as far as I am concerned. Bucks like to move in inclement conditions.

Scanning my surroundings I glanced behind me at about 8:30. Standing there about 50 yards to the east was a buck working a licking branch, just emerging from some thick cover. His antlers were mostly blocked by foliage, but I could tell he had a big body, so I reached around and picked up my bow. When I turned my attention back to the buck he was walking straight toward me, and I could see he wasn't very wide. Initially, I thought he might not be a mature buck, but then he covered the distance to about 25 yards and abruptly turned left. It was then that I noticed the row of long tines and the matching split G-2s. Good enough.

The buck casually took a few more steps and I drew just before he stepped into my shooting lane. I blatted to stop him, but he didn't hear me the first time. So I blatted again. He stopped but took a step beyond where I wanted him. His head and shoulders were shaded by buckthorn branches. I quickly selected a small hole to shoot through and let fly. My arrow deflected just slightly and my shot was a little bit forward, but it did the job. With a broken front shoulder the buck plowed 40 yards and collapsed. My gamble to wait for the rain paid off. 🦌

Grunt calls

We do not cold call with grunt calls. We only use them to attempt to entice a distant buck in that is not coming our way. If the buck is far away, we use an exhale grunt call, and if he is close, we use our softer toned inhale grunt call. We have also used doe bleats for the same purpose. On one hunt in 2005, John used a Bleat-in-Heat can to entice a distant doe into an active scrape area. The doe was being relentlessly hounded by a mature buck, and John thinks the doe came in to maybe take some pressure off her. The buck followed her in and ended up with John's tag on his antlers.

Decoys

While we have taken a couple bucks over decoys in Michigan, we have given up on them at home. We have spooked more deer with them than we have coaxed in. Since the ratio of mature bucks to does is so out of proportion in the areas we hunt, the does rarely react to decoys in a positive manner, and the bucks we pursue often follow behind does. We no longer use decoys in pressured areas.

Decoys, however, work great in low-pressure areas. On our out-of-state hunts we have had excellent success using decoys and rattling in wide draws, low-lying areas of scattered brush and tall weeds, mature timber with some undergrowth, and even along perimeters of short crop fields. John has taken two bucks using decoys and four bucks by rattling in these types of areas. In lower pressure, more open areas, bucks tend to wander in search of does. Since these

When the situation is right, we use decoys, like this Montana doe decoy.

bucks move through areas, and haven't had negative consequences with previous hunter encounters, they fall easily for fake deer and rattling. It is amazing how well tactics work in lightly hunted areas compared to heavily pressured areas. Any tactic that works in a pressured area will work in a lightly hunted area even better; whereas the opposite is definitely not the case.

If you are hunting an area that does not receive a lot of pressure and you want to use a decoy, set it up upwind of your hunting location within a comfortable shooting distance and in a somewhat open area where it is easy for deer to see. If you are setting it up as a doe decoy, set it up quartering away from your tree as a buck will swing around it from behind. As a buck decoy, set it up broadside or maybe a bit quartering to you because a buck will come in to it from head-on and offer a quartering away shot. Never have a decoy facing you because sometimes, especially when a doe comes in, it will want to know what the decoy is so intensely looking at and look toward you and pick you off. Also always wear carbon-lined gloves when setting up, and spray the decoy down with a scent killer once set up.

Scents

We limit scent use mostly to priming a primary scrape area, as described previously. Another way we use scent, though, is a natural scent drag. We collect tarsal glands off of the deer we kill, vacuum-pack them, and freeze them. During the prerut, we then use the tarsal glands as a scent drag. After attaching the tarsal to a string, we pull it behind us a couple hundred yards to our stands, being careful to cross any route a buck might take. We then hang it on a branch within shooting distance. Usually we only attempt this only after a clean hunt or two. So far our experience with most commercial scents as a pure random attractant has been overwhelmingly negative on pressured deer. More deer have been spooked than drawn in by them. If you are hunting in a destination location that the deer are using anyway, there is no sense mucking up the situation.

Where and when

Within a bedding area, use tactics more frequently. Bucks in these areas may be coming or going at any time during their search for does, so if the bedding area is large enough that you cannot see or hear everything in it, perform two sparring sequences, as described earlier, about every two hours. You can also try a couple doe bleats as before, every two hours, between sparring sequences. Another tactic within a bedding area is dragging a thawed out doe tarsal gland to your location.

At funnels within transition routes between bedding areas and at other significant locations, you can perform sparring sequences and doe bleats as you would within bedding areas. If you are sitting during midday, make your sparring sequences loud enough so that a buck in the connecting bedding areas can hear them.

We never use calls or tactics of any sort when hunting a rut staging area because the way these areas work is not conducive to them. As a rule, bucks come into these locations before daylight and linger, so using a scent drag would be counterproductive. Any scent or visual tactics will only cause a buck to prematurely come in (before daylight), linger at your tactic for a few minutes, and leave the area before you can see to shoot. Performing a noise tactic could also be counterproductive if the buck is staged after daybreak in a location where he can see the area and knows nothing is there.

Stopping a buck

Bucks are often on the move as they step into your shooting lane, and you can often bleat to stop them. Just before the buck steps into the open, draw your bow and anchor. As soon as the buck is where he needs to be, bleat to stop him, and then immediately take the shot at the now-motionless deer. Make this vocal doe bleat by pushing the front of your tongue up against the roof of your mouth, just behind your front teeth, and slurring the word "mat." This call has never spooked a deer for us. You may, however, need to bleat more than once to get a buck's attention. Whistling or calling "hey" can send a deer bolting, and grunting can cause the buck to turn in your direction. A soft bleat is a neutral sound that stops them every time.

Summary

Prerut is when your chances at waylaying a big mature buck are best. It is the time to hunt your best spots, and put in some serious hours on stand. The bucks are on their feet, and although they are searching for the first estrous does, they remain relatively true to their core areas. What more could a bowhunter ask for than daytime buck movement in a small area?

14

RUT

Most bowhunters consider the main rut breeding period to be the high-point of the hunting season. It is a good time to hunt, but definitely not the best. The reason many think it is the ultimate bowhunting time is that anything can happen to anyone. If a hot doe passes by a hunter, even if he is doing everything wrong, a mature buck may show up. Every year we hear of inexperienced or not-so-serious bowhunters who connect with huge bucks at this time. The rut somewhat levels the playing field as far as skill level is concerned, because there is an element of unpredictability. We have all heard of that huge buck spotted while crossing a wide open field during the rut, or at least in a spot where he wouldn't normally be seen. But this is the exception and not the rule, especially in pressured areas. There is also some confusion among hunters about what happens in each of the rut phases.

One of the main difficulties with hunting the rut is the doe in estrus lockdown. This is the period when most does enter their estrous cycle. At this point the mature bucks spend most of their time with does in the breeding mode. According to studies, a buck and doe will pair up for up to thirty-six hours. Most of this takes place in the security of cover, where mature bucks attempt to keep the doe until its cycle is over. On several occasions, we have witnessed mature bucks guide a doe back into cover when she wanted to move elsewhere. If bucks do follow does out into more open areas, it will generally not be until well after dark. Normal movement patterns of does and bucks come to a screeching halt. The frenzied chasing that we are led to believe in most hunting media is the norm most of the time just doesn't materialize, especially in pressured areas where few mature bucks compete for breeding rights.

We have witnessed matriarch does near their estrous cycles seek out the area's dominant buck within the depths of his core area. Both does and bucks know the other deer that share the same core areas, and their normal habits and travel routes. We have often witnessed does gravitating toward well used primary scrape areas, and actually waiting for mature bucks to show. Estrous does change their routines and head for cover to seek their sires. The ensuing

John connected with this big buck as it was cruising for does during the rut.

chasing, defending, and breeding is as often more of a slow dance than a mad, frenzied chase. Most breeding takes place well within the confines of good cover. If you don't believe this, count the times you have witnessed a buck breed a doe. This time frame is far different than the late prerut period when the bucks are seeking the first does to come into estrus and the competition for those does is intense.

If you are an astute observer of the deer you are hunting you will notice a sudden overall decline in both mature buck and mature doe activity usually around the second week of November. This is a good indication that the main breeding phase of the rut has begun. A good indication of this is when single fawns or pairs of fawns start moving around by themselves. Fawns are basically set out on their own for a couple days while their does are in estrus and together with a buck.

Hunting the Rut

We made the peak rut situation sounds almost grim, but there are some definite behavioral patterns that are huntable. Your hunting locations and daily timing during the main breeding portion of the rut should remain the same as during the prerut. Mature bucks that are not paired up with does, or are between does, will revert to the same routine that they used during the prerut with the goal of finding another receptive female. Their routine involves the same staging and scent-checking procedure we described during the prerut. Since your prerut locations are in high-traffic areas, there is always the possibility, during the rut, of an estrous doe passing through followed by a mature buck, or of a buck coming in while scent checking for another doe. You might also intercept an interloping buck from another area at this time. During the rut, mature bucks may expand their breeding areas well beyond their normal core area.

Other than within bedding areas, the order of locations we hunt is exactly the same as during the prerut. We continue to hunt active primary scrape and staging areas, isolated preferred mast and fruit trees that are still dropping food, isolated water sources, and funnels between bedding areas, and we do so in accordance with the activity we witnessed during the prerut. One thing you will notice is that

Good timing, dragging a tarsal gland, and rattling during the rut helped take this tall-tined Michigan buck.

scraping activity at these locations may decrease, and it may appear that scrapes aren't being hit at all. This lack of marking is real, but the bucks will use them when they are not with a doe. Bucks will sometimes cruise by a scrape on the downwind side and scent-check in passing. Don't be too concerned if apparent activity lessens somewhat during the rut. This is completely normal. Spending a lot of time on stand is as paramount now as it was before the peak rut.

Hunting a Buck's Bedroom

A highly effective option at this time is hunting inside bedding areas. Much of the chasing, courting, and especially breeding that takes place during the rut is within the confines of a buck's or doe's principal bedding area. Most bedding areas will have a network of trails, thick areas and more open areas, and even dry islands can serve as centers of activity. Keying on these areas may be your best hunting option during the rut.

Hunting inside bedding areas must always be approached with extreme caution. The best way to muck up your hunting area is to carelessly hunt inside a bedding area and spread your scent around. For decades we were very aware of some furious rut bedding area activity, by witnessing it or hearing it from the edges, but knew we couldn't go in. We had learned that our scent control regimen was not adequate enough for the unpredictable movements within bedding areas, because we couldn't count on deer to stay upwind of us. We used the best scent control items available, but nothing did the job. After several hunts, where bucks would chase does to the downwind side of our location and spook, we quit hunting in bedding areas.

Then in the mid-90s we stumbled onto activated carbon clothing, and it totally changed the way, and where, we could hunt. Once we learned how to properly care for it and use other items in conjunction with it, we could hunt anywhere, including inside bedding areas. Hunting buck sanctuaries, as they are becoming known in hunting literature, requires planning and perfect execution for success.

Solid buck bedding areas will be fairly constant in most areas, so once you get a spot just the way you want it, you can pretty much count on deer using it the same way year after year after year. Avoid the temptation to visit these spots to check for activity as every intrusion will lower your chances of success there dramatically and possibly cause deer to use other bedding areas that you may not have access to. Hunting a buck's core bedding area is basically an all or nothing hunting option. Either do it right, or don't do it.

Bedding area hunting requires all-day hunts, at least if you plan on hunting that area again later. Arrive at your stand a couple hours before first light, and plan on sitting as long as it takes. Do not leave until at least half an hour after dark. The late departure allows the deer you are hunting to move out before you leave your stand. All-day hunts can be grueling, but if you do this tactically, you might not need more than a day or two. Plan all-day hunts for a couple specific locations during special periods of the season. When you have other prime locations on a given property, wait to hunt the interiors of the bedding areas until just before gun season, sort of as a last resort.

John arrowed this buck in a bedding area during the rut.

Gun scouting pressure actually begins about a week before gun season, when most gun hunters prepare their spots in the days leading up to the season. This sudden influx of hunter activity negatively affects the daytime deer movement just prior to gun season. This type of pressure generally makes bowhunting in bedding areas more productive. In areas of extreme pressure, such as public lands, adjust your hunting to make sure you take advantage of secluded areas only accessible by waders, hip boots, canoe, or boat. Preseason scouting for gun season will push more deer back into these remote areas.

Deer don't just spend the day lying around, but rather move quite a lot. Between stints of bedding and breeding, there will be some chasing, and any buck with a doe will attempt to drive off rivals. The commotion of the chase combined with the distance the doe travels while in estrus, leaving behind her scent, will attract other bucks in the area, and this somewhat ensures that the most dominant buck that is available during her cycle will get breeding rights.

Gun Season and the Rut

In our home state of Michigan the gun season opener coincides with the middle of the rut. Nothing changes the game in heavily hunted areas quite like the gun season opener. The approximately 700,000 hunters that walk into the woods on a single day put a good amount of pressure on the deer, to express it mildly. Even though the gun hunting pressure has in certain ways decreased in the last decade, still the vast majority of antlered bucks are killed on opening day. The decrease isn't necessarily in the amount of hunters or the time they spend in the woods. In Michigan, the number of hunters who pass on yearling bucks is increasing. This certainly isn't even approaching a majority, but this trend does leave a slightly higher percentage of yearling bucks to live to their second year in some areas. It is extremely rare for hunters anywhere in Michigan to pass on $2^1/_2$-year-old bucks. Compare this to fifteen to twenty years ago, when virtually no gun hunter in Michigan voluntarily allowed a legal antlered buck to pass.

Jon killed this eight-pointer in Kansas during the rut, while gun season was in progress back home in Michigan.

Chris's 2008 Kansas Buck

I arrived for my first hunt in Kansas in mid-November and did a day of freelance scouting. I prepped a handful of spots and began hunting my rotation, and although the bucks were really moving, which was obvious by the many big mature bucks I saw while driving and scouting, apart from a single two-year-old that crossed under my tree on my very first hunt, there just wasn't much activity at my spots, despite good sign. Three solid days of hunting had passed. It was time to adjust.

The farm that I had gained permission to hunt was quite large and divided into several parcels, and there were a couple distant, relatively unlikely looking areas that I hadn't been to yet. At midday I arrived at a parcel that on the map looked like nothing more than a thin strip of trees through a section. There didn't seem to be much cover that would actually hold bucks. Not expecting much I walked across a grass field up a slight rise and peeked over the edge at the widest spot in the trees, where the creek turned. My jaw just about dropped. Standing on the other side of the strip of trees were two really big bucks in a patch of tall big blue stem. Both of them carried tall bone-white racks. All I could see was their heads and antlers as they slowly moved off and eventually vanished in what turned out to be about 40 acres of bedding. This bedding area was just grass, and not identifiable as such on maps, nor topo photos, and it was hidden from view from the road.

I waited for about a half an hour to allow the bucks to move off before walking down to the line of trees. Within fifteen minutes I had selected a tree, prepped it for my saddle, and was on my way back to my van. The spot was crisscrossed with runways, and there were a few scrapes and several shredded rubs. The area was sizzling hot.

The following morning I wanted to be plenty early, so I arrived at my new tree and was set up more than two hours before daylight. Nothing happened until daybreak when suddenly there was a buck closing fast on a runway that crossed literally within feet of my tree. It was a tall tined eight-pointer, probably in the mid-140 category. The buck seemed in a hurry to get somewhere and was coming straight toward me. Though I had my bow in hand there was no shot on the way in. The buck stopped at the base of my tree and smelled it briefly before walking straight away, never presenting even a fair shot. A bit baffled at the situation, which almost never happens while hunting from a saddle, I waited for the buck to get about 50 yards away just to the edge of the big blue stem bedding area before turning over my doe-in-estrus can.

Chris killed this buck on his first ever hunt in Kansas during the rut.

Instantly the buck turned and started back. He had only come about 10 yards before another buck stepped out of the grass, this one a lot bigger. The two bucks shadowed one another as they both cut straight to my tree. Each of them seemed fully concentrated on the other, while searching for the source of the doe bleat. Literally within seconds I had the first buck 20 yards to my right and the second bigger buck 15 yards to my left. The bigger buck stopped and thrashed a bush with his antlers for a couple seconds before raising the hair on his back and taking a single step toward the other buck. At that instant he stepped into my shooting lane and stopped. My arrow was on its way.

The arrow passed through the buck and stuck in the ground behind where he was standing, but instead of running the buck still focused his attention on the other deer. The buck started walking toward the other buck, but then turned sharply toward the bedding area, took two bounds in that direction, and fell over. A couple minutes later I was wrapping my fingers around the biggest buck I have ever seen while hunting. Out-of-state freelance hunts to areas with little hunting pressure can be fun. 🦌

You have three options when the gun season arrives. The first and most obvious is to go gun hunting. Second, you can travel to another state where gun season is not yet in progress but bowhunting is. We usually wait until the evening before gun season before leaving to hunt out of state with our bows. The third option is to bowhunt during gun season. When hunting in a heavily pressured areas, connecting on a mature buck with a bow during gun season has odds similar to winning the lottery. You can study local patterns of hunting pressure, locate escape routes, locate escape destination areas, try to get permission in a bordering area where gun hunting is not allowed, or hunt in suburbia if you can get the permission. If we stayed in Michigan and bowhunted, that's what we would do. But we don't, and we suggest that if you can afford it—and it's not that expensive on a do-it-yourself hunt—go someplace else.

Some other gun season bowhunting options are based on the QDM effect. Many landowners are practicing QDM, and since bowhunting is becoming more and more prevalent in Michigan, there are fewer gun hunters on these properties. This means that if the area is large enough, any gun season disturbance will be minimum in and around these areas. Two things happen in this case. The deer that live on the property will most likely continue moving as normal throughout the gun season. And second, deer from surrounding areas will shift their movement to these properties. As an opportunistic bowhunting predator, you should plan on hunting as close to these properties as you can during the gun season. The best situation, other than having permission on it, is to have permission on property directly next door. If this is the case, plan on hunting in the typical manner as described above.

The other gun season option works for years when the corn is still standing at the beginning of gun season. When the corn is left standing into gun season, the overall deer harvest will be down, and the mature buck harvest will be even lower. When gun hunting starts, mature bucks, even those that are not already bedding in the corn, will head for the safety of it. As we discuss in the corn and scouting chapters, you should have spots prepared in cornfields, and if the corn is still standing, some of the very best time to hunt there is during the rut phases during gun season. When gun hunting pressure hits the woods, almost all of the rut activity shifts into standing cornfields and other dense bedding areas.

15

POSTRUT AND LATE RUT

The prefixes "pre" and "post" generally mean before something starts and after something ends, but since the main rut has no definitive starting or ending date, our reference to postrut simply means the main phase of the rut is over and the majority of does have been bred. Throughout most of the country by the last week in November the main rut is over. The change from the rut lock-down to the postrut phase is quite sudden, which is to be expected since the rut is a synchronic event and most does come into estrus during the same two- to three-week period. That most does will have been bred creates a postrut situation that closely resembles the prerut. Instead of seeking the first does to enter estrus, the bucks will be cruising for the last few late does to enter their cycle.

In a few states where gun season doesn't open until December or in large areas of light gun hunting pressure, there will be more noticeable mature buck movement during the postrut than the prerut or main rut because the bucks have thrown their typical, more nocturnal movement habits to the wind while breeding for the past couple weeks. In areas where gun season took place during the main rut and hunting pressure was heavy, mature bucks that survived gun season will have adjusted their movement patterns to a severely nocturnal time frame. The severely nocturnal movement habits are what we are accustomed to in the areas we hunt in Michigan during postrut.

Hunting the postrut means reverting back to the same hunting pattern and many of the same locations as the prerut. Any bucks that left their core areas will return and resume cruising the same areas as they did during the prerut for the same reason, to find a female. You may notice some renewed scraping activity at primary scrape areas that may have been mostly untouched during the core rut period. Since bucks are less and less likely to find an estrous doe, they have more time to signpost. In pressured areas, this is only if a mature buck or two has survived. Mature bucks that survive the gun season there will not only move less during daylight hours than they did prior to it, they will move with more caution and stick tight to security cover.

This Iowa buck fell to John's arrow during the late rut as it was cruising for does. It fell for John's doe decoy tactic.

If you didn't hunt your primary scrape areas during the main rut, because of a changed rut pattern, return to those spots and again start with an evening hunt so that you can check the area for confirmed new activity before hunting. If there is activity, hunt it as described in the prerut chapter. If there isn't any fresh activity rotate to another area. Because of gun hunter activity, dead bucks, and possible change in preferred feeding areas, most of the scrapes will be untouched. Nearly all isolated mast and fruit trees will have dropped all their food, and it will likely have been consumed. If there were active scrapes at these locations during prerut and the food is now gone, does will have no reason to go there, so bucks abandon the scrapes. When we find a spot with scrape activity, that is where we concentrate our efforts.

The north usually has some snow on the ground by postrut, making fresh runways and scrape activity obvious. Some in-season speed scouting at this time will confirm activity, but stay out of any bedding areas. Scout your funnels within transition zones between bedding and feeding areas, and even though the food will likely be gone, also check your isolated food source locations. Look for signposting or other sign that says "hunt here." Use the same time frames for your hunts as you did during the prerut.

Occasionally you may locate an isolated, slightly used, out of the way runway through some heavy cover. This runway may be so subtle that it was not apparent during your postseason scouting ventures when there wasn't any snow on the ground. If the runway has large tracks in it, a buck likely left them. John once killed a big Michigan twelve-pointer in mid-December that had made this adjustment. The buck was using a route within dense cover that crossed through a more open woodlot. There were well-used runways through the open woods that the other deer were using. The only thing that indicated that a buck used that specific trail was a single, small, fresh scrape along it. John took that buck on his third and last consecutive evening hunt.

If you have locations set up in bedding areas, hunt them as you would during the prerut and main rut. If you witness deer activity on such a hunt, stay an hour or so after it subsides before leaving, and then sneak out. While hunting all day might lead to success, at this time of season in Michigan, the chances are so low that we usually do not sit all day.

The main buck activity level during postrut lasts approximately a week before it gets to a point where there just aren't any more does coming into estrus. At this point rut activity basically ceases, and the deer suddenly revert to a winter routine. The main concern the deer now have is finding the most prevalent and accessible food source. Mature bucks have a brief period of heavy feeding to replenish some of the body weight they lost while pursuing does during the rut phases. They feed like this before the onset of the seasonal slowing of their metabolism for the winter, and before the snow gets deep.

In agricultural areas, picked cornfields, alfalfa, soybeans, and acorns and apples if still available, are the primary food sources for deer. In big timber areas, all oaks that dropped acorns, undergrowth browse, and cedar swamps become primary feeding locations. While white oak acorns are still preferred over reds, the deer are less fussy and will eat both. You need to find locations between bedding and feeding areas where you can enter and exit undetected.

Late Rut

Starting around the second week of December, some places have a very light second rut, when does that weren't bred in their first cycle come into estrus again and early doe fawns come into estrus. Does come into estrus again most often in areas with a severely out-of-balance deer heard that favors does. In areas with sufficient numbers of mature bucks, this almost never happens, as bucks tend to be quite effective at breeding all the does in a herd. Targeting this situation is almost impossible, as it is more a random occurrence than the norm. It's more

John killed this big Missouri buck after sitting from daylight to dark in the rain for three days during the late rut. He was taken on the fourth morning.

likely that early doe fawns come into estrus, most of the time in agricultural areas where doe fawns are well nourished and born relatively early in the season. Doe fawns are only capable of having an estrous cycle in their first year when they reach a certain size. This means that the second rut is more likely in areas with high-quality habitat and a deer population in balance with the carrying capacity of the land on which they live.

We have never encountered a second rut phase with blazing hot action. Most of the rut and breeding activity will simply take place along the feeding-to-bedding routes that are dictated by the onset of winter. We assume this rut is naturally low-key as a survival mechanism. The bucks can't expend too much energy after a long and arduous fall. Hunt the same bedding-to-feeding travel routes as you normally would at this time. Some of these routes will incorporate your primary scrape areas, where you may be able to decipher if any rut activity is taking place.

In mid-December in both 2007 and 2008, John took weeklong trips to Illinois to hunt public land. On those postrut hunts, every mature buck he saw was still searching for does. John killed a nice buck both years. He hunted from a mast tree that was dropping food. The snow beneath the trees was noticeably disheveled from deer searching for food. On both occasions, the bucks he killed were scent-checking for does instead of feeding.

John's 2007 Illinois Public-Land Buck

In December 2007 I tried hunting Illinois park lands for the first time. Earlier that spring I applied for a non-resident archery tag. In preparation for this hunt I visited the Illinois DNR website to find information on hunting state parks. I called a couple park headquarters before deciding which park to hunt. Every park I called managed their deer herds. Most had draws for early season bow permits and gun season permits, but after gun season the parks were open to hunting without a permit.

The park I selected had some special rules concerning parking lots. There are over thirty parking lots scattered throughout the park designated for hikers and hunters. All hunters were required to sign in prior to hunting. After signing in a hunter received a parking pass for the parking lot selected. The rules also stated that each hunter in a vehicle must also sign in and take a parking pass. If a hunter wanted to change areas, he had to return to the sign-in building and check out of the previous lot and into the next. At the end of each day each hunter must check out. Well after dark a park ranger would check all the passes, if any were missing, and the vehicle was still in the lot, a search would ensue.

On December 15 a snowstorm passed through central Illinois and dropped 8 inches of snow. On Monday December 17 the weather forecast predicted bitter cold for the remainder of the week. The main rut had been over for several weeks and although there may be some late rut activity, the bucks would be primarily in a bedding-area-to-feeding-area routine. With snow on the ground their movement patterns would be easy to figure out. Early on Tuesday morning I was on my way south armed with my set of aerial photos taken off the Internet. I arrived at the park right at daybreak.

Two of the employees I had spoken with mentioned that the southernmost portion of the park received the least amount of pressure, so that is where I scouted first. That portion of the park was a bit rugged but not nearly as bad as they made it sound. The timber contained several deep gorges that drained into a nearby river. Going down the hills was rather simple in the deep snow, but climbing them was a task. At the very back of the property, very close to where it dropped nearly straight down into the river, I spooked several deer. There I found a small area, perhaps 2 acres, of thick briars still holding onto leaves. All of the timber I had walked through was relatively open with little browse and deer sign, but this area had good deer sign and even a few new rubs. Unfortunately there was absolutely no way of getting into that location without spooking the deer, because they were feeding and bedding in the same spot. I set up a tree in the middle of the briars anyway.

John's 2007 Illinois Public-Land Buck continued

After my first scouting foray I checked into a different area, based on my aerial photos. I scoured a large area before finding a good location. A patch of timber was positioned in the middle of several fields of tall thick weeds. It was obvious by the numerous runways that gun hunters had pushed the deer into the cover of the tall weed fields. The weeds were so tall and dense that they were nearly impossible to hunt with any weapons. Even a pop-up blind was basically useless because the special park hunting rules did not allow any vegetation to be cut. In the patch of timber I found a couple prickly locust trees under which the snow was really churned up. Locust trees grow long dark beans. Under normal circumstances locust beans are a secondary food source, but with the deep snow covering other browse they became a primary food source. I set up a tree next to the locust and left just before dark.

My first hunt was from the first tree I set up. Even though it was a mile walk I arrived at the briar patch an hour and a half before daybreak. Just as I surmised deer spooked when I arrived. By 10 a.m. I never saw a deer, so I left. I checked out of that parking lot, signed into the other, ate lunch and took a short nap before heading into the woods at 2:45 p.m. About an hour before dark a respectable eight-point appeared and fed a mere 8 yards away on locust beans. He was a nice buck but not quite what I was looking for in this hunt. It was interesting to watch him feed. Each time he pawed the ground several beans popped up from the snow. He picked them up and chewed them from one end to the other, similar to watching a kid slurping up spaghetti.

As nightfall approached the eight-pointer suddenly stared into the timber. I followed his stare to see a bigger buck slowly meandering toward us. The buck moved in to within 30 yards and started feeding, but he was facing directly toward me. I could see five points on his right side, but because of the angle couldn't clearly see what was on the left side. Each time he pawed the snow he took a step forward. Soon he was within 20 yards, and finally I could make out four intact points on his left beam. Slowly I pulled my bow off its hanger and got ready for the shot. He soon turned broadside and began walking. Immediately I came to full

Heavily vs. Lightly Hunted Areas

Whereas mature bucks in pressured areas are extremely cautious and rarely ever move during daylight after gun season, mature bucks in lightly hunted areas move quite a bit early in the mornings and late in the evenings. On several occasions, our out-of-state November hunts lasted beyond the main rut period and into the postrut. On those hunts, we noticed a major spike in buck sightings

172

This buck was feeding on locust beans when John arrowed it.

draw and blatted to stop him, but he didn't stop. My second blat was a bit louder and he stopped at 18 yards, unfortunately behind some small saplings. Time slows down at moments like this, and I scoured the saplings for a hole to shoot through for what seemed like forever. Finally finding a slot, I released my arrow. It found its mark right behind the shoulder. The buck zoomed out of sight.

To my surprise, the buck covered about 300 yards before expiring. The snow, however, made for easy tracking. It turned out that the buck was quartering slightly toward me. My arrow entered right behind the shoulder, but I only hit one lung and passed through the liver. The buck carried nine points and had a 16-inch inside spread. I was very pleased to take such a nice buck on public land in the snow several days after gun season. 🦌

and signposting activity during the last week of the month. The bucks were rarely with does and had reverted back to their prerut routines. The bucks became much more reactive to tactics such as rattling and decoys than they had been just a few days earlier. It was almost as if someone flipped a switch. After all, these bucks had been chasing and breeding does for a couple weeks and weren't concerned about hunters.

Due to the lack of hunting pressure, there are a lot of mature bucks, and those bucks compete very aggressively for breeding rights, both by fighting and constantly moving during the prerut and main rut. The side effect of the battles and constant searching is worn-down bucks. When you encounter postrut bucks, you can almost see the fatigue in their eyes. You also may notice that they are less attentive, as bucks move through the woods with an almost reckless abandon. We have experienced bucks that at times seemed as if they were oblivious to anything other than what they were doing. The exact opposite is what we are used to in Michigan during the same time frame.

If it weren't for Thanksgiving, and late November family commitments, John would plan his out-of-state hunts for the postrut, not the main rut. In lightly hunted states where the gun season opener falls in December, the postrut period is every bit as good as the prerut period, maybe even better.

16

LATE-SEASON
WINTER HUNTING

Sometime around late December in the north, most rut activity will come to an end. The temperatures sink, buck testosterone levels subside, and mature buck activity changes from centering on rut activity to feeding. The frigid temperatures combined with loss of foliage leave the deer with little protection from frequent arctic blasts. Food, security cover, and shelter from the wind are the key elements for hunting at this time.

Migration

In northern regions when weather conditions become severe, deer will often migrate some distance to better wintering conditions. Migration is nothing new in northern big woods regions where winter deer yarding areas are common knowledge to locals. In some northern wilderness regions, deer have been known to travel more than 30 miles to a specific cedar swamp yarding area. Cedar swamps and most areas that offer dense cover and browse are generally in low-lying areas where the ground holds more moisture and is suited for rapid summer growth, which equates to more winter browse. These low areas usually provide the best winter browse and protection from frigid winds.

One big woods area that John hunted in the late '70s and early '80s contained a long, narrow cedar swamp. By late December most of the deer from the surrounding area would be yarded in the cedars. The winter of 1978-1979 was severe with above average snowfall. In the spring of 1979, John counted well over fifty deer carcasses along a half-mile stretch of creek through the cedars. In big timber areas, the beneficial thermal conditions of deer yards generally keep a lot of deer alive. However, when the deer populations become too large for the winter carrying capacity of those same yards, they can become bone yards. This is especially true during winters with heavy snow. When the browse is gone and the snow is deep, the deer are essentially stuck there.

Many deer make short migrations when the snow arrives.

Northern agricultural areas often have a movement shift, or shorter migration, as well. Depending on the type of terrain, the migration could be simply changing travel direction to an easier-to-access winter food source, or a shift to a lower lying, sheltered, or denser bedding area. Sometimes the migration is annual, based on long-term habits and prevailing conditions. One agricultural area we hunted from the late '70s into the '90s was devoid of deer by late December. Most of the deer in an area of nearly four square miles migrated to a large, dense cedar swamp, and more abundant remnant crops farther out, about a mile and a half from where we hunted, sometimes despite light winters. The tendency for deer to migrate from an area that offered food in the form of crops was puzzling to us for the first couple years, but we finally realized that the area we hunted was at a slightly higher elevation and its bedding areas offered little protection from winter winds. That migration was strongly entrenched in the local deer herd. We abandoned that area for late December hunting.

Many agricultural areas have low-lying protected areas where deer can bed and get out of the wind. When an area has protected bedding, the second reason deer migrate is for accessible food. A standing cornfield is a deer magnet because it provides both food and protection from the wind. If a field is large enough, it can draw deer from several miles away and become a wintering area. This was common across the entire Midwest during the winter of 2009. The extremely wet fall meant a lot of corn was left standing. Winter cornfields are great hunting locations. (See chapter 23.)

John's 2008 Illinois December Twelve-Pointer

After bowhunting from trees for over forty years without incident my big fall took place in my driveway. In February 2008 I slipped on a patch of ice while shoveling snow. Falling forward onto the concrete I turned my right shoulder into the impact to avoid landing on my face. As it turned out I might have been better off taking the hit to my face. At impact I felt, and heard, a rip, coupled with severe pain. The muscle group on the front of my shoulder and the accompanying tendon tore completely off the bone. I stood and tried to make the few steps to the house, but couldn't make it. Sliding the door of my minivan open I temporarily passed out. Being fifty-seven years old at the time, I was getting to the point where I needed rotator cuff surgery anyway, but this was way beyond that. After arthroscopic surgery to repair the typical rotator cuff issues, my shoulder was opened up and four screws were used to hold the muscles and tendons in place. The doctor also tied my entire upper arm and shoulder muscles together with what looked like tiny blue rope, so that it could not move. The pictures reminded me of knots I tied as a boy scout.

After fourteen weeks in a sling I started physical therapy. When I held my arm out to make a muscle, my skin drooped because all my muscles shrunk. Therapy went well with minimal pain, but it was obvious I wasn't going to be able to pull my 60-pound Mathews Conquest bow by the October 1 Michigan opener. I had to come up with a bow I could handle. I called Mathews and begged them to make me a 30- to 40-pound draw weight, 60 percent let-off, super-soft cam, Conquest bow. For arrows I had a dozen Carbon Express-Maxima Hunter 150s fletched with feathers. I also switched broadheads. I decided to go with 100-grain, $1^1/_8$-inch cut, fixed blade Strikers. This combination shot great and was all that I could handle. I got the green light to bowhunt from my doctor a few weeks before the season opener, and by then I worked my draw weight up to the bow's maximum weight.

Since I was so focused on rehabilitation, I didn't do any scouting before the season, and since my physical activity was completely limited I was also as out of shape as I had been in my entire life. I don't think I have ever gone into a hunting season so completely unprepared. Climbing trees was really difficult as I struggled to hold and pull my body weight with my right arm. I also moved slowly and carefully so as not to pull everything loose and have to start the whole procedure over again. I hunted through Michigan's bow season the best I could, but in a month and a half of hunting I didn't even see a buck that would score over a hundred inches. I was thankful, though, to be able to hunt at all. And as the season progressed I was gaining strength and feeling a little better about the chances of full recovery.

On November 21 I traveled to Kansas with my son Jon. My muscles were working better, but they were still not quite right, and I couldn't hunt like normal. On that hunt Jon killed a giant eight-pointer. I went home empty-handed, never get-

177

ting a shot opportunity at a good buck. My handicap was beginning to get me down. I hunted for two months and had yet to fire an arrow. This had to change. Upon arrival back in Michigan it was time to get some venison. I shot a doe for the freezer. My shoulder and equipment worked perfectly.

I had applied for an Illinois tag in hopes of being physically able to do a December bowhunt. I was physically getting better every day, but mentally I was about to call it quits. If the hunt hadn't been planned with a good friend of mine, I probably would have stayed home. On December 14 (the last day of the Illinois gun season) the extended weather forecast for central Illinois was for snow, extreme winds, and extreme cold. Perfect weather conditions for a winter hunt, so Russ Clark and I packed our gear and headed to Illinois.

We arrived at the park at 10:00 a.m. and scouted the entire day. We found three hunting locations. Two spots were in bedding areas and one was a locust tree where deer had been feeding on the dropped locust beans. We weren't completely happy with our three locations, so we didn't hunt the next morning so we could do some more scouting. After we found two more hunting spots that morning we returned to the hotel, cleaned up, and went hunting. To say the weather was absolutely miserable would be an understatement. The temperature was seven degrees, there was a biting wind, and it was snowing sideways. We knew what we were getting into and were totally prepared. My Rivers West suit blocked the wind and kept me dry. I had five Grabber Adhesive Body Warmers strategically placed around my body to keep my core body temperature and head toasty warm.

I decided to hunt the locust tree location because the year before I had taken a nine-pointer from a different Illinois state park in December that was feeding on locust beans. I was perched about 30 feet up a maple tree, 20 yards from the locust. The mobility of the saddle allowed me to swing around the tree and place my nose against the trunk, which blocked the wind from my face. The wind was so strong that I rarely pulled my face away to look for approaching deer. My focus was on a single point beneath the locust tree. Initially the deer didn't seem to be moving. Then about a half hour before dark I heard a twig snap directly below me. Turning my face into the wind I saw a three- and a six-pointer, followed closely by an eight-pointer. They passed through and meandered out of sight into the timber. By the time I put my head back behind the trunk my eyes were watering profusely. No sooner did the group of bucks disappear a respectable ten-pointer suddenly stepped beneath the locust tree. He didn't eat any beans, but was sniffing as if scent checking for a receptive doe. I was amazed that suddenly all these bucks were on the move during such poor weather conditions. I was considering taking the 20 yard shot at the ten-pointer when another deer caught my attention. Through the whiteout I could just make out another buck, and three does, moving toward the locust. This was unbelievable. I was on state land only two days after

John endured some daunting obstacles and a very long season before he killed this great winter twelve-pointer.

gun season and this was the fifth buck of the evening. As he got closer it was clear that he was a shooter.

Swinging back to the shooting position, I pulled my hands out of my hand muff and slowly lifted my bow off its hanger. The buck steadily progressed and within thirty seconds was 18 yards and slightly quartering to me. I came to full draw and blatted to stop him, but due to the strong wind he didn't hear me. I blatted again a bit louder, and no response. He was now 14 yards away, broadside, and still moving. Two more steps would put him behind brush. My last vocal bleat was loud, he heard it, stopped abruptly, and looked around for the source of the sound. I waited a long time for this opportunity. In my haste to stop the buck I forgot to check my bulky clothing for string clearance once at full draw. Fortunately the clearance was fine and the arrow flew true, finding its mark right behind the buck's shoulder. The buck shot through the timber and just when I thought he would disappear into the blizzard he dropped.

I immediately lowered my equipment and practically floated over to see what he was. In those few brief minutes he was already covered with a blanket of snow. His left antler had six tines, and when I pulled his head out of the snow, the other side was a perfect match, a perfectly typical twelve-pointer. A long, hard, and sometimes painful year culminated with this success on a single afternoon hunt. Sometimes bowhunting for whitetails is about persevering.

Russ hunted for two more days without seeing anything he wanted to shoot. His hunt was then cut short by a severe ice storm. 🦌

Winter Bedding and Feeding

Although the odds at connecting with a mature buck remain low overall after gun season in pressured areas, the chances improve when the bucks' routines change from postrut and late rut patterns to a winter bedding and feeding pattern. Now is the time to hunt those locations that you set up immediately after the previous season. The postseason scouting chapter has more on scouting plans and what to look for when setting up late season locations.

If you don't have any late season spots ready, winter scouting is fairly straightforward. Set up on well-used runways and keep your eyes open for runs with large sets of tracks. The best locations are along transition routes between bedding and feeding areas that provide the best cover. Stay away from field edges. Deer group in winter and often travel single file. They slow down as they near fields to scour for danger. It is difficult enough to fool a single deer while sitting along a field edge with an open sky background, let alone several. Pressured deer will not be fooled by field edge hunting.

By deep winter most acorns will be long gone; however in some big timber areas, where there is an abundance of oaks, acorns may still be on the ground. By this late in the season, the urge to feed is so great that mature bucks may feed on acorns in open timber, where they wouldn't have earlier in the season. When available acorns are a primary food source, look for a hunting location. Big woods winter acorn spots should be hunted in the evening. They are destination points, and deer often spend entire nights nearby, making morning hunts impossible.

Any spot with winter acorns in agricultural areas are also prime locations. And if you have a proper entry and exit route, you can hunt both mornings and evenings. There is a chance on morning hunts that deer will feed in crop fields until just before daybreak before returning to the woods and feeding at the oaks on their way back in to bed. If you have multiple fruit trees, such as late season apples, you can hunt them in exactly the same manner as the oaks. Old orchards are good late winter locations, which you should have been hunting throughout the rut phases, as they receive more traffic as browse and other food sources become scarce.

Another winter hunting option is to freelance-hunt inside bedding areas. Freelance hunting is necessary because it is not wise to scout the bedding areas if you plan to hunt there in the near future. If there is snow on the ground, enter a bedding area several hours before daylight. Your eyes will quickly adjust to the conditions, and you will easily be able to recognize runways and how well traveled they are. Take the least invasive route and set up in a location where several runways converge. Don't get carried away with trimming and lane clearing because you want to leave as little human scent as possible. Hunt just as you would during the postrut and second rut, and remain on stand at least an hour after the morning deer traffic ceases.

It is enjoyable to hunt and watch deer during the late season. These deer are fully alert as they enter an exposed area to feed.

Dense cedar swamp deer yards are yet another potential winter hunting spot. These are both feeding and bedding areas where deer reside all day and night. No matter when you enter them, you will likely spook deer. Most of these swamps are large, and while mornings and evenings are the premier time frames to hunt, due to the security of the dense cedars, they offer secure feeding opportunities and can be hunted at any time of day. If you have a deer yard to hunt, spend a day or two hunting there and then leave the area completely alone. Stressing yarded deer too much can be detrimental to their winter survival.

We enjoy hunting the late season because there are few hunters to compete with, the deer are concentrated, and we know how to comfortably dress for bitter cold. During the winter, we usually concentrate on filling our freezers with venison, if they aren't full already.

Severe Cold Weather Clothing for Stand Hunting

The most challenging part of winter hunting is sticking it out in below freezing temperatures. We are both small-framed individuals with little body fat, and when not dressed properly, we get cold easily. We remember the old days when winter hunting meant shivering, chattering teeth, and blue fingers. Fortunately, being tough has nothing more to do with winter hunting. New clothing and other technological developments have made winter hunting more comfortable and enjoyable than ever before. Though we have always been fairly determined while bowhunting, and have been known to hunt in conditions where most other hunters wouldn't, the truth is we are prepared for the elements. We always try to have the clothing and tools to stay warm and comfortable on stand for an entire day, no matter the conditions. To use an old cliché: There is no bad weather, just bad clothing. Starting at the bottom and working up, this is how we keep warm.

Feet

Most insulated boots come with temperature ratings that are rather meaningless because they are walking ratings, not sitting ratings. Many companies make knee-high rubber boots with up to 2,000 grams of insulation in the body of the boot. For sitting long hours in bitter cold weather, these boots simply don't keep our feet warm. We use knee-high rubber boots with insulation in the body of the boot and removable insulated liners. The thickness of the insulated liner puts more space between the bottom of your foot and the rubber sole of the boot, making them warmer and more comfortable. We have some old rubber pack boots made by Red Ball, LaCrosse, Rocky, and Northern, but unfortunately Red Ball is out of business and the others abandoned the rubber/liner boot category. We also own a pair each of Baffin's and Ranger's rubber/liner boots and a pair of LaCrosse Alpha boots, which don't have a removable liner. Baffin's Titan pack boots are our first choice, LaCrosse Alpha (the model with neoprene/ 2,000-gram Thinsulate) are our second choice, and Ranger's Glacier Bay our third.

We wear knee-high rubber boots because they don't breathe and, therefore, trap our foot odor. Unfortunately in cold weather, the lack of breathability, coupled with long walks to your stand, can mean more foot perspiration. Perspiration will wick into your socks and liner, causing your feet to get cold faster than if they were dry. Back in the '80s John came up with an inexpensive solution to this problem on a late December bowhunt on federal land. He was hunting a little more than 2 miles from the parking area, and by the time he arrived on stand his socks and liners were soaking wet. After sitting just a short while, the single digit temperatures took a toll on his feet, and he was forced to abandon his all-day hunting plans.

The next day he packed two pairs of wool socks in his pack. For his hike in he wore a pair of ordinary socks covered with plastic grocery bags inside his boots. This kept moisture away from his boot liners. At the base of the tree he removed the bag and socks and donned his woolens. He then had dry boots, liners, socks, and feet, and was able to stay in the field all day.

To help your feet stay warm, wear socks that have a blend of at least 3 to 5 percent Spandex and 40 to 70 percent wool. The wool will wick moisture away from your feet, and the Spandex will keep your socks in place. Wool is a unique fabric that retains heat when it is damp or wet.

In extreme cold, or when we are on stand for long periods, we also use Grabber's adhesive air-activated toe warmers on our socks over our toes, or place an

The right clothes and gear are the key to comfortable winter hunting.

air-activated foot warmer in the soles of our boots. Because the only air these warmers receive has to come in through the top of the boot, they do not get as warm as when they are used in a breathable leather or Cordura boot. If you are walking long distances, put the toe warmers on once you reach your destination or a couple hundred yards away.

Body

Layering is the best way to keep your core body temperature under control from the moment you leave the vehicle until you return to it. We carry most of our upper body layering garments in our backpacks. Layering allows you to walk comfortably to your stand without overheating, and once on stand when your body cools down, you put on the other layers of clothing stored in your backpack.

On stand we wear either Scent-Lok's ClimaFleece or High-Loft BaseSlayers as our bottom layer. Over this we base our layering on temperature and weather variables such as wind and rain. Options include military wool sweaters, fleece vests, Duofold insulated turtlenecks, and garments specifically made for insulated layering. A deep-knapped fleece or down vest is great for layering because it helps keep your core body warm while allowing you to move your arms freely.

On cold windy days, the wind will eventually penetrate your insulated clothing, no matter how many layers, unless one of the outer layers is waterproof or windproof. We wear a midweight Rivers West waterproof suit, or waterproof vest, under our Scent-Lok fleece exterior suits during cold, windy conditions. Rivers West garments have a dense, high-loft fleece exterior that makes them quieter than most other waterproof garments. Most waterproof garments have short-

Late season button buck.

napped, microfleece exteriors that do not sufficiently mask the noise of the waterproof polyurethane or Teflon membranes. As temperatures drop, the membranes in the garments become much noisier than they were in the 70-degree store. Without any foliage to absorb sounds, every noise seems as if it passes through an amplifier.

If you are walking long distances, keep your windproof or waterproof upper body layering garments in your pack until you get close to your stand. Forget the waterproof/breathable label; no waterproof garment breathes enough to keep you from overheating on long walks. If a garment keeps water out, it also keeps your perspiration and body heat in.

The strategy for remaining warm on stand starts with not overheating on the way to the stand. This is very important. Wear as little as possible on your upper body for the walk in, and then fully dress either a short distance from your tree or while in the tree. Store all the clothes you change out of in airtight bags so they do not emit any scent while you are hunting.

Hands

Heavy insulated gloves aren't practical for bowhunting because they severely limit your sense of touch. We normally wear Gobbler gloves by Manzella while on stand. Manzella's Gobbler gloves are thin, they stretch, and they fit like a second skin. We wear a hand warmer muff with a waist strap and an air-activated hand warmer inside to keep our hands warm. On the way to our stands, we always wear Scent-Lok insulated gloves for scent control, and then we change into our Gobbler's after we are in our saddles.

Head

We wear a Scent-Lok fleece headcover during our walks to our stands. After we arrive, we pull on a mesh Spand-O-Flage facemask and wear the Scent-Lok fleece headcover over top. The Scent-Lok fleece headcover comes with drop down earflaps. For brutally cold, windy weather, we also pack a waterproof Rivers West radial hat that blocks the wind better.

Air-activated warmers

An item we have been using for many years is Grabber's air-activated adhesive body warmers. They were introduced into the medical market for people with arthritis, and unlike Grabber's hand, toe, mega, and ultra warmers, the temperatures of which fluctuate according to the amount of air they receive, these gems maintain a temperature between 130 and 145 degrees at all times no matter how much air they are exposed to. When properly and strategically placed, they will keep you toasty warm and extend your hunting time until you get tired of sitting. We couldn't stay on stand as long as we do without these adhesive body warmers.

We adhere the body warmers to the outside of our bottom layer of clothing when we feel the slightest bit cold. Depending on the severity of the weather and wind, we use as many as five at a time, but usually we only use two. Typically we will stick one on each side of our ribcage. In severe conditions we wear one over each kidney, one over the sternum, one on the lower back, and one at the base of the neck. We also use Grabber's hand warmers. Each adhesive body warmer usually lasts two to three hunts because we peel them off before exiting the tree, stick them together (perpendicular to each other so they are easy to separate on the next hunt), and slide them into a quart-size Ziploc freezer bag. This cuts off the air supply so they can be used again.

17

Short-Term Hunts

What could be more exciting than stepping into a completely new area with a short amount of time to figure things out and connect on a mature buck? Traveling away from home to hunt far-away areas is quite a way to chase whitetails. In the last decade or so we have done more and more of this kind of hunting, mostly for the sheer fun it provides, but also to test our hunting style and skills in completely new terrain. We have refined our freelance style and have come up with a system that will work just about anywhere.

Access

Access to good property is far easier to acquire in less-populated western states than in heavily populated, heavily hunted eastern states. Even though big buck mania has locked things up a lot tighter than a mere ten years ago, there are still avenues that can lead to good hunting permission in distant territory. And compared to heavily hunted areas like the Northeast, Pennsylvania, or Michigan, there is also public land that provides hunting as good, or better, than most private property around home.

The best way to gain access to hunting land in far-off states is the same as around home: through networking. Most of us have family and friends around the country. These relatives and friends are the best source for seeking permission. Perhaps your uncle out West doesn't own any property, but if he is a local, he probably knows someone who does. Chris has gained permission to several great tracts of hunting land from friends he met in college. John gained his first out-of-state permission through talking to a customer service rep in California who had a brother who owned land in Kansas.

Another way to gain permission is by contacting farmers and landowners directly. This may seem daunting considering the distance from home, but the chances of gaining permission in lightly hunted areas are far higher than around home, and the farmers are less standoffish. If you don't have friends or family in a location, you have to decide where you want to hunt before taking the first

This giant Iowa buck fell to John's arrow on a short-term freelance hunt.

step. Initially we planned our hunting locations in areas that we could drive to in a single day, to states with known populations of big bucks. Our first trips were to Ohio, Wisconsin, and Iowa.

Look for areas not yet on the big buck map. Trying to land free permission in famous areas like Buffalo County, Wisconsin, or Pike County, Illinois, is nearly impossible unless you already know someone. Lesser known areas can provide hunting almost as spectacular as famous areas, and it is far easier to get permission. It will take a little upfront work to acquire hunting permission, but once you make the effort, it is not that difficult. And if you currently live and hunt in a heavily hunted area, once you make the first trip, you will wonder why you didn't take the time to do it years ago.

The first step is to buy a DeLorme atlas of the state you would like to hunt. These maps usually show every piece of state and federal land that are open to hunting as well as all creeks, rivers, and lakes. Knowing where all the public hunting properties are is important because it will give you a backup plan if you get there and your current plan isn't working out. Look for counties that have a lot of creeks and rivers. The next step is to obtain a plat book of that county. These are almost always available from the county clerk's office. Many plat books in western states list both the addresses and phone numbers of the landowners, along with the location and size of their property. When your plat book arrives, compare property ownership to the maps in the atlas. Find out who owns property along the creeks and rivers and nearby timber areas. You might consider the property along a small creek bottom through an area that is otherwise completely open. Sometimes places like this are real sleepers, that other out-of-state hunters wouldn't think of hunting because more typical habitat exists elsewhere. Landowners who own such properties probably aren't often asked for hunting permission.

Locate several different areas that potentially hold deer, and then compare the landownership according to your plat map to aerial photos on your computer. Make a list of the landowners to ask. The next step is the phone call. Cold calling is sometimes tough business, but we have had fairly good luck in states like Iowa, Missouri, Kansas, Nebraska, and North Dakota.

If you have the time, a spring trip to the area you would like to hunt is a great idea. Just like gaining permission around home, a personal visit can help your cause. It is easy nowadays for people to say no over the phone, but in person, requests are more difficult to decline. Asking for permission on the spot also allows you to show you are a respectful and serious hunter. Find the local lunch locale, or morning coffee hangout, that most nearby farmers use. Quite often local taverns are the best places to eat lunch or dinner because they have a more open atmosphere than the local diner. Striking up conversations at places like this can be enough to land permission or at least get a couple of leads to follow up on.

Once you have permission to hunt and established a relationship with a landowner in a particular area, your chances for expanding your permission increase. If you show that you are a serious hunter, and take the time to establish a relationship with the permission-granting landowners, they will often tell you about other farmers in the area who may grant permission.

Homework

Before heading to any new hunting area, do your homework. Through the process of gaining permission, you should already have general maps and aerial photos of the areas you intend to hunt. The next step is to print out aerial photos and maps in the closest format possible. Scour the area for potential hunting spots from home, pinpointing the areas that need to be scouted intensely and others that you can either ignore or quickly cruise through. Mark areas of interest, such as obvious funnels, travel corridors, bedding areas, and feeding areas. Occasionally you can basically select a tree to hunt from the combinations of maps and aerial photos. You should still look at everything a piece of property has to offer, but doing this kind of homework shortens the footwork and gives an overview of a new area that was impossible before computer technology.

John's 2009 Kansas Buck

Even though I didn't kill a buck in Michigan in 2009 I considered it a good season. It was the first year since 1999 that I saw three different Pope and Young class bucks before gun season in Michigan. In 2008 I never even saw a 100-inch buck in my home state. My son Jon and I always plan an out-of-state bowhunt beginning around the Michigan gun opener. This year we met our good friend Bryan Schupbach in Kansas on November 15.

On the last day of our Kansas hunt the year before, Jon and I knocked on some doors for permission and acquired three new properties for 2009. Because it was our last day we couldn't scout them. So as soon as we arrived we hurriedly prepped some of our old stand locations and began scouting our new ones. Two of the new tracts were fair, but one was excellent. It was a long wide draw with a small creek running through it. The draw was lined with mature timber, and was full of dense brush and wild grasses. All around the draw in every direction for several miles was nothing but picked crop fields. With the crops down this was the only available cover in the area. About half a mile off the road the draw narrowed to its tightest point. There we found several active scrapes and fresh rubs everywhere, and to make things even better there was a large multi-trunked cottonwood exactly in the center. This was definitely the spot.

The three of us spent about two hours getting this stand just right, because we were sure someone would get an opportunity at a good buck. After the shooting lanes were cleared we hung a Lone Wolf stand about 20 feet up the straightest trunk for Bryan, and prepared a spot for an Ambush saddle about 30 feet up another crooked trunk. The next morning Bryan was in his stand well before first light. Just after daybreak a wide buck walked right into one of the shooting lanes. The buck carried a really wide rack with many tines. Bryan decided to shoot. He made a perfect shot and watched the buck run 30 yards and fall over. Bryan glassed the dead buck and could see that it had very short tines, but there were twelve of them. Since it was still early he decided to sit for a while and enjoy the remainder of the morning. To Bryan's dismay it wasn't even an hour later that an absolute bruiser ten-pointer sauntered in. He claimed the buck would have made an excellent magazine cover photo, because it was perfectly symmetrical with tall white tines. It hung around the area for a long time, worked a scrape, and made a new rub. The buck edged his way over to the dead twelve-point, sniffed it briefly, and meandered off.

This area was so hot that even though we had disturbed it for several hours when we scouted it, and dragged a buck out the next day, I decided to hunt there the following morning, something I would never do at home in Michigan. Sitting in my saddle well before first light I could hear several deer pass through. Just after daybreak a couple six-pointers started sparring nearby. They put on quite a show,

190

This buck had been a real fighter—every one of its tines was broken.

and gave me some ideas for future rattling sequence attempts. Before they finished another bigger buck stepped into the scene. He was cruising the edge of the funnel along the opposite side of the draw from where the bucks were sparring. He heard them and changed course to check out the action. I happened to be right in between the big mature buck and the youngsters. As he got closer I glanced at his rack. It was bone-white with a couple large tines. Immediately I assumed this was the buck Bryan saw and concentrated solely on making the shot. There was no way three big bucks could be using the same travel corridor. I didn't even glance at the rack again. The buck moved steadily toward the yearlings and within seconds was at 8 yards. When I came to full draw he stopped and looked up at me. I thought I was totally busted, but this was Kansas not Michigan and a moment later he lowered his head and kept walking. The buck took a few more steps and gave me a broadside shot. At the impact of the arrow he bounded about 40 yards and collapsed.

I packed my gear up, lowered my bow, and walked over to see just how perfect the ten-point was. The ten-point might indeed have been perfect, but the nine-point lying at my feet certainly wasn't.

He had seriously massive main beams and the looks of a big non-typical, but every point on the rack was broken. Five points were missing right at the main beam, and one of the main beams was busted. At least 6 inches were missing, along with who knows how many points. I had just shot one messed up heavy-antlered buck. I was surprised and initially felt a twinge of disappointment, but that feeling quickly changed to elation at having killed a mature uniquely antlered warrior. I sure would like to see all the bucks he battled with to break tines like that. 🦌

Timing

The rut phases are the best time for out-of-state trips. Most crops are harvested by the end of October, removing large bedding areas in the form of standing corn, milo, and even some taller soybean fields. As crops are harvested, the deer that were bedded in them have no alternative but to move to another bedding area. This concentrates the deer in wooded areas. The foliage drop also concentrates deer. The testosterone levels in bucks peak, and they move more during daylight. It is common for creeks and rivers to be lined with excellent bedding or transition cover. Once the crops are harvested and the foliage has dropped, these are often the only areas that offer any security cover, making hunting rather easy.

Driving

When you arrive at a new area, the first thing to do is take a drive around the area. This is a form of scouting. As you drive, compare the actual conditions on the ground to those on the map. For instance, you can see that there are fields on maps and photos, but you can't tell what is growing there, whether crop is standing or has already been harvested. The drive will give you a more precise starting point for your upcoming scouting. You may have located a travel corridor on your maps that leads to a field, but when you arrive you find the field is plowed dirt. You can pretty much assume that that corridor is not seeing much use and can concentrate your initial scouting efforts elsewhere, perhaps on another, less-obvious travel route to a food source. The initial drive will give you a feel for the overall condition of the area.

You should also stop at the landowner's house, if you are hunting private property, to thank the landowner in advance for allowing you to hunt. Always take a few minutes to establish a relationship or firm up an already existing relationship. Farmers and landowners want to put a face to the people they grant permission to, and they oftentimes are a wealth of information regarding what has been happening on their property. They might tell you where a big buck has been spotted or, even better, has been seen often, and who or what human activity has taken place on the property. A conversation like this can help you plan your next steps.

Speed Scouting

The biggest mistake hunters make on short-term hunts is hunting too soon. Most guys hit the woods and immediately start hunting. After driving eighteen hours to get someplace, no wonder. However, don't hunt until you get a good overview of the deer activity in the area. Speed scouting is the answer. You will

A freelance pack should contain everything you need to prep a single tree.

increase your chances of success dramatically if you take at least one whole day to scout the entire property or properties you will be hunting.

Try to schedule your trip so that you arrive early in the morning and can scout that first full day. Put on your scent control scouting attire and take every precaution that you do while hunting. Even though you will be hunting deer that experience far less hunting pressure than back home, leaving loads of scent will have a negative effect on buck movement. Try not to broadcast your intentions by leaving a large amount of scent in the woods.

Take one loaded freelance fanny pack and put enough steps and bow holders in your regular scouting backpack to prepare at least three trees. Load your freelance fanny pack with everything you need to prepare a single hunting location for a tree saddle: twenty screw-in or strap-on steps (depending on where we are hunting), white reflective tacks and ties, folding handsaw, rope, and three bow holders. Make sure you also take your extension saw.

Then following the maps, head straight to the locations you pinpointed on your maps as the best, paying close attention to everything you walk past for mature buck sign. When you find a premier location, such as a primary scrape area, staging area, or well-used travel corridor, immediately prepare it just as you would at home and remove the bottom six steps from the tree when finished.

Then move to the next location until you have covered the entire property. By removing the bottom six steps, you will have enough to do a fourth tree, and if things go well, you will have cleared out four good spots on the first day. Order the spots you have prepared from best to worst.

Hunting

Starting the following morning, hunt the best morning spot from the day before. Just like hunting a premier hunting location around home, arrive at least an hour and a half before the crack of daylight with the intention of sitting at least until noon or 2:00 p.m. After this first morning hunt, you should have a feel for the deer movement in that particular spot, and you should be able to make a decision: Either stay put or move to another tree for the afternoon. If you experienced hot action, return to the same spot the following morning. If the deer movement wasn't quite what you expected, hunt another spot. By rotating like this, you will have enough spots for at least four days of hunting. By taking a single day to speed-scout at the beginning of your hunt, you hunt more effectively than you would had you just walked in the woods and set up at the first interesting location you found.

Remember, though, that you must be willing to adjust immediately. If deer activity in your hunting spots just doesn't match the sign, or you see deer movement through another area, simply pull your steps and change locations. Freelance hunting like this requires balancing carefully planned tactics with on-the-fly adjustment. The beauty of hunting out of a saddle system is that adjusting spots is easy and quiet.

Hunt just as you would back home. If you are in an active primary scrape area, hunt it clean on the first hunt or two before attempting any tactics. Staging areas are strictly for morning hunts. Limit hunting inside bedding areas to morning through midday hunts. Hunt funnels between bedding areas anytime. In low pressure areas, you can occasionally hunt open field edges with decoys. We have watched monster bucks casually walk across several hundred acres of short crop fields trying to find another doe. Compared to Michigan, it is another world.

Hunting Tactics

The wonderful thing about hunting in a lightly hunted area where there are quite a few mature bucks is that just about every type of tactic will work. The mature bucks in these areas have likely never heard a hunter try to fool them before. Also with so many breeding-age bucks, the competition for breeding rights makes them more susceptible to calling.

Rattle more aggressively when out of state because the bucks are accustomed to hearing large bucks fight and the areas are usually more open. Loud rattling attracts the attention of bucks that are farther away. Rattle sequences should last about thirty seconds, with some short three- to five-second silent intervals interspersed between the aggressive rattling. On a morning hunt, rattle a couple times between 8:00 and 9:00 a.m. and between 10:00 and 11:00 a.m. On evening hunts, rattle about half an hour before dark.

Use decoys in locations that can be seen from long distances, such as along a short crop field edge. While we don't hunt along perimeters of short crop fields at home, we occasionally do when we travel. We set up our decoy 15 to 20 yards from our trees in a position where it is most visible to the surrounding area. We have also called bucks in with doe-in-estrus cans and have had bucks follow our tarsal drags to our locations. In some low-pressure areas you can actually rattle and call as seen on TV.

18

HUNTING PUBLIC LAND

Many serious bowhunters avoid hunting public ground. This is a mistake. Some of our biggest bucks have come from public property; every fall we include public land hunting in our hunting mix, and we are always searching for new public land hunting locations. All across the country there are public land gems that can provide you with the opportunity at a big mature buck, even in the heaviest hunted states. Because of the nature of uncontrolled hunting and truly wild wary deer, public land hunting is perhaps the most difficult whitetail hunting out there. Hunting public land successfully certainly isn't easy, and it's rife with surprises, but with some effort, determination, time, and the willingness to go that extra mile, you can be successful.

Public Land Reality

No matter how much hunting pressure the private property parcels in a given area receive, any public land nearby will usually receive more pressure and be more difficult to hunt. We hunt public land in some densely populated regions of southern Michigan, and our hearts go out others across the country who are limited to public lands in heavily populated regions. We know how difficult and frustrating it can be. These properties see tremendous pressure. The hunters there face intense competition. They have zero control and are hunting areas with few mature bucks. The deer are extremely experienced at avoiding hunters. Due to theft, tree stands commonly vanish from the woods. And setting up hunting spots is more difficult because of equipment limitations, such as strap-on steps or sticks only, and restrictive limb-cutting rules. We are not trying to scare anyone off, but public land hunting is as tough as it gets.

Finding Public Property

Public land, and land that is open to the general public, comes in many forms. In Michigan the most common form is state property that is open to hunting.

Land owned by the federal government falls under nearly the same category. Some other possibilities are private property that is open to hunting through government programs that reward the landowners for public hunting access to their property. In some places, municipal property, such as waterworks property, is open to hunting, as are some parks properties. Refuges are another potential location for public hunting access. In every area you intend to hunt, research available public property.

Sometimes access is as simple as parking and walking in, but other times you may have to jump through hoops to get permission. For instance, some city land hunting requires a special permit from the local police, and a refuge or game area might require a short-term permit. Still others have implemented a permit by lottery system. The possibilities are numerous. Inspect all tracts of public land in your area for hunting purposes, no matter how small or how large. We have hunted tracts of public land as small as ten acres and have had a lot of success on a small, forty-acre piece, but we also hunt some areas of several thousand acres. Remember, though, bigger is definitely not always better when it comes to public ground. Use all the resources available to find public ground, and learn how to gain access. Then investigate every piece of public ground within your hunting range. Not every spot will prove worth hunting, but some will, and you may just find a tremendous spot either tucked away well beyond the reach of most other hunters or a small spot overlooked by all others.

Other Hunters

The principal difficulty with hunting public ground is other hunters. Please remember that every person who is hunting public ground has just as much right to be there as you do. There is no such thing as your own spot! Encroachment is normal and to be expected. The land is available for anyone to hunt, and that is the essence of the American hunting system and one of the things that makes American hunting the best in the world. In order for you to be successful in this situation, you simply have to be better than both the deer and the other hunters. Killing mature bucks off of heavy-hunted public land on a regular basis is a supreme test of hunting ability.

When scouting public ground, initially the most important sign to look for is that left by other people so that you can find places the deer go in reaction to the people. Find locations that other hunters are using, but also look for signs of general human use. Most public land use is multifaceted, which means that there might be walking trails, bike trails, or even horse riding. Follow trails to see how they are used. Deer often create a set of deer trails parallel to well-used hiking trails but in thicker cover, and those deer move more in the morning and less during midday and afternoon.

Chris's 2007 North Dakota Public-Land Buck

For the third year in a row I drove halfway across the country for a short early-season hunt with my good friend Dan Maurer in western North Dakota. Dan is an avid bowhunter, Lutheran pastor, would-be cowboy, bird hunter extraordinaire, and the proud owner of a little hunting cabin about as far out in the middle of nowhere as you can get. Located near the edge of Missouri National Grasslands, the terrain around his place is, needless to say, quite a bit different than the verdant woods of Michigan; in fact, finding a tree big enough to hunt out of is a challenge in itself. With the nearest river bottom over 30 miles away, this is legitimate prairie whitetail hunting, not to mention running into cactus isn't unusual. The coulees, draws, and buffalo berry patches in the area are just as likely to hold mule deer and pronghorn as whitetails, but nonetheless there is a healthy population of *Odocoileus virginianus* to chase. I like the challenge the prairie presents, the opportunity to change gears a bit, and to spend time with Dan, who through his otherworldly connections always makes things interesting.

The alarm clock jolted me awake seemingly in the middle of the night. Half grudgingly and half eager I sat up and mechanically made for the shower. It was the seventh day of a ten day hunt and with all the walking and hunting I had been doing I was beginning to get run down. When I start to feel fatigued on a hunt I like to jump in the shower before my morning outings. The warm water wakes me up, warms me, and a prehunt scent-eliminating shower is always a good idea anyway. A few minutes later, now awake and clean, I quickly pulled on my underlayers and grabbed by pack from its airtight tub. Just as I was about to walk out the door Dan popped out of his bedroom. Groggily he said, "Hey, I have to tell you something. I just dreamt that you shot a huge buck with all kinds of points, and its body was so big it reminded me in my dream of a rhino." I think my reply was dismissive and something along the lines of "Okay Dan, that's great, now get up and go hunting."

A step out the door I had already forgotten about Dan's premonition. I had a long walk and potentially a long hunt ahead of me. So far in my week of hunting things were fair but not extraordinary. The very first evening on a hunt from the ground a 120-class eight-pointer walked within 20 yards, but catching me a little by surprise I was a millisecond too late on the shot. At full draw with my pin on the buck's chest I was just about to drop my finger as the buck spun and bolted, leaving me standing there in wonder at the keenness of a whitetail's peripheral vision. Although I had seen many deer and a couple more decent bucks, I hadn't had another good buck even close to within bow range. What I did encounter during the week, however, was far more hunting pressure than I anticipated. Every morning and evening there were several pickups parked along the public land access road. This morning, however, I was full of optimism.

The long walk was worth it for this big North Dakota public-land buck.

Two days earlier after a morning hunt I decided that it was time to get away from the other hunters. Like everywhere else, most of the hunting pressure on this public land was within a quarter mile of the roads. Donning my scouting pack I hiked a mile and half back into the public land over a couple of long bluffs. It was there that I discovered the best spot I had seen since my arrival. Off the end of a bluff was an oval-shaped patch of aspens about an acre in size. Immediately I noticed the many runways that crossed through the aspens, and around both ends, and a couple of obvious rubs. My attention piqued, I inspected the situation a little closer. To the east of the aspen patch was a thick draw that proved to be clearly a bedding area. However, to the west, at least in close proximity, was nothing but mostly open prairie. Standing on the west side of the aspens I scanned the grass-land with my binoculars and about a mile away discovered a rancher's wheat stub-ble field. The situation instantly became clear. The deer were bedding in the draw and making a nightly trek to that wheat stubble field. On their way they crossed through the aspens, both in the evening and morning. The deer in their travels to and from the cut wheat could remain almost a mile from the nearest road, and be-hind the bluffs, well out of sight of both road-hugging hunters and road poachers. (Only a day earlier I found a poached mule deer with its head cut off.)

This was a great funnel. The best thing about this spot though was that right on the east edge of the patch stood an aspen big enough to hunt out of, only the third tree I had found with such stature. And it was in good cover to boot. Within fifteen minutes I had the tree prepped for my Ambush saddle and left the scene.

Chris's 2007 North Dakota Public-Land Buck continued

Arriving at the parking spot I donned the last of my scent control armour and began my hour long hike to my promising aspen. Normally, I walk to my stands without the aid of a flashlight, and this particular October morning it struck me that it was extremely dark. There was neither moon nor stars. A thick blanket of cloud cover had rolled in during the night. About halfway to my tree it got even darker when incredibly thick fog suddenly enveloped me. Covering the remainder of my walk mostly by feel I made it to my tree over an hour before first light. Within a few minutes of my arrival I was sitting comfortably in my Ambush saddle.

For an hour I half-dozed, with an ear open, futilely attempting to audibly detect any approaching deer. As daybreak arrived I couldn't help but wonder at the fog. The air was so full of moisture the fog was actually more like a mist, and I couldn't see 40 yards. Silently holding a conversation with myself I was just thinking that I would have to be on high alert, because the deer will be on top of me before can react, when suddenly standing in my shooting lane a mere 20 yards away was a huge buck. One split-second glance was all it took to decide it was big enough.

The buck was ghosting steadily by, so hurriedly I pulled my bow from its hanger, attached my release, and drew. The few seconds it took to do this was too long, and by the time I had drawn the buck crossed just out of my shooting lane, so I let back up. I must have made a tiny bit of noise because just past my lane the buck froze. Now he was standing a mere 10 yards away completely blocked by undergrowth. He stood completely motionless for what seemed like an eternity. Once I even had to look away, and then back, to reassure myself that he was still there. The buck had two options: Either he could continue on his chosen path, which would give me a 9-yard shot in two more steps, or he could turn and walk straight away into the draw, where there was no shot. With a quick flip of his tail the buck took a step forward. Immediately I moved around the tree, drew, anchored, and selected a hole to shoot through. The buck took that second step, and though my only open shot would put my arrow a touch high on his chest, I decided that it was now or never, and let fly.

The buck folded to the ground, falling straightaway, but in a rolling flash he was back up and bolted straight under my tree, and within two seconds collapsed in a crashing heap only 25 yards behind me. He didn't make another move, not even a single kick. I have never seen a deer die so fast in my entire life. Slumping back in my saddle I was in a mild state of disbelief. The way the buck was lying, right in the middle of the aspen patch, I was unable to see his antlers from my tree. After that initial glance at his rack I was so concentrated on making the shot that I hadn't even peeked again. My thought was simply, "I sure hope he is as big as I thought he was."

After gathering my gear, along with my composure, I scaled down the tree and walked over to the buck. His antlers were no disappointment—they were actually bigger than I expected, fourteen points and long tines. Reaching into my pack I pulled out my camera and snapped a few quick shots, and then got busy gutting. Still wondering at the sudden collapse I inspected the buck's lungs. The arrow cut through the entry side lung right at the top, down over the heart and straight through the middle of the exit side lung. A definite double-lunger, but even so a buck this big shouldn't have collapsed that fast. Looking a little closer, and sticking my fingers through the holes to get an idea of the arrow's path I noticed the main artery coming up from the heart was sliced with an X. Cut off the oxygen to the brain and the lights go out fast. But there were still other questions that had to be answered. Why did the buck run back under my tree and what was the loud crack on impact? This was a little more straight forward. My arrow hit the opposite lower leg bone and shattered it. The broadhead stopped just under the skin in the opposite shoulder.

As soon as I was finished I grabbed my gear and hiked back to my van. With such a long drag ahead of me I went to ask Dan to come and help me. I drove to the spot where he was supposed to be hunting, but his truck wasn't there, so I continued on to the cabin. There I found Dan still in bed. "Dan, get up!" "Did you get one?" "Yeah!" "How big is he?" " He's alright. Take a look." I handed Dan my camera. "That's the buck out of my dream—you got the rhino buck!" It was only then that I remembered Pastor Dan's dream. I guess when your hunting partner has otherworldly connections you should listen to his premonitions. 🦌

The best public land locations are usually those where motorized vehicles are prohibited. Most hunters, and people in general, will not walk very far. In areas where vehicles aren't allowed, most hunting pressure will be relatively close to the access points. The majority of hunters hunt within 250 yards from a trail, road, or access point, and very few will venture farther than 400 yards into a trailless forest. Mark every hunting location of other hunters on your maps when you walk a tract of public ground. Marking these spots carefully will sometimes create a noticeable pattern of hunting pressure. When a pattern becomes apparent, the solution is to find the gaps the other hunters leave. The deer certainly are aware of these. When you find a tree stand or prepped tree, always give the spot a quick inspection to try to decipher the quality of the hunter. How high is the stand? Why is he hunting there? Is he using bait? What would be the best time and condition to hunt this spot? Does he have a reasonable chance at killing a mature buck? Answering these questions can help you create a hunting plan for

Gaining as much knowledge about other hunters on a piece of property is just as important as scouting for deer sign. Here John is inspecting another hunter's stand location.

the area that takes this hunter into consideration. You must know how he will affect the deer movement and either avoid him or use him to your advantage.

Most hunters choose public land because they don't have any private land to hunt. This means that they most likely aren't that serious. You will generally encounter hunters with average to below average hunting skill and knowledge, who have an average amount of time to hunt. A lot of these guys are more like deer movement deflectors rather than hunters. The less serious a hunter is the less likely he is to implement a scent control program, so he telegraphs both his intentions and presence to the local deer. Unless he uses bait, most deer will avoid his locations immediately after they are set up or at the latest after a couple of hunts. This is particularly true of mature bucks. The main tenant of public land hunting is to figure out how the deer react to this pressure.

Sometimes you will find zones of lower human pressure, such as across rivers, streams, lakes, creeks, marshes, or simply farther back in the woods than most people are willing to walk. Use every tool available to reach places like this. Hip boots and waders are integral components of your hunting gear. It is amazing how much difference crossing a hip-deep creek can make in deer sign and activity, simply because most hunters don't go through the effort to carry a pair of waders a short distance into the woods. Carry your waders to the river, pull them on, cross, and then hide your waders on the other side. Canoes are another tool you can use to access some exceptional public areas devoid of other hunters.

We know of several landlocked tracts of public land only available by water. Whenever you canoe, or boat, into a landlocked piece of public property, make sure you take a couple maps. Adjoining landowners are protective of such properties. We have been confronted by neighboring landowners and been accused of trespassing on a couple occasions. Producing a plat map of the property, and offering to call the warden yourself, will usually lead to a bit of backpedaling on the accuser's part.

In areas with trails and no access for motorized vehicles, a mountain bike is an important tool. This is no real secret anymore, and a lot of other hunters are using bikes to reach far into such tracts, which means that even after riding a bike a couple miles into the woods, you might encounter other hunters with the same idea. Still, we jump on our bikes wherever we find a suitable spot, such as within some tightly controlled state game areas or refuges.

The opposite of getting way back into the public ground is hunting extremely close to roads or access points. Make sure that when you scout a piece of public property you include the first hundred yards from any road; the more traffic and larger the road, the better. Most hunters overlook the areas closest to highways and shoot across the first hundred yards of woods. They don't like to chance being seen by passing motorists. Several of our hunting locations are virtually a stone's throw from traffic, and we have killed some really nice bucks on public ground just across the fence from major highways.

Beware of Deception

If you've read this far in this book, you know that we concentrate our hunting efforts largely on the morning and midday periods. This is even more true in public land. If you can't find any zones that aren't hunted or far-off, hard-to-get-to spots, but deer are still active in the area, a way to capitalize on the situation is to hunt primarily mornings into midday. Our anecdotal hunting experience tells us that apart from the opening couple of days of season, at least 90 percent of the hunting takes place in the evenings. Driving to hunting areas and counting vehicles during season in both morning and evenings will give you an idea of the difference between typical morning and evening hunting pressure.

Although we have killed mature bucks on both morning and evening hunts, the majority of our mature bucks have fallen from morning into midday. We have far more mature buck encounters during morning and midday hunts than on evening hunts. Also in researching this point, we found that some states record time of kill for their deer and that there was about a fifty-fifty split between bucks killed in the morning compared to those killed in the evening. Correlating this to daily hunting pressure implies that roughly 10 percent of all hunters hunt in the morning, but they kill 50 percent of the bucks. The chances of killing a mature buck are greater during morning hunts.

Earlier chapters described the timing and behavior you capitalize on during morning hunts. Typical public land hunters who hunt in the evening condition deer to heavy evening hunting pressure, with a major influx of pressure on the weekends. Adjusting your hunting to mornings later in the week can be key to public land hunting success.

The nature of public land hunting competition means you will encounter some other tactics aimed more at you than the deer. One thing we run into regularly on public land is dummy stands. The idea is simply to create the impression that a particular area is crawling with hunters. For this purpose other hunters will sometimes hang several stands—we have seen up to a dozen—at very obvious spots, often close to common access points. There may even be large ground blinds set up. Most hunters who step into such a spot for the first time will immediately see all the stands and think that the area is being slammed. This might indeed be the case, but it is worth the effort to investigate these stands to see whether or not they are getting real hunting pressure. If you pass through an overabundance of not very well placed stands and suddenly get to overall less obvious pressure or perhaps better positioned stands, you will know what is going on. Someone may have a great hunting spot that they are trying to keep everyone else out of.

There are other methods hunters use to give investigating hunters the impression of really heavy pressure. Ribbons and tacks are the most common. When we find ribbons or tacks, we always follow them to their destination. If you find a couple rows of ribbon or tacks that lead nowhere, it is obvious what is going on. Another more deceitful method to keep other people from hunting public ground is simply posting the property. Unfortunately this is more common than it should be. Most often, neighboring landowners post public ground. One public area we hunt contains an easement through the property to private land behind it. The easement is posted as private property, and the land is shaped in such a manner that the easement entrance is close to neighboring private land. By posting all along the easement and on the neighboring property, landowners give the impression that there is no public land in this location at all. Without very closely investigating property lines and maps, we never would have discovered this spot.

Another trick that landowners use is to hang posted signs on their side of the fence facing the wrong direction. We hunt another small piece of property that has three small, 1-acre parcels along the front. Along its flank, it is posted as we have just described, and the signs are visible from the road. Without closely inspecting the property lines and maps, we never would have thought that behind the houses and signs lay public ground. The landowners didn't break any laws, but they made a clear effort to deceive in this case.

Another thing we have been encountering more and more is non-hunting or anti-hunting neighbors, perhaps not even adjacent landowners, simply posting the public property. On one occasion, we found a public land tract cut in half by no trespassing signs. On another, the property of a friend of ours was completely posted by anti-hunting neighbors. He even had no trespassing signs tacked to the base of his stand sites. On yet another occasion, an older anti-hunting woman walked back and forth down a trail continually blowing a whistle. And on another, whenever the bordering private property neighbor saw a parked vehicle, he would walk over to the fence line every hour or so and shoot three shots from his 12-guage shotgun, just to keep the deer from moving. This man was trying to save the deer until gun season, when he might get an opportunity.

Take a close look at all property lines and sizes when you are scouting public property. Often all is not what it seems at first glance.

Hunting Tactics

About the only tactics we use on public lands in pressured areas are subtle sparring sequences and doe bleats. Because we are generally within some sort of bedding area where deer feel secure, a mature buck may succumb to a gentle sparring sequence or bleat. Any sequence or bleat must be subtle enough that if a buck hears them and doesn't respond, it will not spook or alarm him. When he does get up to move, he may even move in that direction out of curiosity.

19

RAIN, SNOW, AND WIND

Nothing keeps hunters out of the woods better than a good steady rain. And who can blame anyone for not wanting to potentially get soaking wet, become uncomfortable, and perhaps even catch a cold. Not to mention that in most hunting literature and media the best weather conditions recommended for hunting are almost always dry, calm, and cold. It's no wonder that most guys decide to hang out around home during rain and snow.

Contrary to the dry, cold, and calm that most other bowhunters prefer, we love to hunt in the rain, snow, and even wind. Hunting in these adverse conditions doesn't make us masochistic. Being wet and cold used to be just as uncomfortable for us as it is for anyone else. It is the potential reward of intercepting a roaming mature buck that drives us to make an extra effort to get into the woods during what normally would be considered bad conditions.

Bucks on the Move

Through the course of our hunting lives, initially through coincidental encounters, it became clear that pressured mature bucks move more during daylight with increased precipitation. During the early stages of our hunting careers, raingear wasn't nearly as good as it is today, and we too avoided hunting during hard steady rain. Sometimes, however, we were either already hunting when the rain began, or we were stubborn and hunted no matter what, even if it meant getting soaked to the bone. This was sometimes the case in light drizzle conditions during the rut phases. Despite the fact that rain accounted for only a small percentage of our overall hunts, the number of mature bucks we saw during these hunts often rivaled the total from all other conditions over the span of an entire season. Soon we were going out of the way to hunt during rain, and we began to notice some general tendencies that we began to key on.

Though there is no way to be sure of the reasons mature bucks move more during rain, we surmise that this is caused by a number of factors. The first is probably simply the wet factor. What animal just lies around when it is raining?

They can't go inside, so what difference does it make to them whether they are bedded or up and moving? Most deer will remain bedded during a heavy downpour but will rise shortly thereafter or if it subsides to a light rain, if for no other reason than to merely shake off. Another reason we believe bucks are on their feet more during rain is the reduced light. Daylight comes later during overcast skies, and overall, it remains a bit darker during rain. A third reason we believe mature bucks move more during precipitation is perhaps a learned survival behavior because it is far more prevalent in heavily pressured areas than in lightly hunted areas. Few hunters are likely to be in the woods during this time. If a deer goes through much of his life without encountering hunters during wet weather, he may become conditioned. The deer also seem to know that they can move silently through wet surroundings and that wet conditions help their sense of smell. Whatever the exact reasons may be, we are certain that your chances at having an encounter with a mature buck are better during rainy conditions than otherwise.

Type of Rain

Not all precipitation is the same. Some types of rain are far better for hunting in than others. Obviously, never hunt when the sky is lit up with lightning. No buck is worth risking your life, and under those extreme conditions deer hunker down. The best conditions are steady drizzle to light rain, followed by a sudden change in conditions. For instance, after a long dry spell nothing gets deer on their feet

John hunted this Michigan fourteen-pointer for four years before finally connecting right after a sudden heavy midday November snow squall.

like a good soaking rain. Often you will notice that the deer will appear just after a strong initial downpour. When the weather forecast calls for these conditions, we try to plan for a hunt.

Hunting in the rain is an exception to the overall hunting plan. No matter what time of season it is, during steady rains, or sudden changes in conditions, you can hunt some of your very best spots. Hunt those primary scrape areas, travel routes from bedding area to bedding area, or especially those within bedding areas. It is, of course, best to hunt such conditions in the morning, but we also recommend sitting through midday, as mature bucks will be more active during the rut phases. Stay all day if possible. We have often witnessed bucks re-working scrapes during late morning and midday lulls in rain. In 1996 during the October lull, in a torrential downpour, John went out at about 10:00 a.m. to prepare a new location on the back side of a standing cornfield. By the time the location was finished it was about noon and John was drenched. On his way out, when he got to the corner of the field, 40 yards in front of him stood the huge buck he was pursuing, freshening up a scrape in the still-pouring rain. They made eye contact, and after a few seconds, the buck vanished into the woods. John saw that buck only three times in four seasons and two of those times it was raining. And the day he finally killed the fourteen-pointer, it had just stopped snowing.

Keeping Dry

One of the main reasons that we are so excited about hunting in the rain nowadays is the developments in raingear. Soft microfabric polyester technology fabrics used in conjunction with waterproof Teflon and or polyurethane membranes have came a long way in the last fifteen years, making it possible to remain dry and hunt comfortably in some downright deluge conditions. Before these technological developments, hunting in the rain meant simply suffering. Wool was about the only material out there quiet enough to wear bowhunting, but it also meant getting wet. PVC-lined rain suits just were just too noisy and stiff to be practical for bowhunting.

We wore microfabric/waterproof membrane raingear but still had issues with noise. When Rivers West began selling raingear, we were ecstatic about the increased potential to take advantage of rainy weather deer movement and remain comfortable and, most importantly, quiet. Rivers West uses similar waterproof membranes as everyone else, but they mask the noise of the membrane with a deep exterior fleece. Rivers West uses three different depths of fleece in their product line, APF (lightest), LAW (midweight), and H2P (most dense and deep). Our favorite suit from Rivers West is their Ambush jacket and Trail pants, and both have the H2P exterior fabric and are by far the quietest rainwear we have ever owned.

Chris's 2005 Wisconsin Fog Buck

It was the first week of November and the cold was more piercing than I antici-pated, so for the first time that season I used some adhesive body warmers, stick-ing one over each kidney and another on my chest. There is nothing worse than freezing on a hunt, not to mention that the shooting ability of most people, in-cluding myself, sinks in direct relation to how chilled one is. Tucking in under my Rivers West gear, which is windproof and very warm, I knew I would be comfort-able for the entire morning and could probably hunt all day if necessary. The com-bination of body warmers and a warm windproof outer shell has extended my comfortable time on stand exponentially. I used to think it was normal to shiver while bowhunting, but fortunately those days are over. I slipped into my half-awake predaylight hunting trance, and a couple hours passed, until the dull gray of break-ing light, and the opportunity to begin using my eyes, snapped me to full alertness. The clear sky promised sunshine soon.

My tree was along the top edge of a big western Wisconsin bluff. The distance between the ploughed crop field and the edge of the precipice was about 30 yards. The narrow top of the bluff served as a funnel between two bedding areas that bucks used to avoid open terrain during daylight. To the east an overgrown fence line separated a small secluded alfalfa field from sight of the road and fun-nelled deer from the bedding area on the other side right to me. To the west a block of open timber was between the funnel and a thick southwest-facing sloped bedding area. A perfect location to catch cruising midday bucks.

Just after daylight a deer topped the ridge about 80 yards away. A split-second streak of antler got me looking closer, but the buck was out of sight so fast that I was unable to judge its size. Reaching for my doe-in-estrus can, I flipped it over a couple times, hoping at least to catch a confirming glimpse. To my pleasant sur-prise the buck turned back in my direction. Within a few steps I saw all I need to see, a yearling eight-point. He stared in my direction for a bit before losing interest and returning to his previous course. What struck me about this buck was that he crested the ridge at nearly its steepest point, which is almost a cliff. If you were to kick a rock over the edge, it might roll for a couple hundred yards. I never expected a deer to climb up right there. It is interesting that a deer will walk up an almost ver-tical ridge but will often walk several hundred yards out of its way to cross through a hole in a fence.

From one instant to the next the conditions changed. Out of nowhere thick fog enveloped the hilltop and woods. My view of the valley below was completely obscured, as was my view of the old farmhouse on top of the bluff. I could only see about 60 yards. The sudden change had an eerie touch to it and reminded me

Chris's 2005 Wisconsin Fog Buck continued

of the Lake Michigan fogbanks that I encountered as a teenager helping out on a salmon charter boat, fogs that seem to arise out of nowhere, tossing one into a slippery and dangerous world devoid of orientation, where other boats, rocks, and shores unseen present a real danger. Fortunately I wasn't in a boat on the big lake and was quite aware that mature bucks tend to move in foggy wet conditions. For another two hours I sat in the hazy gray soup, senses peaked, because if a deer indeed appeared, it would be very close before I could see it.

Just after 9:00 a.m. the fog simply vanished. As quickly as it came it was gone. The only detectable meteorological difference was a faint breath of wind. A quick inspection of my surroundings revealed it devoid of deer, so with the coast clear I munched down a chocolate bar. I hadn't dared to move and make noise opening a plastic wrapper as long as I couldn't see whether any deer were on the approach. Sated, warm, and content I adjusted my saddle and settled in for at least three more hours of hunting.

As luck would have it, I didn't have to sit for hours. Mere minutes later I glanced to my left toward the hidden alfalfa field, and standing there, on top of the ridge about 70 yards away, was a tall tined buck. I didn't need to look twice to know that this was a nice deer, especially considering the ten or so other hunters on this farm, so I immediately reached for my bow. Moving steadily the buck dropped down into a low spot. With him briefly out of sight I took the opportunity to shift to my left, edging around on my treesteps into position for a shot. Seconds later he reappeared, and without any hesitation footed it directly toward my shooting lane. When he was two steps from the opening I drew. The instant the buck's chest filled the lane I let out a short low-toned nasal, "mat." He immediately put on the brakes, lifted his head, but stared forward, unsure of where the sound came from. Con-

Rain Precautions

Shooting and blood trails are two major concerns about hunting in the rain. Before you consider hunting in the rain, take the time to practice with your bow under similar conditions. Heavy rain and moisture can have an effect on your arrow flight, particularly if you are using real feathers. In really heavy rain, you should notice that your arrows fly a bit low. Knowing how your equipment reacts to these conditions is paramount in deciding when to shoot or not.

If it is raining hard, or the forecast predicts heavy rain, it is critical to take only the shortest, best shots possible. We shorten our shooting distances during

Thick fog had this buck returning to its bedding area later than normal.

centrating on a single point in the middle of his chest I let my arrow free. My point of concentration became the point of impact. The buck spun and bounded three times back in the direction he came from and then stopped. He stood for a few seconds with his tail twitching and spinning in erratic circles. In an attempt to run he took two more bounds but stopped a second time. For another second he stood still, before falling over and sliding about 15 yards down the bluff. The base of an ancient gnarly maple kept the buck from sliding even farther. This buck was moving toward a bedding area within minutes of a dense fog lifting. I'll take fog, rain, or snow for hunting anytime.

hard rain, but there are no set distance limitations. These should be based on your personal shooting capabilities. Take short shots that you are absolutely certain you can make. Don't attempt shots at the far end of your range. This should be everyone's mantra in taking shots in the first place, but unfortunately isn't always the case. The last thing you want to do is take a tough, perhaps marginal shot, make a marginal hit, and lose the blood trail when it's washed away by rain. Broadside to quartering away short shots where you can hit both lungs are a must if you want to take advantage of the opportunity that hunting in the rain provides. Double-lung hit deer rarely travel more than 100 yards before expiring and should be easily recovered even with a poor, partially washed-out blood trail.

Snow

Hunting in the snow is just like rain, except that it is colder. The best snow is a light to moderate fall with little wind, basically a frozen drizzle. Just like during rain, mature bucks will be on their feet in these conditions for the exact same reasons. If it is later in the season, the main movement pattern will probably be from bedding to feeding and vice versa, rather than scrape, staging, and other rut activity.

Wind

For decades, heavy wind was the one type of weather that had us completely baffled, and it is still our least preferred condition to hunt in. Unlike rain, where deer's senses are probably not diminished, heavy wind causes problems for deer. Heavy wind swirls scent around quickly and unpredictably, it causes a great deal of movement in the woods, and it is loud. It is obvious why deer don't move as well in heavy wind as in other conditions. After all, all three of their main defenses against predators are impaired. Interestingly, we have noticed that we see more predators like foxes and coyotes when the wind is really howling. Predators move during windy conditions to take advantage of prey animals' diminished ability to detect them.

Deer simply don't move much during high winds, but they sometimes do, and sometimes it is enough of an opportunity that if we have the time, we hunt in winds as high as 40 mph. Instead of sitting home, we try to make the best of every situation. In 2007, John took a big twelve-pointer during blizzard conditions. It was seven degrees, snowing hard, with a steady 30 to 40 mph wind. There is only one guarantee in hunting: If you're not out there, you can't kill anything.

Like every other condition, you should have a plan and specific locations for hunting in high winds. One spot that Chris heads to every time the wind is really blowing is at the bottom of a steep bank that borders a cornfield on the top. Through a coincidental outing, where the wind kicked up after a very hot day and he just about froze, he noticed a lot of deer activity. The local deer were passing heavily from woods to corn while using the wind-protected bottom as a travel route. This movement is almost always present during heavy winds in the area. Deer do move during high winds, but you must be in a sheltered location to take advantage of it.

Proper clothing during cold, windy conditions is an absolute must. We don't care how much insulation you have on, if your exterior or first layer under it doesn't block the wind, it will penetrate through your permeable insulation within a short period of time and freeze you. We use our Rivers West Ambush jacket and Trail pants as exterior garments during extremely cold and windy conditions.

The plan for hunting high winds is simple. Hunt low-lying areas that offer some shelter from the wind, such as within bedding areas or the bottom, downwind sides of ridges. Just as with rain, you need to shorten your shot distances during windy conditions. Strong crosswind can cause erratic flight that can affect accuracy more than rain.

Morning and evening wind lulls

Another aspect of high winds is that there is almost always a lull in the wind both in the evening and morning. How many times have you decided not to hunt because of heavy wind, only to have it stop about half an hour before dark? As soon as the wind stops like this, the deer tend to start moving, sometimes with a determination not seen otherwise. They seem to know that they have a window of time where their sensory defense will work before the wind picks up again. We have both killed mature bucks in situations like this. John killed one of his most prized Michigan bucks on a day that the wind was really blowing. In fact, the buck was bedded very close to his tree when he arrived there. He probably was only able to get into the tree and set up without alerting the buck because the wind covered the noise of his approach. Just as the wind slowed, the buck stepped out of the patch of red willows within shooting range.

Your chances are diminished during high winds, but anything can happen. Like hunting in the rain and cold, hunting in the wind can take a lot of determination. Stick it out and something good may happen.

20

SUBURBS AND EXURBS

L ike it or not, hunting in suburbs and exurbs is going to play a big role in the future of bowhunting. If you aren't hunting areas such as this already, you probably will in the future. These areas sometimes provide tremendous hunting, but they also have potential for personal and political conflict. Knowing how to handle the situation is very important for hunting success, avoiding conflict, and retaining your hunting permission. The concept of suburbs, and urban sprawl, has been around for decades, and suburban hunting is generally associated with areas close to mid-sized to large cities. Immediately your thoughts should turn to the land surrounding major cities such as New York, Detroit, Chicago, Kansas City, Columbus, or any other large city. The main traits of suburbs are copious human population and mostly small properties. Suburbs with high deer populations will often border parks, remnant farms, golf courses, or larger private estates. The best suburbs for hunting are also usually those with more exclusive and wealthy residents. In areas like this the property sizes are a bit bigger, and deer have more room to live between the houses. These areas will have a much higher than average non-hunting resident population and usually more anti-hunters as well.

Exurbs are similar to suburbs except that they can turn up just about anywhere, even in otherwise rural areas. Lake associations often form a sort of exurb. These may lie within overall agricultural areas, but with houses and neighborhoods close together around and near the lake they form a patchwork of landownership very similar to suburbs, with a mixture of protected and hunted areas. In areas like this you will often find deer bedding in backyards and feeding on ornamental shrubs. Exurbs are growing around even small rural towns. The trend in building in the United States is outward into what was once the country. Many areas that we hunted as pure farmland ten and twenty years ago are now subdivided and split into a patchwork of tracts, ranging from 40 acres down to single lots.

Both suburbs and exurbs create a patchwork of property ownership and a network of safe areas for deer, either through no-hunting ordinances or simply

214

*Above: Deer moving through a Michigan
exurb in the winter. Due to tight travel
corridors, well-used runways such as this
are common.*
*Right: A small buck in a suburban back-
yard has the potential to reach maturity
due to the lack of hunting pressure.*

private properties that don't allow hunting. Because of the high human density,
gun hunting is often either frowned
upon, illegal, or completely impossible in such areas. From a bowhunting stand-
point this allows for two important things to happen: Bucks have a chance to
reach maturity and the deer population will grow rapidly. We know of several
hunters who routinely kill giant bucks every year off tiny suburban tracts of land,
and we know of places where the suburban deer population is very high, well
above that of nearby farm country.

Deer behavior in these settings is somewhat different than in traditional
rural areas. The principal difference is that deer are more accustomed to human
activity. It isn't uncommon for deer to bed in yards where people walk by, or
work in their lawns a couple houses over, without the deer spooking in the least.
In some neighborhoods deer become a common sight and allow humans in
close proximity. This creates a notion in a lot of resident's heads that all deer are
then tame. This certainly isn't the case. These deer have been conditioned to accept the normal activity in the area. The instant that the human activity is beyond

its normal parameters the deer go on high alert and react in a similar fashion, though not as severe, to deer in a more natural setting. This means that the deer will spook when a hunter is nearby in a tree stand, but may not when the homeowner takes his garbage out to the curb on Monday morning. The deer can differentiate between types of human activity. Despite this, the advantage for the bowhunter is that deer are used to humans. There is residual human scent all around, which allows hunters a little leeway in their efforts.

The very confines that make gaining access in suburban and exurban areas so difficult are exactly what can make hunting there so good. Quite often that which remains of the woods or cover in these areas are the only travel routes the deer have at their disposal. For example, a wooded strip along a stream that separates a woodlot from agricultural land a mile upstream may be the only path deer have to take. Another example is a buffer of woods between a subdivision and a highway. For a couple years we had access to an area like this until it was further developed. At one end there was a swamp and at the other end there were some fields. In situations like this every deer in a local herd will use these routes eventually. Hunting becomes simply a matter of spending enough time there until a mature buck shows up. Finding a transition route that is the only one available for the deer to use in a suburban area that holds mature bucks is like hitting the jackpot. Getting access to such a spot is rare, but not unheard of. The major difficulty with such hunting is definitely not the hunting, but gaining access to the suburban location, and then keeping that access over a period of time.

This great buck lived in a suburb, often frequenting a small park surrounded by houses.

Access

Most suburban hunting spots are gained by simply living in the neighborhood. Other than that, you usually have to know someone quite well to gain access. For instance, Chris got permission to hunt in a subdivision after a friend's parents were unable to grow a garden. Only after several attempts to stop the deer with various fencing styles did they seek the help of a hunter and allow Chris to hunt their ten acres. When they moved into the place, they loved the deer, and hated hunters, but that changed when the deer began costing them money. Unfortunately, hunters don't have a very good image in the urban non-hunting scene. The pitiful Hollywood-based image these people have of hunters is a group of twisted backwoods cretins out to kill Bambi. As hunters it is in our best interest that we present ourselves as respectable individuals. Knocking on doors in suburban areas for hunting permission is very difficult at best. When you attempt this, follow the guidelines in the access chapter (chapter 2) of this book. Present yourself as professionally as possible and be ready for denial. Keep seeking for that special spot, never give up, and you may eventually be rewarded for your effort.

Small Tracts

Almost all suburban and exurban hunting will be on small tracts generally ranging from just a couple acres to perhaps forty. The scouting and setup procedure for small tracts is exactly the same as we have already outlined in this book. Because the property is small you should have no problem walking every inch of it. The main difference is that small tracts will by nature be missing some elements found in larger areas. It is probably impossible to have bedding, feeding, travel routes, and primary scrape areas on ten acres. What you will have on a small tract is a tiny fragment of a deer's home range. You must be able to determine when and how a mature buck is using the property and adjust your hunting accordingly. The best possible situation is, as we have already mentioned, a tight funnel that all the deer in the area have to use. You may have part of a bedding area, or just a yard that is used for feeding, or even a single apple tree that is used as a primary scrape area. Spots like this should only be hunted when absolutely ready. Timing and planning are essential to regular success, even in the suburbs.

Never Leave a Trace

One of the most difficult aspects of suburban and exurban hunting is the non-hunting and anti-hunting people. Nothing can cause you to lose your hunting permission than it becoming obvious that you are hunting in a suburb. We have several acquaintances who gained permission to hunt great suburban pieces of

Sights like this are becoming more and more common across the whitetail's range.

property only to lose permission because neighbors disapproved of having any hunting going on around their property. A couple of them lost their permission before they ever had an opportunity to hunt the locations they set up. As unfair as it seems, a single complaining neighbor is likely to cause you to lose permission, even though you are not even hunting on their property. This is just the unfortunate nature of the situation. Most of the time, it is more important for a landowner to keep neighborly peace than to please a hunter. We have also heard of several cases where either the police or the local conservation officer was called because non-hunting or anti-hunting neighbors noticed a hunter. Although you are doing something completely legal, it is best to keep a low profile while hunting both suburban and exurban areas. Having to disguise your intentions isn't always comfortable and may not sit well with dyed-in-the-wool hunters, but we are merely reporting on the state of things and the possibility of dealing with it. This book is about being successful at bowhunting and not propagating the profound meaning of the importance of hunting. There are other arenas and ways to be successful at that.

Keeping a low profile means approaching hunting in these more urban areas in a certain way. The main idea is to never leave a trace. You should be able to hunt suburban areas without the locals even knowing you are there. We learned this lesson the hard way, several times over. Chris once hunted a spot where whenever his vehicle was parked there, a neighbor would walk his dog through the woods. John hunted a spot where the neighbors liked to drive quads and shoot guns next door every time his van was parked there. Whenever you gain permission to a suburban or exurban tract make sure to sit down with the landowner and discuss how the neighbors feel about hunting. Make sure to ask whether any neighbors are vegetarians or anti-hunters. Also arrange a parking spot that blends into the area. While parking in a landowner's driveway may not attract any attention at all, parking in a two track along the back edge will certainly get noticed. In one spot we hunt we park behind a pole barn, and in another we park right in the driveway.

Sticking to the subject of vehicles, when you hunt areas like this, try to drive an inconspicuous vehicle. Nothing will attract more attention in a majority non-hunting neighborhood than a big Ford plastered with hunting stickers. We certainly don't object to hanging out the "I'm a bowhunter" banner, but when hunting in tight quarters it really isn't a good idea. Our minivans are completely devoid of conspicuous hunting advertising.

When we scout these types of areas we initially wear street clothes like jeans and long-sleeved shirts. We also try our absolute best to only scout and prepare locations in these types of areas during a rainstorm when people will be inside or maybe in very windy conditions that will mask any noise we might make. We might even carry a camera with us, just in case we happen to run into someone. And we make sure we are not noticed. We prepare all of our stand locations so that they are unnoticeable to the casual observer. It is also important not to leave tree stands in trees. Since we hunt mostly out of tree saddles this isn't a problem for us. You never know who will be walking through the woods while you aren't there, and a tree stand is a telltale sign of hunter activity.

Hunting areas like this requires a plan for getting in and out of the woods. This may mean nothing more than getting dressed at your parking spot behind the garage. Since our hunting vehicles are minivans with the back seats removed, we simply change in the back of them. However, some other situations require more careful action. For instance, the neighbors next door to one small spot we hunt are staunch anti-hunters, and they have a clear view of some of the property we hunt. When we hunt this location we hunt only in the morning, arriving before they are up and getting ready for work. They are at home most afternoons, so we simply don't hunt then. When we arrive back at our vehicle after a morning hunt we are careful to change out of our hunting clothing before departing. This way we look like typical suburban visitors.

Taking shots in suburban areas is an exercise in extreme caution. You simply have to take good easy short shots. The last thing you want to do is try to track a poorly hit deer through a suburb. Ideally you want them to drop within sight. If you do have to track a deer, do it during midday when most people are at work, and while you are wearing street clothes. Speaking of work, it is very important to be able to hunt these locations during the week when the kids are at school and the adults are at work. Weekends are not good times to hunt such areas.

Chris's 2008 Minnesota Suburb Buck

Finally, after a couple years of trying I landed hunting permission on 10 acres just outside the Twin Cities. The parents of a good friend of mine had grown weary of the deer decimating their garden and flowers and shrubs. The property was located at the far outskirts of the cities and was in an area with enormous houses. Each house was situated on at least 5 acres, and properties were as large as 20 acres. Nearby there were also some larger tracts and even a couple farms. The entire area was classic suburb/exurb.

My permission came quite unexpectedly during the season already in progress, so my hopes for the place weren't that high. While returning from a trip to North Dakota I stopped in with the intention of scouting for perhaps later in the season or the following season. On my only previous visit to the place I never set foot outside the yard, though I knew from my friend that the area had a very high deer population and that there were good bucks there.

Arriving at midday I immediately began scouting. It only took me an hour to find and prep two locations. One was a primary scrape area in a meadow of sorts. There were nine scrapes under an apple tree, three of them the size of a car hood. A nearby Scotch pine was nearly perfect, and all I had to do was run my steps up the tree. There was no clearing involved. The second spot wasn't much more difficult. A funnel of spruce trees forced the local deer to cross the property near the house. In just a few minutes I had one of the spruce trees ready to go. Adjacent to the property was a large bedding area, which is why this particular land had so much deer traffic. The primary scrape area was being hit so hard that I decided to hunt the next day, instead of continuing on my ride back home.

The following morning found me in my saddle above that primary scrape area. Nothing happened until a lone six-pointer meandered through at about 9 o'clock.

Don't forget about gut piles. If you do kill a deer, don't simply leave a gut pile in the woods. Gut piles in the woods can attract a lot of negative attention. All it takes is someone walking a dog to find a gut pile for an entire neighborhood to be alerted to someone hunting nearby. It doesn't matter how you do it—put it in a stump, hide it in a thicket—just make that gut pile vanish. If you place a gut pile in a hard to get to location, the raccoons, opossums, and other scavengers will consume it quickly.

Getting deer out of the woods is another challenge. To use the same example as before, in the area we hunt with the anti-hunting neighbors we basically

Like it or not, suburban and exurban hunting will become more and more common in the future. Chris killed this buck on his first hunt on a small suburban tract of land.

Half an hour later a doe and two fawns emerged out of the bedding area, obviously with someone on their tails. A couple minutes behind them a good eight pointer appeared, with his nose to the ground. The doe and fawns crossed under my tree at about 20 yards. The buck did the same. I blatted to stop him. My arrow was a bit high, but it found the spine and the buck went down. This was the first time I ever hunted in Minnesota and one of my shortest hunts ever. It was a classic suburban hunt. 🦌

drag any deer we kill up to the landowner's back porch and load them in our vans behind the house. In most other situations we have had to wait until after dark to drag deer out of suburban areas. You must consider all the areas where you could be noticed and think about how you can get around them.

All of these things may sound extreme, and they are compared to normal hunting situations, but suburbs and exurbs are not typical situations. We have described the most extreme case. Usually you will be able to hunt suburbs and exurbs somewhat normally, but you should always be mentally prepared for the worst case scenario and be ready to find the solution. Finding a good suburban

This mature doe is quite comfortable bedding at the edge of a backyard.

or exurban hunting location is rare and could be a ticket to regular, rather easy, success with mature bucks. The last thing you want to do is lose access to such a location due to negative attitudes toward hunters.

When you are careful hunting suburban areas, good things can happen. We actually gained more permission in a suburb because the landowner was impressed with our success and elusiveness. When another neighbor began talking of too many deer in his yard at a summer barbecue, our landowner confided that he had hunters on his place who did a good clean job. The guy complaining was amazed that he had hunters nearby and had never seen or noticed them. Our permission was then immediately expanded by five more acres.

21

HUNTING FROM
THE GROUND

The majority of our hunting takes place from trees. And wherever suitable trees are available, that is where you will find us. There are, however, situations where hunting from the ground is the only option. If the sign is right, we don't hesitate a second to keep our feet firmly planted on terra firma.

Most areas that require ground blinds are obvious, because there are no trees that offer adequate cover at a decent height. Yet it amazes us how many stand sites we encounter that are around 15 feet high and offer absolutely no foliage or background cover. These types of locations may be acceptable in some lightly hunted areas but definitely not in pressured areas. We can only assume that these hunters don't know any better. They would be better off hunting from the ground.

In our search for land to hunt we don't exclude any type of property. This means occasionally we land permission in areas that are devoid of trees, which consist purely of fields, or where the best hunting locations are far from suitable trees. Some typical habitat types where we hunt from the ground are cattail marshes, standing cornfields, large autumn olive patches, red willow swamps, isolated swales, newly overgrown clear-cuts, overgrown fencerows between fields, and grassy CRP fields.

Setup

Ground blind hunting is often presented as walking out into the woods and simply throwing out a pop-up blind in a bit of background cover. Simple pop-up blind ground hunting definitely works in the land of lightly hunted or micromanaged deer herds. All you have to do is watch TV shows or videos to verify it. Unfortunately, in places that receive heavy hunting pressure, this type of simple ground hunting will not work with any consistency, probably not at all. It is rare for a mature buck, or doe, in a pressured area not to immediately notice such a large out-of-place object in its core living area. Usually the buck will react by immediately leaving the scene.

A good ground blind fits naturally into its surroundings. This spot was made by clearing out the inside of an existing thicket.

We have encountered quite a few pop-up blinds sitting basically in the wide open along field edges or pushed up against some brush in the woods. They stick out like sore thumbs and are usually noticeable immediately and from quite a distance. Often their camouflage patterns do not even match the surroundings. Pop-up blinds are great tools, but you have to use them correctly. This means adjusting to the hunting intensity in your area and using some natural debris from the area as concealment for the blind. If a mature deer is able to detect your silhouette sticking off the side of a leafless tree while sitting well above its head, just imagine how easily it will notice a pop-up blind that doesn't blend with its surroundings.

Deer's sensory perception at ground level is simply amazing. They can detect the slightest movement. At ground level they are truly in tune with their surroundings, and just as importantly they notice when things are out of place in their core territories. This means that ground blind locations have to be well concealed so that they literally become part of the terrain, and must also be made so that it is possible to draw and shoot undetected. There must be enough cover so that non-target deer can pass by undisturbed. Properly setting up a pop-up blind location makes a big difference in your chances for success.

The first step is to select a location that is a compromise on distance. You need to be as far away as possible from the target point where you expect deer to be, so that they can both come in and pass undisturbed, as necessary, but you must also be close enough so that you feel comfortable making the shot. Chris likes to set up his ground blind spots for a 20- to 35-yard shot. John likes his a little closer. The main problem is that the vast majority of the time any mature deer that gets inside the 20-yard mark will see you, even if you don't twitch a muscle, and no matter how well you are camouflaged. Since mature bucks commonly appear after other deer, this presents a real problem. Anyone who tells you they kill mature bucks regularly by sitting behind trees on a stool is probably stretching the truth a bit. We have hunted enough from the ground to know that it is extremely difficult to kill mature bucks with a bow from the ground.

We divide our ground blind spots into two categories: There are blinds that are annual, meaning that they must be made anew every year, and there are semi-permanent ground blinds that only need touching up from year to year. The annual ground blinds are in cattail marshes, standing cornfields, and perhaps in overgrown CRP fields. The more permanent blinds are typically in more wooded areas like fresh clear-cuts, autumn olive thickets, brown brush bedding areas, and along overgrown fencerows.

Though ground blind hunting situations are always site-specific, two areas that remain relatively constant are cattail marshes and cornfields. These must be cleared out after the cattails, or corn, have reached full height, which means just prior to, or during, season. It is imperative that you implement your complete scent control routine whenever making these spots. Ground hunting within cattail marshes is really only practical in years that the marsh is relatively dry during the fall or has small dry humps or islands within it that are large enough to bed on during years the rest of the marsh is wet.

We look for well-used entry points, exit points, or travel routes within the marsh. A standard ground blind setup can be made just outside the marsh at any entry/exit location, but when setting up within a marsh we follow the best runway until it intersects with another runway and set up where we can take advantage of the converging routes.

A ground blind in a marsh can be made from the cattails themselves, or we set up cut cattails against a similar colored pop-up blind for added concealment. When using pop-up blinds we literally bury them in cattails. Plopping down a dark-colored pop-up blind in a cattail marsh is simply asking for extra attention. The blind must become part of the marsh to be effective. When setting up either, make sure the floor within the blind is bare dirt and free of any dry debris that could potentially make noise at the wrong moment.

Create your shooting lanes by cutting, or bending, cattails so that about two feet of each stem remains intact. This will aid in concealing the lane. The cattails will be short enough not to impede shot. Make these lanes about 24 to 30 inches wide. The wider the lane, the more apt a deer is to stop and look down it and notice your setup or drawing movement. You will want to make two shooting lanes in a V shape to the runway. V-shaped lanes will allow you to see a deer pass through the first lane and allow time to prepare for the shot at the second lane. On a quiet hunt in a cattail marsh you should be able to hear any deer moving toward your location and be able to prepare for the shot before they get there.

Chris's 2010 Massachusetts Public-Land Buck

Massachusetts couldn't really be considered a destination spot when it comes to chasing big whitetails. Sure some big bucks are killed there every fall, but when compared to more renowned big buck states it has far more hunting pressure and generally lacks the big agriculture that helps to crank out oversized racks. As far as I am concerned, a mature buck is a mature buck no matter what it scores. So when my friend Ben invited me on a mid-November hunt to a new area, he discovered an area right along the leading edge of the eastern seaboard I couldn't resist. If there is one thing I like to do, it's step into new terrain with bow in hand and try to connect with a mature buck. The area we would hunt was right on the coast, and I mean so close you could actually hear the surf. This was going to be an ex-ploratory hunt—Ben had never hunted this area and in fact only paid it one brief visit before the day we began hunting.

We arrived with the rain midday on Sunday, which thanks to anachronistic blue laws is a no-hunting day in Massachusetts. The rain was light and predicted to move out into the Atlantic late that afternoon. Immediately we started ex-ploratory scouting. This meant we drove around with map in hand identifying tracts of public land and other land open to hunters. In a few miles I became aware that this would be a slightly different kind of hunting. The entire area was thick, al-most impenetrable brush, a mix of various briars, abundant poison ivy, scrub oak, and junipers interspersed by a few pines, almost none of which big enough to hunt from. Any hunting would have to take place from the ground. The second obvious difference was that the entire area was basically a bedding area. The brush was so thick in most places that a deer could be standing 10 yards away and you wouldn't be able to see it. And to make matters even more difficult, there were no agricultural feeding areas. The deer mostly fed in nicely groomed yards, which were common in the area. This also meant that the deer movement would be random. The positive side of the coin is that because of those conditions the deer were rel-atively numerous, and bucks had potential to live to maturity due to the extremely thick cover. This assumption was underscored by many good rubs strewn about. By nightfall we had discovered a couple decent public-land spots and set up a few makeshift ground blinds.

Despite the forecast, the rain didn't stop, and instead the weather got much worse. The wind picked up and was blowing between 25 and 40 mph, with gusts occasionally over 50 mph. The rain was coming in horizontally from the northeast. Because time was short, however, we began hunting mornings and evenings while spending midday searching for new hunting areas and speed scouting. By Wednesday morning I had yet to see a deer while hunting, though I had seen a

Chris killed this East Coast buck from the ground on a short-term hunt.

few while driving. The only things that seemed to be moving were the branches and brush from the heavy winds. Ben faired slightly better and had seen four deer while on stand, including a spike buck. Wednesday during a midday scouting foray we discovered a tiny patch of public land, approximately 10 acres. A ditch at one end of the property served as a decent funnel that led to some small fallow fields, and it contained a small crab apple tree where the deer had obviously been feeding. Ben decided to set up at the crab apple tree. At the other corner of the property was a small opening interspersed with a couple junipers and pines that showed good potential due to several good rubs and a lot of fresh track. A small brush-covered hill offered a good natural ground blind overlooking the small bowl, with a view to another grassy opening on top. Though I couldn't find any scrapes,

Chris's 2010 Massachusetts Public-Land Buck continued

the terrain had the look of both a rut staging area and a primary scrape area. These two spots were the best we had found so far, despite the four other hunters' locations between our stands. About an hour after discovering the spots we started hunting. Ben managed to set a stand about 10 feet up in a tree in the funnel while I plunked down on the ground hidden in a bush at the crest of the small hill. From my spot I could shoot to the small bowl and across the opening on top.

For several hours nothing happened. The wind kept on howling, and despite my impervious windproof raingear I began to question attempting to hunt in such high winds. Deer's three principle defenses are limited in such conditions. They can't see as well because of the constant movement all around, they can't hear as well because of the wind, and scent is blown about so rapidly that they can't smell as well either. Most of the time deer simply move less when autumn gales are blowing.

One thing about hunting whitetails is that about the time you come up with a behavior rule you think is solid, the deer will go and prove you wrong, or at least prove there are always exceptions to rules. About fifteen minutes before dark I was sitting there wishing the wind would stop, when a single doe sprinted right in and stopped about 5 yards away on top of the hill. She glanced back for a split second and bounced off. Since it was the second week of November I knew what this meant and picked up my bow. Scouring the small opening with my eyes, I waited for the buck to step out. For ten minutes nothing happened. But then, just at the edge of darkness, the buck angled out of the brush across the opening, and immediately turned and was angling straight away. It was a good buck for the area and looked to be about a hundred inch eight-pointer with a really good mass. Although the buck was only 30 yards away I had no shot. He stood still for a second and then began walking away.

The gusts had picked up right before dark to at least 40 mph and the wind was straight from the buck to me. On impulse I instantly stood up and strode directly toward the buck. While walking I drew my bow. The gap closed fast and in a couple seconds I was standing with my bow drawn about 20 yards directly behind the buck. Still he had no idea I was there, although I was in the wide open. And still I had no shot. To get a better angle I took two steps to my right, hoping for a hard quartering away shot before he made it to the cover a few steps in front of him. The instant I took those steps the buck twisted his neck and looked right at me. Now concentrating on making the shot, I anchored and aimed at his back rib. The same instant my finger was dropping for my release the buck simply bounded forward and my arrow flew harmlessly right where he had just been standing. A half a second faster and I may have connected. The shot was on the razor's edge, but unfortunately for me, barely on the wrong side of the edge. While hunting from the ground, milliseconds can make the difference between a good hit and not hitting a deer at all.

Motivated by that encounter, I was hunkered on the little hill again the next morning, knowing full well that a repeat appearance of the buck from the night before would be very unlikely. The wind and rain hadn't skipped a beat. For the first hour of light I studied the grassy top, mentally preparing for a repeat of the previous evening's action, glancing occasionally in the little bowl. It was just after 7:00 a.m. when above the sound of the gale I heard what sounded like two sticks being slapped together directly behind me. Slowly I turned and peaked over the bush I was hiding in into the bowl to see a mature buck working a thick licking branch over a scrape that hadn't been there five minutes earlier. He was straight downwind. The sound was from his antlers slapping the branches. Very carefully I lifted my bow off the ground. Still squatting behind the cover I drew and anchored. At full draw I stood up. Immediately the buck spun from quartering hard away to slightly quartering to me. The instant the buck stopped, my arrow was on its way. At the hit the buck lunged forward about 10 yards and stopped for a couple seconds in a patch of brush. He then dropped his head and scuttled about 20 yards across the bowl and disappeared into a wall of thick stuff. A second later the last sound I heard above the wind was a large snapping branch.

I waited about forty minutes before walking to where the buck was standing at the shot. From the point of impact ample blood was easy to follow. A few minutes later I discovered the buck just inside the brush where I had last seen him. He was mature buck, at least $4^1/_2$ years old, with a tall dark eight-point rack. My shot was low but just clipped the heart. This time I was right on the razor's edge.

We continued to hunt the remainder of the week while scouting for new spots at midday. I never saw another buck. On the last day we hunted a new area, and Ben had his own very close encounter with a big mature buck, milliseconds making the difference once again. It was a great initial exploratory hunt in totally new terrain. Hopefully, we get a chance to hunt the leading edge again sometime. 🦌

During spring scouting ventures is when you should locate and start to prepare cattail marsh locations. If you discover a location, cut your shooting lanes, and pull the root systems from within the blind setup area, you will not have as much work to do when you return prior to season to do the final preparation. Your spring work will mean less work and scent prior to season. You can set up the same way in standing cornfields and some overgrown CRP fields. Make sure that you get explicit permission from the farmer before you do this in a cornfield.

More permanent ground blinds can be built in clear cuts, fencerows, and autumn olive thickets. Whenever possible it is best to incorporate your ground blinds into existing structures. For instance in clear-cuts it is best to place your blinds in leftover tops, or piles of slash. The point is that the deer are already used to seeing these structures, and changing them and then sitting there will not attract as much attention as altering an area more dramatically. When you make your ground blinds, get the majority of the work done in the spring, when you are clearing out your trees. Just like in the cattails, the first step is to clear a patch down to the bare dirt, either big enough to sit and shoot comfortably, or place a pop-up blind. Following this, stack up cover all around, leaving just enough opening to shoot through. Make sure that you don't leave any gaps that the deer could see movement through. Just prior to season, return to your spot and touch it up while implementing a complete scent control routine.

We hunt a couple areas where there are autumn olive thickets that are quite large. If you have never been inside an autumn olive thicket you don't know what you are missing. The short trees with low drooping branches often create a thick maze of tunnels that are impossible to walk through. In order to get from one point to another it is sometimes necessary to crawl on all fours. For deer this provides almost absolute security because people rarely venture inside such thickets and simply struggle to do so with conventional hang-ons or climbers strapped to their backs. The interesting thing about these thickets is that there are often small openings inside them. We have found a couple places like this that were used as primary scrape areas. The only way to hunt them was from the ground. The fortunate aspect for us was that we could easily make a natural ground blind that melts into the autumn olives and have a primary scrape area to shoot to. If you have any hunting property that contains a large patch of autumn olives make sure you explore it for the possibility of ground hunting.

We are extra conscious of detail when clearing our shooting lanes when hunting from ground level. When hunting from trees many hunters neglect cutting tall weeds and other small stuff because they can shoot over it. When shooting parallel to the ground, any small vegetation left in a shooting lane can deflect an arrow, so it must be cut. Also, just as with tree locations we choose our entry and exit routes carefully and mark them with reflective tacks as necessary.

For hunting in a ground blind you will need a comfortable chair, preferably with a backrest. Be certain that you can sit and twist around in the chair and open and close it without it making any noise. You may also consider purchasing an HME or Allen ground stake or a Gorilla Tundra Tuff bow holder. These bow holders stick in the ground and hold your bow upright while hunting. There is no way to effectively conceal even the best of natural ground blinds from other hunters. On public land you can almost be guaranteed that someone else will hunt from it, especially during gun season.

How well you remain concealed and how well you practice scent control are the two big questions when hunting from the ground. Your blinds must hide you completely, yet be inconspicuous enough so that deer don't pay extra attention to them. Proper preparation, timing, and diligent scent control remain the deciding factors. Select your hunting spots according to sign, as we outlined already. Use your imagination and you will find places and conditions for good ground blind locations.

22

QDM AND BAIT

The quality deer management concept (QDM) has grown tremendously in popularity in the last decade. The results of this speak for themselves. There are more big bucks killed every year than ever before, even in pressured states like Michigan and areas in the northeast. This is great for landowners and people with enough cash to lock up tracts of land, and there is nothing wrong with a landowner managing his property for his own recreational pleasure. For the not so deep pocketed, or connected, quality deer management can be both a curse and a blessing. The curse is, of course, the privatization of deer and the locking out of a lot of bowhunters. In many areas where free permission to hunt was commonplace ten to fifteen years ago it is now nearly impossible to gain access. Another negative aspect of QDM is that it cheapens the accomplishments of truly skilled bowhunters. A 100-inch buck taken off public land or in a heavily pressured area doesn't even warrant a close look nowadays, even though such a deer is usually far more difficult to kill than a four- or five-year-old 150-incher off of highly managed property. We can lament the situation all we want, but the trend towards QDM will definitely continue, despite backlash. As a bowhunter you have to remain pragmatic and adjust to the situation. QDM simply raises the bar on what a mature buck should look like and brings bowhunters new challenges and new rewards.

The blessing of QDM is that there are more mature bucks to hunt, and they are easier to hunt than super-pressured deer from the era of every buck seen is down. Most leaseholders and landowners who implement the program are not the best hunters in the world. By providing excellent habitat on their land, and passing small bucks, they attempt to make their own hunting easier. This increases the number of mature bucks in the area, therefore increasing your chances of connecting. The good news for guys like us is that bucks roam, and most property owners don't own enough property to keep animals entirely on their land, despite their best efforts to do so.

Key QDM Concepts

We do not own or lease any hunting property, do not manage property, and don't have permission on any property that is heavily manipulated for deer. Chris has done a lot of research on QDM, trophy buck management (TBM), and deer micromanagement to gain a better understanding of what is involved, and the potential consequences it will have on the future of deer hunting. Deer micromanagement isn't going away anytime soon, so it is a good idea to at least understand the basic principles to know how to adapt.

Allowing young bucks like this to mature is key to any deer management system.

Though official QDM praises general habitat management that is good for deer and other wildlife over large areas, in a lot of cases it has morphed into trophy buck management. This started innocently enough as planting food plots here and there to beef up nutrition and perhaps doing a few forest cuttings to thicken cover. Better nutrition and cover combined with passing on younger bucks naturally led to an increased number of mature bucks with big antlers. Many of these bucks, however, were then subsequently killed on neighboring properties, by neighbors who didn't necessarily agree with QDM principles. To counter this, more recent developments have concentrated on keeping bucks in the smallest areas possible, particularly in more pressured regions, and manipulating buck movement to make them more predictable and easier to kill. This latest version of deer manipulation has many names. We will call it deer micromanagement.

The concept of concentrating deer on a particular piece of property involves the key ingredients: food, cover, and water. The basic thought is to modify a piece of property so that a deer's every need is met, and it has no reason to go elsewhere, particularly during hunting season. Most people immediately think linearly: bedding area to feeding area with a travel route in between. This is a good start, but to keep deer true to a certain area there is more to it than that. To manage buck movement in a controlled manner one needs to be more of a landscape architect than a hunter.

Buck bedding sanctuary

One of the first steps to hunting landscape architecture is buck bedding areas. On most large properties these are already present as traditional bedding areas, such as swamps, or overgrown CRP fields. Sometimes, however, a bedding area can be created by the land manager by planting tall grasses, such as big bluestem, in former fields, or through select cuttings to open up the canopy. The general idea is to have a safe area for deer on a property. The rule is for hunters to remain completely out of these areas unless blood-trailing a buck. A buck should never be disturbed in his safe zone. This is basic conditioning.

Safe feeding area

The second part of the equation is a safe feeding area. This will generally be the largest food plot on a tract of managed property and is often centrally located and surrounded by woods or other cover so it cannot be seen from any road or neighboring property. These are the nutritional centers and destination locations for most of the deer in an area. A common theme is to keep the cover around these plots open so deer can see them from a distance. Deer can feed comfortably and see any approaching danger from afar. This is often a safe feeding area where no hunting is allowed. It is also important in this system to plant food types that are preferred during the fall hunting period. There is plenty of literature on this subject, so we won't get into what those particular plants are, nor how to go about working food plots.

Numerous small food plots

Closer to the security of the buck bedding sanctuary it is common practice to place numerous smaller food plots. These serve several purposes. Small food plots function like bait because deer are opportunistic and will hit such areas both on their way to and from bedding. They may also be used as primary scrape areas during the rut phases, sometimes doubling as staging areas. These are primary hunting spots in the deer micromanagement hunting system. What the micromanagers have done is design almost the exact type of hunting areas that have been our main focus for decades: primary scrape areas and staging areas near a food source that occurs naturally.

Numerous small bedding areas

By creating as much thick cover as possible, small bedding areas are established. Numerous bedding opportunities ultimately cause a property to hold more deer. Small feeding areas and bedding areas spread does across the property, and this prompts bucks to be on their feet more during the rut. More does mean more bucks during the rut. These strategically placed bedding areas and food plots create a solid travel route for cruising fall bucks. The combination of providing safe feeding and bedding areas, numerous small food plots, and plenty of diverse bedding with very controlled and limited hunting pressure will make it normal for mature bucks to be on their feet in daylight during the prerut and rut. This is the main goal of buck micromanagement. However, deer manipulation has been taken even further.

Trails to food plots

Creating travel routes to and from the main food source is also an element of this system. Making a travel corridor can be as simple as opening up the canopy and allowing the undergrowth to shoot up between the main bedding area and food plot. Since deer are edge animals, they will naturally use this route, creating a funnel for the land managing hunter. It is along this route to the main areas that hunting stands are established, along with stands at the smaller food plots. Sometimes trails are made that connect the smaller food plots. The most serious land manipulators even make trails that follow circuitous routes so that it takes longer for a buck to get from one point to another. The idea is to make the over- all distance a buck has to cover longer. The more distance a buck has to cover, the higher the chances are of catching him on his feet during daylight. Yet oth- ers mow trails for the deer to walk on. We know people who mow trails through bedding areas that lead to a specific point, usually a particular hunting stand. When deer aren't disturbed they almost always take the path of least resistance. Making a route that is easy to walk on into and through a bedding area provides a good opportunity to connect with a mature buck.

Raked trails to stands

Another important aspect of this plan is planned entry routes to stands that avoid feeding areas. These are usually mowed trails that are raked to allow quick, silent access. Quick and silent entry and exit to stand locations is critical to suc- cess on micromanaged properties. The deer will be spread out across most of these properties and all entry and exit routes have to be planned so as not to spook the deer.

No hunting until prerut

The last general component of the micromanagement plan is not to hunt until the late prerut, when the bucks are up moving during daylight. And since they haven't experienced any pressure there is no reason for them to be nocturnal. This combined with the fact that bucks in this sort of situation aren't targeted at an early age, even though they have countless human encounters, lead to bucks that have no aversion to moving in full daylight, and not much aversion to hunters either, especially when they know the scent of the principal land man- ager. Exceptions to prerut hunting are sometimes made through the constant surveillance of scouting cameras. We know some people who have a series of cameras with live twenty-four-hour feed to computers strictly for monitoring deer. By using scouting cameras, you can sometimes pinpoint a buck's move- ments at certain points regularly during the day. The exception is usually then made to hunt early.

John and Jon's 2010 Kansas Scrape Bucks

In 2010 John and Jon traveled to Kansas for their annual out-of-state hunt. On this hunt they both killed bucks from a small 40-acre property. For Kansas, this is a tiny piece of land. In the area they were hunting, most properties are at least a quarter section. This piece of land, however, had all the ingredients necessary for deer activity. About two-thirds of the property consisted of mature timber and with dense brush and the other third was prairie grass. The dense brush made this parcel exceptional, as it provided a dense secure bedding area. Large open fields and prairie surround the tract for miles. Near the property line at the end of the timber was a primary scrape area with five well-used scrapes. At the corner of the prairie grass adjacent to the timber and plum brush was another large scrape and several rubbed fence posts. And in a small clearing bordering the largest stand of plum brush was yet another primary scrape area.

At the scrape area in the timber John and Jon prepped a long-needled locust tree that was within 20 yards of all the scrapes. As anyone who has ever set up a stand in a long-needled locust tree knows, removing clusters of long pointed needles is anything but enjoyable, but it was the tree that had to be done. At the single scrape near the corner of the weed field they also prepped a big cottonwood. The trunk was at least 3 feet in diameter and there was a lot of cover, so this stand was low by Eberhart standards, around 25 feet up. They also prepped a tree at the second primary scrape area. With three trees ready, the work on this piece of property was done and it was time to hunt.

On their initial morning hunt Jon was perched in the scrape area near the plum brush. At the crack of daylight Jon saw a huge buck pass through well out of range and eventually disappear into the bedding area. He attempted a short sparring sequence and some vocal doe bleats in an attempt to lure the buck within range. The buck responded and covered about half the distance to Jon's tree, but wouldn't come any closer. Over the next hour two more good bucks passed through the scrape area, an eight-point in the 125-inch class and a larger buck with a broken main beam. Jon passed on both. It wasn't long before a nice ten-point walked in and stood broadside in the middle of the scrape area. Jon has killed a couple nine-points, but to this point had never killed a ten-pointer. He drew back his bow and took the 12-yard shot. Jon's arrow perfectly passed through both lungs, yet despite the pneumo-thorax the buck dashed 150 yards before falling.

The next morning John sat in the locust tree. About half an hour before daybreak the huge buck that Jon saw the day before passed right through the center of the scrape area, a mere 8 yards from the base of the tree. In the starlight John

Both Jon and John killed these bucks off a piece of property after the landowner prohibited other hunters from baiting and deer movement returned to a more normal routine.

John and Jon's 2010 Kansas Scrape Bucks *continued*

could easily make out the huge white antler frame, but it was too dark to distinctly see a body outline and it was also before legal shooting hours. The buck headed directly toward the plum brush bedding area near where Jon was sitting the day before.

At around 7:45 a.m. deer movement began in earnest. Several does and fawns, a couple yearling bucks, and the nice eight-point Jon had seen the day before all passed through the scrape area. For the next hour there was constant activity. The bucks were chasing, the does were being chased, and the fawns were just confused about the entire situation. It was obvious to me that none of the does were in estrus.

After a brief pause in activity a nice buck moved in. He was alone and if John hadn't seen the huge buck earlier he probably would have shot. The buck freshened three of the scrapes, putting him a mere 20 yards away for a couple minutes. The deer was a big eight-point that John estimated to be in the 150 category. After the buck left, John couldn't believe that he had let such a giant pass; after all this was not TV or video fantasy land, this was regular ask-for-permission property.

As hunting typically goes, hindsight is keen. John hunted hard for the next four days without a shot opportunity at a decent buck. On one morning hunt John sat in a steady hard freezing rain accompanied by 25 mile per hour winds for six hours. It seemed as though all the does had entered their estrous cycle at the exact same time, and all the mature bucks were tied up with them. All the scrape areas on the three properties he was hunting were still being worked, but the large tracks in the scrapes were suddenly absent. John watched lots of small bucks chasing and mature does consistently loitering near scrape areas, both signs that the mature bucks were with estrous does and not having to move much. John was really starting to question his own stupidity for passing up that eight-point.

On the seventh morning John sat in the cottonwood near the single scrape for the first time. Shortly after daybreak the 125-inch-class eight-point passed through, while chasing a couple does around. He was relentless in his pursuit even though it was obvious neither doe was in heat. They all eventually headed toward the bedding area. Shortly thereafter the large half rack that Jon had seen also walked through. He was heading for the plum brush as well. Two more does with two fawns passed by at 8:15 and also headed the same direction. At 8:30 another group of two does and two fawns were following the same runway the half rack had taken. The lead doe abruptly stopped and stared toward the scrape. John followed her stare and to his surprise saw the eight-point he had passed on earlier in the week. The buck had come in from the bedding area and was working one of the licking branches over the scrape.

John knew the does weren't going to continue toward the buck, so he prepared for a shot to the spot where the does were standing. The does turned and retraced their steps back into the timber. As if on cue the buck immediately left the scrape and strutted toward them. Within a few seconds, he was standing perfectly broadside at 20 yards. After bringing his Mathews Conquest to full draw, John waited for the buck to step into the open before vocally blatting to stop him. The arrow found its mark and disappeared perfectly behind the buck's shoulder. Even with a perfect hit, the buck sprinted about 200 yards before dropping.

Upon recovering the buck, John found that it was a nine-point. It had a $5^1/_2$-inch antler with its own separate pedicle between the two main beams. His original guess of 150 was pretty close, with the extra antler the buck grossed 156 inches. Both of those hunts are perfect examples of how bucks and does gravitate to, and use, primary scrape areas. When primary scrape areas are located within or close to some form of perimeter security cover they are daytime hunting hot spots during the rut phases. 🦌

This Stuff Works

Does this stuff work? You bet it does. Video whitetail hunters prove its effectiveness year after year. There are a lot of hunters out there experiencing amazing big buck success by implementing similar systems of management. The main principle is to make killing a mature buck as easy and predictable as possible. The problem is that some people have taken the manipulation way too far. One landowner and outdoor writer in Michigan actually clear cut and burned a section of his woods to keep deer from moving onto the neighbor's property after it was purchased by a group of hunters. We have read of people using bulldozers to make earthen banks to guide deer movement, and of hunters building wooden fences to guide deer through a certain point. Whether deer manipulation to this extent is a form of hunting or more animal husbandry is something you have to decide for yourself. We look at the entire situation pragmatically as a simple matter of fact that we have to deal with. We're not happy with it, because this kind of manipulation takes a lot of the magic out of whitetail hunting and degrades magnificent animals. These practices are unfortunately leading toward a European-style hunting system.

Capitalizing on QDM

Fortunately, deer still roam, so this keeps the micromanagement deer-growing crew from locking the bucks up completely and opens a window of opportunity on neighboring properties. For our purposes here let us assume that you do not have access to the micromanaged property on which the hunting is totally planned. Our interest is in the average guy next door. Remember, the land manipulator doesn't want you to kill any of *his* mature bucks, so he isn't doing you any direct favors, so don't worry about doing him any either. Capitalizing on bucks coming off of managed property requires knowing the principles of management, how the land is hunted, and when and why mature bucks will leave the managed property.

Behavioral Differences of QDM Bucks

Bucks that grow to maturity in overwhelmingly QDM areas are simply less wary than bucks in pressured areas, despite the fact that overall hunting pressure might be fairly heavy. This is simply a matter of conditioning. Bucks are most vulnerable at the yearling stage. During their first season without their mothers, and their first rut, they move a lot during the fall. As they continually move they undoubtedly encounter hunters. Since these bucks are no longer targeted they experience no negative consequences. Through this positive conditioning they don't react as severely to the presence of hunters later in their lives. This doesn't mean the bucks are stupid and prancing around during daylight without a care, but there is a behavioral difference between managed bucks and bucks that receive heavy consequential hunting pressure. Even managed bucks become more nocturnal and shy as they age. The key point for the bowhunter next door is that there is a population of mature bucks that moves during daylight.

Watch the Path Back Home

Although the biggest and most dominant buck in the area will perhaps take up residence in the most managed areas, that same buck will push rivals to outlying areas. And remember, even the smallest range of a mature buck is a bit more than a square mile, and most of the time much larger than that, especially during the rut. This range almost always overlaps several sections. Even though much of this larger range is used mostly after dark, this allows an opportunity to intercept mature bucks as they return to their safe zones in the morning. This is also where the increased tendency for managed deer to move during daylight comes into play. Instead of moving through your property before daylight, a more protected mature buck might not return until after daylight. This creates an opportunity for killing one of these bucks as it follows a route across your property. Hunting along key travel routes, funnels, and even fencerows leading toward the managed property are possibilities for such an ambush.

Acorns and Apples

Natural food sources are the scourge of the micromanagement crowd. No matter what they plant, a good crop of acorns, particularly white oak acorns, will draw deer from food plots and managed property. In years with good acorn crops we have often had many acquaintances complain that the deer ignored both food plots and even bait. Let us imagine, for example, that you have permission to hunt 20 acres, next to a half section of managed property, with a stand of mature white oaks on it. It may be an out-of-the-way corner that sees little activity in most years, but during a good acorn crop the deer will be on this property. If there is cover and a negotiable travel route, the deer will even use the property during daylight. The task becomes simply monitoring the oaks on a yearly basis. In those falls when there are acorns this spot must be in your hunting rotation. The same thing goes for apple trees, or any other preferred food source. The chances of a buck coming off micromanaged property for better food is good, especially early in the season.

Hunt the Bedding Areas

Buck bedding areas, as they are often referred to by deer micromanagers, are generally the largest, thickest, and most natural bedding areas. If the bedding areas or swamp is large enough, it will often be shared by numerous landowners. If you happen to have access to a portion of the bedding area bordering the managed property, you are in luck. As we mentioned these thick areas are mostly off limits to hunting and considered sanctuaries. In such a case you should really consider developing a plan to hunt right in the midst of the bedding area. (See page 150 for more on hunting bedding areas.) Look for the key ingredients we mention and plan a couple all-day sits. Mature bucks often bed in the same spot day after day, and they move during the day within the secure cover of their sanctuary during the rut. By setting up in an opening in a swamp, you could be putting yourself in a position to intercept even the most mature and dominant buck from the managed property. Hunt a spot like this very sparingly, perhaps only a couple times a season. Remember, bedding area hunts always require perfect scent control and timing.

Cornfields and Micromanaged Property

No matter how micromanaged a piece of property is, cornfields change the game. Corn draws deer in just as acorns and apples do. Once corn has reached its full height, and as long as it is standing, it not only attracts deer, but it attracts mature bucks as well. Almost every large cornfield will have a mature buck using it, and quite often bucks will set up residence there. Open spots, fencerows, rock piles, strips of grass between fields, and especially fingers of woods jutting out into the corn are key positions for intercepting mature bucks. Stalking on windy days is also a possibility. Rattling from a fencerow or single tree in the corn is another. Even if you only receive permission to hunt a field, it could be your opportunity to kill that big micromanaged buck. Corn levels the hunting playing field and frustrates the deer manipulation crowd. Cornfields aren't necessarily the easiest places to hunt, but they are an option that shouldn't be ignored.

Hunt Early and Late

Many of these highly managed properties are designed to be hunted primarily during the rut phases. During the early season there is often abundant food on neighboring land, and deer use these food sources until they are pushed onto the managed land by scouting and hunting pressure. This means that if you have access to land near highly managed property, you should plan a few early-season outings to intercept a buck that is not yet aware that hunting season has opened. The window of opportunity is usually pretty short, but a well-planned hunt can be worth it.

Because managed properties are designed for hunting during the rut phases, bucks will often change their routine, and locales, after the cold of winter arrives. Postrut situations offer the opportunity to hunt travel routes to far-off food sources, such as a faraway picked cornfield. Late-season hunting can provide opportunities at bucks that otherwise primarily live on off-limits property. Hunting near highly managed property is like hunting near almost any off-limits piece of property that holds deer. With a carefully implemented plan it is possible to score on a nice buck even though you aren't allowed to set foot in the heart of the area.

Baiting

Baiting was the less-sophisticated precursor to QDM and micromanagement practices. Baiting is common in much of the whitetail's range, legal in some places and illegal in others. We have encountered baiting almost everywhere we have hunted. In Michigan baiting was essentially the norm for about the last twenty years, until it was made illegal in 2008. Despite the fact that it is currently illegal bait is sold at just about every rural gas station across the state. There is still an enormous amount of baiting going on and the Department of Natural Resources seems mostly to ignore it.

Baiting is a popular method of hunting because it allows hunters with little deer hunting knowledge to be successful. All it takes is to find an area that holds deer and bait it long enough for them to become accustomed to feeding there. You don't even need to know what a deer trail looks like, because if you put bait out, they will come. Most bait hunters we know simply seek the best tree for their stands and place bait there. Baiting is also an opportunity for people who only have marginal hunting property to kill deer. Add some food to the mix and deer will be drawn in from other areas. An example of this is a 40-acre parcel that we have hunted for decades. A guy bought 10 acres next door, where the deer essentially never set foot, and started putting out truckloads of various bait. After a couple years, much of the deer movement shifted. Instead of the deer crossing the 40 to get to surrounding crops, their main destination became the 10 acres. Essentially, one baiter altered the main deer movement pattern in half a section. This sort of thing has happened to us on countless properties in Michigan and on public land elsewhere. Baiting has led hunters in a lot of areas in Michigan to feel like they must competitively bait in order to keep some deer traffic on their property. In fact, a lot of hunters took up baiting in earnest simply to hold deer on their property.

John's experience hunting in Kansas showed us how baiting can affect normal hunting. In 2004 when John took his first trip to Kansas he was unaware that baiting was legal there. That year he received permission to hunt a 40-acre parcel of timber that bordered another 20 acres of timber. The surrounding area was crop fields and open prairie for at least a mile in every direction.

That small parcel was a real gem, especially once the nearby crops were down. John killed a good buck there on his very first morning hunt and was really excited about returning. However, when he returned the following season his excitement turned into disappointment. He found another hunter's setup about 50 yards across the fence. The stand was set up in typical television fashion with two 20-foot ladder stands placed side by side overlooking a 55-gallon corn feeder. The obligatory remote camera was pointed at the feeder. John found out later that this was a hunting location of a high profile TV personality.

From 2005 through 2009 John checked the 40 acres each season. During those seasons the TV baiting location across the fence was always there. That feeder totally altered the deer traffic on the 40, almost eliminating daytime buck activity. John never hunted that location during those seasons.

During the long ride home from his 2009 hunting trip John decided to call the owner of the bordering property to discuss the situation. The landowner was unaware that the TV guys were baiting. He was a non-hunting farmer who didn't have much time to walk his timber. The landowner expressed immediate concern with what he considered an unethical hunting practice. He followed up by informing the hunters that they could continue to hunt his property but had to remove any form of bait. The TV personality pulled up stakes and left the property. When John returned in 2010, the deer movement on the 40 acres had reverted back to the way it was initially. Two primary scrape areas that were there in 2004 reappeared and the property was finally worth hunting again.

We've noticed in the last few years while on out-of-state hunts that a lot of guides use bait so their client's can be assured of seeing deer. Though baiting is very prevalent on guided hunts, most hunters don't like to claim they shot their buck over corn because they know it would diminish their accomplishment. Baiting is a common practice, and is often a method that is used by video hunters (though not commonly shown on TV), particularly in Canada, Kansas, and Texas. Most of the time the stands are placed along a travel route to the bait. This allows the hunter to intercept the buck before it actually arrives there. For filming purposes we have also found double stand sites where the bait was actually placed on the back side of stands so that it wouldn't appear in the video.

Because we hunt in Michigan, where baiting was legal for decades, we have witnessed every conceivable baiting practice. Although we are very aware of how effective baiting can be we do not bait, nor do we recommend baiting. But like deer management practices, it is important to know how baiting works to be able to readily react to it.

Baiting for mature bucks requires a little knowledge of deer behavior and an understanding of proper seasonal hunting timing. The bait is placed in a location where bucks feel secure, perhaps in a travel route between bedding areas or close to a bedding area. The location is continuously baited throughout the season, so that does, fawns, and young bucks feel completely comfortable feeding there during daylight. The key for mature buck success is seasonal timing. These spots should then be hunted just as we would hunt a primary scrape area, which means completely leaving them alone until the late prerut. Mature bucks incorporate such areas into their searches for estrous does, and they scent-check bait stations. In fact, these bait zones can become primary scrape areas and staging areas. By completely leaving these spots alone until the prerut, the chances of a mature buck scent-checking them during daylight is pretty good.

Dealing with bait

Dealing with bait and bait hunters is tough, and there are really no pat answers. Sometimes we try to use another hunter's baiting program to our advantage. There are a few tendencies that make this possible. The first is that bait is heavy, costs money, and requires some work to keep up. The consequence of this is that most bait stations are within a hundred yards of a road or two track, and that most hunters only have a few baited stands because the cost and work prohibit hunters from having numerous stands. Also, most bait hunters overhunt their stands. Beyond this, most bait hunters will have a typical hunting routine: They predominantly hunt during the evening, arriving in late afternoon. Generally, in Michigan at least, these guys target the first legal buck that strolls in.

As we already discussed, you should scout an area for all other hunting activity. Sometimes you will find areas that are not being baited, or you'll find travel routes between bedding areas and bait. You can hunt these locations exactly as you would between a bedding area and normal feeding area. It is also possible to hunt within such bedding areas during the rut phases. Since bait is seldom put in bedding areas this is a good option.

Timing is another way to get around bait hunters. By concentrating your hunting during morning and midday during the week you can hunt a lot of areas without coming into conflict with bait hunters. Also due to their traditional routine a lot of these baiters alert the mature bucks of their intentions well before there is a real chance to kill them. Overhunting as well as the scent from baiting often cause scent contamination, and mature bucks will strictly avoid bait stations until well after dark. Young bucks are the most vulnerable at bait stations and are reduced heavily year after year, leaving few to reach maturity. There are almost always fewer mature bucks in heavily hunted baited areas than otherwise. Another option is to simply abandon heavily baited property, if there is no way to hunt around the baiter or the baiting is too intense. Sometimes there is no other reasonable option.

23

CORN

Corn plays such an important role in deer behavior and hunting in our area, and across much whitetail range, that we decided it deserves its own chapter. Corn is one of the few crops that provide nearly everything deer need in the fall. By the time it reaches head height, cornfields can be daytime bedding areas, secure transition routes, escape cover, and feeding locations. Most importantly, depending on the size of the field and how well it is groomed, cornfields become preferred bedding areas that normally attract the mature dominant bucks. This situation alters the hunting in the entire surrounding area. Although this happens everywhere cornfields are found, it is most prevalent in pressured areas. The intense hunting pressure acts to reinforce the tendency, and a large portion of a local deer herd will take advantage of the security corn provides.

How the corn is harvested has a direct impact on your hunting. It is either chopped into silage early in the fall, picked during October or November, or sometimes left standing throughout the hunting season, due to too much moisture.

Silage
Standing corn is usually cut for silage early while the leaves on the stalks are still green. The stalks are cut close to the ground. The entire stalk, ears and all, are ground for livestock. Once a cornfield is cut for silage it loses its bedding area status, and unlike a picked cornfield where there will be corn left on the ground, it also loses its appeal as a feeding location. If you are hunting in an area with a cornfield that has been cut for silage, it should be treated as if it were a barren field. These fields generally have little relevance to your hunting.

Picked
The vast majority of cornfields are picked after the corn is dry enough to sell. After picking there is always some corn left in the field. The quality of the combine will dictate how much corn is left behind. Once picked the field will lose its bedding area quality, but may remain a preferred feeding location. A picked corn-

field should be hunted in the same manner as any other short preferred crop. While deer may feed in these fields during daylight, mature bucks in pressured areas will feel vulnerable entering them before dark.

Standing

There are few types of natural vegetation (cattails and brush) that grow tall enough to totally conceal a moving buck, and none of them double as a food source. Standing corn is a crop that is literally in a class by itself when it comes to deer hunting.

Farmers do not leave corn standing by choice. In years when corn remains standing beyond late November it is usually due to unusually wet weather conditions.

John snapped this picture of a doe while stalking a cornfield.

During seasons when cornfields remain standing general deer sightings will decrease, compared to seasons when the corn is down. General signposting in the nearby timber or anywhere away from the cornfield's edge will also decrease. There should be significant signposting around the perimeter or in close proximity to the cornfields. This is because many of the area's bucks will spend most daylight hours in the corn.

Hunting Standing Corn

No matter the time of season, hunting along, or in, standing corn creates a situation where you will be hunting an area where a mature buck may reside. And you will not be disturbing the rest of the property with your presence. You can experiment with stalking, ground hunting, or hunting along the perimeter without being concerned about altering deer traffic to your rut phase hunting locations.

Perimeter hunting

Mature bucks commonly exit standing cornfields in the evening and enter them in the morning to bed down. This is opposite of deer movement patterns into other crop fields. Perimeter hunting is about taking advantage of this pattern. In pressured areas mature bucks feel secure only when moving in or out of the corn during daylight where there is ample transition cover. Some bordering transition

This deer is entering a cornfield early in the morning at an interface with the woods.

cover examples are woodlots with undergrowth, overgrown ravines or points, areas of thick brown brush, swales, tall-weed fields, thick pines, or another natural bedding area. Find the interface and set up there.

Perimeter oak trees or fruit trees are another solid option. If there is fruit or mast, set up here for evening hunts. These trees drop only so much food each day and sometimes deer just can't resist a first come, first served preferred food source, especially when it is so close to where they have been bedded all day. If a mature buck comes in, it will likely be close to darkness. Don't leave until you can't see your pins.

Whenever you set up a perimeter hunter spot, make a narrow shooting lane into the corn by cutting or knocking down cornstalks. It is common for bucks to scent-check the perimeter of a standing cornfield in search of previous doe traffic. When doing so they often stay several rows within the corn. This is most common when the rows are parallel to the edge you are set up along. Make sure you have the farmer's permission before knocking down or cutting any corn.

If the corn is still standing once the leaves have fallen, deer entering or exiting the field will likely notice your silhouette against an open sky background, if you are hunting too low or exposed in a small diameter tree. In this case you should move higher up the tree in an attempt to get out of their peripheral vision or make sure you have ample background cover.

Stalking

Stalking through standing corn is an excellent way to take deer during the mid-October lull. Whenever the conditions are right, we hit the cornrows in October. There is always a possibility of tagging a big guy this way, before the onset of the rut phases. Also, farmers often request that you take some does and this is an exciting way to do so.

Before you begin there are several important factors to consider. The first is daily timing. Midday, from 10:00 a.m. to 5:00 p.m., is the best time for stalking corn. This is when most deer are bedded. When deer are up and feeding, it is difficult to move into position for a shot opportunity, because they are moving as well. The second is your human odor. You must implement a complete scent control regimen because half of the deer you encounter will be downwind. The third is camouflage. Wear a light beige exterior garment that blends well with corn and that can be worn over your carbon suit. Scent-Lok's Vertigo tan is a pattern that blends well in corn. Also, dress lightly because in this style hunting you are always on the move. The fourth is hunting pressure. The more pressure there is in an area, the more the deer will be pushed into the corn. Hunting pressure on adjoining properties will force deer that may not have been bedding in the corn to do so as the season progresses. Your best odds at a good buck are to hunt the cornfield's perimeter, or elsewhere on the property during the first several days of season, and stalk corn after the pressure has pushed more deer into the corn. The fifth is weather. Weather conditions are absolutely critical to being able to successfully stalk corn. We only stalk on days that are extremely windy, during a hard rain, or a combination of both. The wind should be blowing at least 25 miles an hour; the more noise and movement, the better your odds.

Beginning a stalk

You always stalk through the cornfield perpendicular to its rows. Start at a corner of the field and walk about 50 yards up the side parallel to the rows. Begin stalking by slowly poking your head through each row and looking both right and left for bedded deer. If there aren't any deer, scan forward through the rows for deer bedded in front of you. When stepping through a row, plant your boot next to the root of a stalk and push the stalk sideways with your knee. Then slowly step through the gap. If the wind is blowing in gusts, you will need to remain stationary and wait for the next gust before continuing to stalk forward. Continue this process until you have completed a pass through the field. Then move 50 yards down the field edge and stalk back through to the side you began on. Exactly how far you move down the side of the field after each pass depends on how far down the rows you can see. For example, if you can see 30 yards in each direction down each row, you would move 60 yards down the edge before making your next pass. It is best to carry your bow in a sling of some sort while doing this. Do not attempt to stalk corn with a nocked arrow.

Sometimes you encounter other animals in the corn. John stalked to within five yards of this napping coyote.

When you see a deer it will usually be bedded. If the deer is a doe or a fawn, other deer will normally be bedded nearby. If the deer is one that you want to shoot, estimate how far away it is, and then back up five rows and check the wind. Take your time. The deer is not going anywhere. Now sneak down the row you are in, in the direction necessary to get downwind of the deer. Count your footsteps as you go and keep a sharp lookout for other deer that may be bedded nearby. Once you are in a downwind position at a comfortable shooting distance from where the deer is bedded, nock an arrow and slowly stalk back through four rows until you are one row from the row the deer is bedded in. Slowly poke your head into the stalks and wait for its attention to be elsewhere before stepping into the row for the shot.

In well-groomed fields with wide cornrows and no interspersed weeds, if you are right-handed and the deer is going to be on your right side once downwind, you may want to consider following this procedure before taking a shot. As previously described back up five rows but move twenty or so steps farther down that row than previously described (counting every step). This should put you far enough away from the deer so that you can cross the row the deer is in without being detected. Then turn and move four rows back toward the row the deer is in, stick your head into the row the deer is in (the fifth row) and look to make sure you can cross that row without being seen. Cross the row the deer is in and move down that row back toward the deer. You are now in the row on the other side of the row the deer is in. Move back toward the deer, counting the extra footsteps you took to move farther down the field, and then peek into the row the deer is in. If the deer is too close or far, adjust your distance, wait for an opportune time (noise wise), slide your head in the row, and when the time is right, slide your bow arm and chest into the row, and make the shot. This minor adjustment will make it easier to get a shot off without spooking the deer because you won't have to get your entire body into the row before turning and taking a shot. Southpaws should do the opposite if needed.

If the bedded deer is one you do not want to shoot, move a couple rows back, sneak far enough away from the deer (counting your steps) so you can cross the row the deer is in without being detected, cross the row, count your steps back to your original position, and return to stalking. At this point be extra cautious for other deer bedded near the one you just passed on.

Stalking corn requires patience because you may cover a lot of field before seeing anything. In areas with numerous fields you may not see a deer in a particular field. Do not get overanxious and move too quickly through the field due to lack of sightings.

Stand hunting inside cornfields

This method is likely your best bet if pursuing only mature bucks. Just like in a typical bedding area, mature bucks will move during daylight in a cornfield in which they bed.

Stand hunting within a field requires you to walk the entire field edge in search of the most used runways into or out of it. Since these runways can be used during the security of darkness by mature bucks to enter or exit the corn, the runways you look for do not have to be within or close to bordering transition cover, as is the case while perimeter hunting a standing cornfield. For example, the heaviest runway may lead into an adjoining open hayfield.

Once that is done, follow the best runways into the corn and try to find a location where other deer traffic converges. You can also stalk the field looking for the rows that have the most traffic. It is common to find a row that is wider than the rest, and that row usually will have the most traffic. Once you have found the best location, using cut cornstalks, set up a makeshift ground blind about 20 yards to the side of the most of the activity. You can also use a pop-up blind of similar color to the corn and stand the cornstalks you cut while setting it up against it for added concealment. When setting up a ground blind, make sure the floor of the blind is bare dirt.

Once the blind is done, make your shooting lane or lanes by cutting or bending over cornstalks to the target area. Leave about 24 inches of each stalk sticking up (bottom of chest level on a mature deer). This will aid in concealing the lane. Unlike the wide shooting lanes you would make in the woods, make these lanes only about 24 to 30 inches wide. The wider the lane, the more apt a deer is to stop and look down it. You may also consider making two shooting lanes in a V shape to the runway. V-shaped lanes will allow you to see a deer pass through the first lane and allow time to prepare for the shot at the second lane. When the corn is dry and there is no wind, if there are deer feeding on corn anywhere near you, you will be able to hear the cornstalks move as the deer bite kernels from the ears. You should also be able to hear any deer moving toward your location as they brush by the cornstalks.

Another feature to look for when stalking corn is old rock piles or small weed-filled openings that were too wet for the corn to grow or for the tractor to plant. Usually the edges of these openings will be well traveled, and if you locate such an area, you can set it up in the exactly the same manner.

John's 2005 Iowa Buck

The fall of 2005 was a tough season. Due to business commitments, and work on my Bowhunting Pressured Whitetails DVD series, I didn't bowhunt at all in Michigan. I applied for an Iowa tag earlier in the year and expected to be done with the video project by the time hunting season rolled around, but that didn't happen. My plan was to lower my expectations a bit in hopes of getting back to Michigan to wrap up the DVD project.

In previous years my typical routine in Iowa was to initially hunt a farm that included an island in a large river system. The island can hold some giant bucks, but depending on the crops in the area, deer activity there varies. Some years it is great, others not so much. If the island spot doesn't work out, I then move to another farm, to a spot I call the Hole. On this trip, however I skipped the island and made straight for the Hole. The Hole is a wide stretch of bottomland that lies below a steep bluff along the Iowa River. The woods consist mainly of mature maples and tall weeds, interspersed with brush. The property I have permission to hunt on is quite small, but the same type of terrain stretches along the river for miles. I hadn't set foot in the Hole since 2003, but the scrape areas and runways hadn't changed a bit since my last visit. Above the bluff, fields extend for miles in all directions. When the crops are cut it forces the deer to concentrate along the river and in the bottomland where I was hunting.

The tree I chose the first afternoon was about 150 yards from the bottom of the bluff in some scattered brush and tall weeds. There were scrapes and rubs strewn throughout the area and I was in the center of the sign. During the first several hours, all I saw was a single doe browsing her way toward the bluff. Once she was over the hill, it seemed as though the entire Hole came alive with deer.

Mock scrapes

In any natural opening within a cornfield where there is heavy deer traffic you can also set up a mock scrape/licking branch combo. While implementing a full scent control routine, stand in the location where the deer traffic in the opening is most concentrated and look for the most suitably concealed location within a comfortable shooting distance where a ground blind can be set up.

At least 4 feet into the opening from the edge of the corn, dig a hole and bury a long, straight 2- to 4-inch diameter cut tree into the ground, leaving at least 6 feet of it above the ground. Keep in mind that bucks may rub their antlers on whatever you use and it must be deep enough and sturdy enough to take some

This buck was killed in an area where deer activity increases tremendously after the corn is cut.

There were deer moving toward the bluff from every direction, and they all seemed to be does and fawns. I counted twenty-two deer before the first buck appeared, and he was a nice one. The buck was closely pursuing a doe who was definitely not playing easy to get. She kept moving toward the bluff and he kept circling in front of her to keep her in cover. Since they circled about a hundred yards away and didn't appear as if they would get any closer, I decided to attempt to call them in. I tried a rattle sequence, and that didn't even arouse their interest. I didn't think grunting would evoke a response, so I tried a doe bleat call. The buck paid no attention to it, but the doe did. She turned and walked toward my tree, with the buck on her heels. She passed within 5 yards of the tree, as did the buck. I waited until he was about 20 yards away before bleating to stop him and take the shot. He didn't travel very far before expiring within sight.

As is often the case, some real work began after the shot. Getting the buck up that steep bluff was going to be a chore. I had the pleasure of trying to get bucks up that hill before, so this time I came prepared with a 100-foot, four-pulley system, block and tackle. Still, it took me a couple hours to get that deer up over that bluff. After that it was straight back to Michigan and back to work. 🦌

punishment and not tip over. When cutting a tree for this, the best option is one with a 3- to 4-foot-long branch sticking off the side that will end up being 5 to 6 feet above ground once the tree is buried and will work as the licking branch.

If no suitable trees are available, you can bury a non-treated 2 x 4 that has been lying outside (scent-free) for a while. Leave 6 feet above the ground. You will have to cut a licking branch at least 3 to 4 feet long that can be mounted to the board and will remain rigid and sturdy enough to take some antler abuse. The branch can also split into multiple licking branches toward its end. The licking branch should be attached so that its end is 5 to 6 feet above the ground over the eventual mock scrape.

Look closely. Deer can be pretty well camouflaged in cornfields.

Using the untouched end of a stick, make a mock scrape below the licking branch and douse it with buck or doe urine. Chris likes to use synthetic scents by Buck Fever Synthetics for this. You can also snap the end of the licking branch and smear some licking branch scent (forehead gland) on its end.

A mock scrape setup should be completed at least a few days before hunting the location. The most opportune seasonal time frame would be just before, or during prerut, when bucks are jockeying for dominance and looking for those first estrous does. If the cornfield is big enough to attract deer as a daytime bedding area, and the scrape becomes naturally active, this location can be hunted at any time of day and several times throughout the rest of the season.

It is imperative that the mock scrape/licking branch setup be far enough into the opening so that the farmer doesn't hit the tree or board while picking the corn. You should also let the farmer know where the setup is so that he is aware of it, in case he combines the corn before you remove it.

Trees and swales in cornfields

There may be swales with trees in cornfields. The edges of these will usually receive deer traffic. If a tree offers suitable cover, set up in it. Sometimes you will find large sprawling oaks in cornfields. During the years the field is in standing corn and the oak has acorns, these are terrific locations to hunt at any time of season. In this situation deer can feed on a preferred food source while remain-

Lone oaks in cornfields can be great hunting locations in years when they produce acorns and the field is in standing corn.

ing within the security cover of the bedding area. You can hunt stands like this any time of day.

Hunting standing corn can be very effective, but by the time the rut phases start you should hope that the corn in your area is down, forcing the deer to confine their bedding areas and travel routes to areas where they are more vulnerable.

24

FINAL THOUGHTS

As we said at the beginning of this book, we simply love to bowhunt white tails. If you are reading these words, you most likely love bowhunting whitetails just as much as we do. You have probably also noticed how much time, effort, passion, and pain we put into our hunting. Chasing wary mature bucks is a way of life, a challenge we crave. Hard work and planning are the key elements of bowhunting whitetails the Eberhart way.

Attitude is critical to pressured whitetail hunting success. Along the way we all encounter setbacks, such as losing permission to hunt good locations, ruined hunts, missed opportunities because of our own errors, and even perhaps injury. These things are all part of the game. Take them all in stride and keep on hunting. A little determination and positive thinking goes a long way in deer hunting. Every minute you are out there, and do things right, the closer you are to that next mature buck.

We are concerned with the trend toward growing and manipulating whitetails. These magnificent wild animals are being degraded more and more by management practices that tend to take much of the challenge, excitement, and mystery out of bowhunting. Euphemisms such as *extreme management* or even *harvest* are code for growing and continued privatization of animals that should never be tamed. We are hunters, which is why we kill our game, not harvest it. Grossly exaggerated hunting ease in the name of entertainment is misleading for young hunters and the non-hunting public, and it is dangerous for the future of bowhunting. Don't be fooled by the images of monster bucks crossing the screens. Mature pressured bucks in most places rarely reach those proportions, and a mature buck is a real trophy no matter the antler size. Bringing whitetail hunting into the technological age and keeping hunting fair-chase and real are big challenges facing the hunting community for decades to come. Hopefully our children and grandchildren will be able to experience hunting truly wild wary whitetails as we have.

It is still possible for the average hunter to bowhunt wild and free whitetails. With careful planning and implementation you can be successful at bowhunting mature bucks, even in some of the most heavily hunted locales in North America. It certainly isn't easy, but maybe it shouldn't be. Get out there, do the work, and kill that big mature buck you have been dreaming about. We hope our way of hunting helps you on your hunter's path.

INDEX

Page numbers in italics indicate illustrations and sidebars.